SPECIAL FORCE
A CHINDIT'S STORY

Me resplendent with Crown Bird hackle, official Chinthé
emblem and unofficial Chindit titles

SPECIAL FORCE
A CHINDIT'S STORY

Jesse Shaw

ALAN SUTTON
1986

Alan Sutton Publishing Limited
Brunswick Road · Gloucester

First published 1986

British Library Cataloguing in Publication Data

Shaw, Jesse
Special Force : a Chindit's story.
1. Great Britain, *Army, South-East Asia
Command, Special Force* 2. World War,
1939–1945—Campaigns—Burma 3. World
War, 1939–1945—Personal narratives, British
I. Title
940.54'25'0924 D767.6

ISBN 0-86299-285-0

JA/80/1128–888/G/161086/3000

Typesetting and origination by
Alan Sutton Publishing Limited
Photoset Palatino 10/11
Printed in Great Britain
by The Guernsey Press Company Limited
Guernsey, C.I.

Contents

CHAPTER ONE

Dad wouldn't let me join the Army

Bow, East London, 1917. A motley group of teenaged boys waited outside their headmaster's room; hated schooldays were nearly over. 'Come in the first,' they heard, and one lanky individual was stared at meaningly.

'In yer go, Sticks,' he was urged.

'Sticks' hung back but, like Uriah the Hittite of old, found himself being thrust to the forefront, except that poor old Uriah offered no resistance. 'Why me first?' hissed the struggling Sticks.

'You're the biggest, an' got boots,' 'explained' one of several barefooted.

'What on earth's going on out there?' shouted Mr Lucas, the head.

The door was wrenched open, revealing plump Mr Broom, Stick's own class master. 'Oh,' he growled sepulchrally, 'it's *you.*'

*   *   *

I stood looking warily at the school committee. All, apart from stately Miss Gunsberg, infants' headmistress, had caned me to little effect, and no doubt were happy at the imminent departure of their *bête noir*. 'Now, Shaw,' began 'Lukey', 'what are you aiming to be?'

'A soldier, sir, like my father.'

'He does not agree. You must wait until you're eighteen.'

'The war will be over long before that, Jesse,' asserted Miss Gunsberg's dark brown voice.

'Your father still in France?' asked Lukey. 'Veterinary Corps, isn't it?'

'No sir, 'e got wounded. Artillery now, in Sussix.'

'What was he before enlistment?'

'Iron plate worker, sir. Said I ain't strong enough for that, not 'eavy enough for me 'eight. Said try to get into the print. Com . . . compositin', I think it was, sir.'

'It could be an idea,' interposed Broomy. 'His spelling's good.'

Lukey looked dubious. 'That's a 'father-to-son' trade. Anyway, we'll do our best for you, Shaw. Send in the next.'

Later, Broomy said goodbye, smiling all over his rubicund face. Lukey gave me an envelope for my mother and another for the Employment Exchange. 'Call in at any time and let us know how you are progressing.'

The bell. As I left with the boisterous crowd, I passed the spot where I'd had my one and only fist fight. A chap had insulted my father, jeering that nobody got wounded in the 'Vetinery Corpse' – a horse must have bitten him. Three blows only were struck – the first on his eye, the next on my conk, and the last, ending the scrap, landed painfully on my ear. It came from my adversary's mother, arriving to collect her offspring. 'You 'it someone yer own size!' she yelled.

Now, by the gate stood the caretaker, who'd once threatened to brain me after I'd nearly brained *him*. I'd dropped the cricket bag from a window to save humping it down three lots of stairs, unaware that the old fellow was in the playground. He now grinned and waved, shouting: 'Good luck!' My eyes smarted as I told myself I'd call often, little knowing that I was passing through that rusty old gate for the very last time.

A mile walk home, accompanied by cheeky sister Esther, aged nine. 'What's this?' asked mother, eyeing her envelope.

'Dunno, mum. Me character, p'raps.'

Looking grim, she began to read aloud: '"James Jesse Shaw has attended this school since infancy. He is intelligent, comes from a good home, and his conduct has been satisfactory".' I remained speechless, but not mother. 'What?' she squeaked. '"Satisfactory"? Satisfactory *and* "intelligent"? I 'ope this doesn't stop Mr Lucas from goin' to 'eaven. Blind ole Riley – what'll yer father say?'

'Dad's said too much already,' I grumbled. 'I can't join the Army.'

'Now don't let me 'ear any more o' that.'

'Jesse-e-e wants to win a V.C.-e-e,' shrilled Esther in high falsetto.

'Shut up, young Tess!' I bawled.

'Shan't. *You* shut up!' was the retort.

'For goodness' sake,' groaned mother wearily, 'shut up the pair of yer!'

*　　*　　*

At the Exchange, mother was at my heels, and a clerk, whose shoulders appeared to be shaking, led us to an office. From a desk the manager looked up and gaped. Narrow as a beanpole, I was nearly six feet tall, and wearing knickerbocker suit, black stockings, Eton collar and bow tie. Fortunately it wasn't summer, or a straw boater would have been topping off that lot. 'Mrs Shaw! Your son must *not* go for any interview dressed like that. Trousers *please*.'

'Oh . . . sorry,' she murmured. 'I'll see to it.'

He read Lukey's letter. 'There's nothing in print. Now —'

'Sir,' I said eagerly, 'is there a job travelling – abroad?'

'Good gracious, lad, you're far too young. Never mind. Here's travelling of a sort, with prospects. An American firm. Their London branch, so I'm afraid your travelling will be done – ha-ha-ha – on foot. Don't forget the trousers, Mrs Shaw.' He handed me a card, and my heart, that had bounded like a yo-yo at the word 'American', dropped like a lump of lead.

*　　*　　*

A year and three jobs later. The first, with the Western Union Telegraph Company, was cut short. On late turn, I was delayed by an air raid, having to walk home. 'Enough o' this,' said mother. 'We'll find something with better hours.' Next a warehouse near St Paul's. Sightseeing in the Cathedral I found a girlfriend, Jean, who was on the till in a City shop managed by her father. One of my new mates was in the South London Cadets – what a chance! My badgered mother gave way, and at the drill hall I was given a cap and belt; the rest would be issued when they found something to fit! Another air alert, and after a lengthy trek I stalked indoors wearing my new ornaments, tossing up a smart salute that was ignored. 'I've been worried stiff,' exclaimed mother. 'You can just take those things back tomorrer.'

'Look,' I protested, 'you and dad stopped me joinin' the Army, but what's wrong with Cadets?'

'Nothing, but I'm not 'avin' you wandering about in air raids.'

'No raid. Only a warnin' tonight. I can't pack up because o' that. I'm supposed to be a soldier.'

'Soldier be blowed!'

'You look more like a bloomin' milkman!' giggled Esther.

'You mind yer own business!' I bawled. 'Mum, I want Jean to see me in these.'

'I'll tell 'er 'ow smart you looked,' chirruped Esther.

No good. I had to persuade my pal to take back the things. The warehouse would lead nowhere; I merely humped parcels. During midday breaks I used to chat with a printer by Dowgate Dock. One day he said that an apprentice was leaving because of a 'barney' with the foreman. 'Any chance?' I asked instantly.

'I've mentioned you. Come along before six.'

I passed a spelling test, and my father obtained a day's leave to sign papers. On my first morning a boy of about twelve accosted me, speaking in a most superior accent: 'And who are you?'

'I'm startin' work 'ere. Waitin' for the foreman.'

'Oh. Well, my daddah *owns* this factory, and those –' he flipped a comprehensive hand – 'are all daddah's machines. Don't touch anything without being told.' He walked away, nose in the air.

My own parent had warned me that a printer's 'devil' was a general factotum, and I would have happily have accepted it had it not been for the surly curmudgeon of a foreman. No wonder my predecessor had been in a barney. The old man hated me, perhaps because I was head and shoulders the taller. On my fifteenth birthday Jean and I argued. 'Stop grumbling,' she said. 'This is the third job since you left school.'

'Easy for you. Your father's the boss. You ain't got my foreman.'

'Don't keep saying "ain't".'

One day I was sent for colour needed urgently. The foreman arrived, grabbed, and the tray fell, missing me but covering his trousers with about a gallon of post office red. Seconds later I realised that I'd never complete seven years' tuition under this man, and after lunch, when I should have been clocking in, I was at a recruiting office.

*   *   *

It's all right, it's all right now.
No need to worry any more.
I saw the Army wasn't strong,
Everything was wrong
'til the day I came along,
Then the band played, they all hoorayed,
The guns fired a salvo of delight;
I joined the Army yesterday,
So the Army of today's all right.

'What can I do for you?' asked the soldier behind the desk.
'I heard I can enlist at fourteen, sir. I'm fifteen.'
'That's right. All you need is your parents' consent. Is that all right?'
'Yes sir. I think so.'
'Think so? Give me the address and I'll send them the form.'
Oh blimey! I'd intended to fill the names in myself. 'Can I take it with me?'
'Just give me the address,' he repeated.
'Er . . . I think I'll ask 'em first and make sure.' I slid out, away from his obvious suspicion, but wasn't finished yet; there was another R.O. in Finsbury Square.
'Yes, lad?'
'I'd like to join the Army, sir.'
'How old are you?'
'Eighteen.'
He looked and sounded sceptical; conscription had begun long before. 'Oh? Then why no call-up?'
I was prepared. 'Bombed out by Zepps and 'ad to move twice.' (True.)
'I see. We haven't caught up with you yet. Any trade?'
'No sir.'
'Just call me "sergeant". By the way, is your father serving?'
'Yes, sergeant,' I answered incautiously. 'In the Royal Field Artillery in Sussix.'
'Sussex? I can possibly get you into his unit.'
What? Roll up at Dad's camp? That *would* be good! 'I'd like to join the Middlesex Regiment, sergeant.'
He smiled. 'That's *my* regiment. Any particular reason?'
'My 'ome's in Middlesex, and my Uncle Wink was in 'em. Got killed.'
'Sorry to hear it, lad.' I left with an envelope and a railway warrant to Mill Hill.

At the barracks I began to wonder what would happen when I failed to arrive home. About to draw a palliasse and blankets, I hesitated. 'Do I 'ave to sleep 'ere tonight?'

'Up to you, mate, as long as you're at the Orderly Room by nine.'

Declining the rough bedding, my season ticket helped on the way home. 'Where the devil 'ave yer been? Yer dinner's ruined.'

'Sorry, mum. Tell yer why in a jiff.' I entered the scullery to wash.

When the meal was in front of me, she stood waiting, arms akimbo and looking impatient. 'Well?'

'I've joined the Army.'

'Eh? Not those bloomin' Cadets again?'

'No. The *real* Army. I've left me job.'

Mother gaped, and sister yelled: 'Hooray! War's over. We've won!'

'Shut up, you!' I shouted. 'Not so cocky when dad volunteered. Cryin' yer eyes out then. Mum, it's fixed. Mill 'ill in the mornin'. Uncle Wink's regiment,' I said impressively.

Down waddled Aunt Lizzie, our lodger on the top floor, followed by Uncle George. 'What's all the rumpus? What's he been up to now?'

'I'm just findin' out,' gritted mother. 'Now look 'ere, 'ow did yer manage to do it?'

'Mum, it's all fixed, I tell yer. Might as well let me go.'

'Not on yer life. I can guess what you've done, an' we'll see what yer father does about it.' She grabbed pen and paper to catch the last collection and I went out looking to Jean for sympathy, but didn't find it. Fed up, I went early to bed.

'For two pins I'd come with yer,' threatened mother next morning, and was capable of doing it. 'You're daft if you think your father'll let this pass.'

At Mill Hill I waited with some young men – would the medical examination end it? My turn came, and I was told to undress behind a screen, and did so. 'Aren't you ready yet?' called the M.O. impatiently.

'Yessir.'

'Well, for Christ's sake come out. D'you think I'm coming in to you?'

'Sorry sir.' As I appeared, he grunted something about the Army putting some food into me; luckily my mother wasn't within earshot.

After a bit of poking and prodding he asked: 'Have you had the usual children's ailments?'

'Think so, sir.'

'What d'you mean – "think so"? Anything serious?'

'No sir.' And then, without so much as a by-your-leave, he gripped one of my testicles and told me to cough. Shocked, I cleared my throat, and he promptly grabbed the other; I felt thankful there were only two. 'Get dressed,' he ordered brusquely. 'A.1.'

My naked feet trod on air back to the screen, and later I was sworn in. Among the kit then issued were long underpants, horrible objects I'd never before worn. Parcelling our civilian clothes now – 'Address them to your next-of-kin, and hurry up,' ordered the Quartermaster, and noticed me hesitating. 'Get on with it, you.'

'Er . . . my next-of-kin's in the Army,' I replied, and someone laughed.

The Q.M. regarded me sourly. 'Send them to your home,' he barked, 'and call me "sir".'

I tied the bundle, with a horrid presentiment that my 'next-of-kin' was at that moment wending his way north – what a chump I'd been to mention Mill Hill. For dinner we had something called 'brown stew', and afterwards I sat wrestling with my kit, trying to smooth the new brass buttons. Then, as I was brushing away energetically, the door was flung open. Someone shouted: 'J.J. Shaw?' and there, behind him, stood Nemesis.

I rose from the bed, knees spongy, as my father crossed the room and spoke very quietly: 'Orderly Room.' I started to pull on my tunic, but he suddenly hissed: 'Just a tick. What the devil 'ave yer been doin' with those puttees?'

'I did 'em as neat as I could.'

'Neat? You've got the tapes at the bottom.'

'Same as yours.'

'I'm not in the Infantry. Put 'em right for Gawd's sake!'

There were half stifled chuckles as I readjusted, then we walked in silence to the Orderly Room. My father waited outside, and when I entered an officer said: 'Are you Shaw?'

'Yessir.'

'Apart from the inconvenience caused us, you've committed an offence.'

'Sorry sir.'

'However, your father agrees to your becoming a boy soldier. All right?'

'Yessir.' (Good old Dad.)

'You'll now be in the Royal Fusiliers.'

A clerk thrust a form in front of me. 'I've already signed one o' those,' I told him.

'Sign again, *Boy* Shaw,' he grinned. 'Your medical category is now A.4.'

My jaw dropped. 'Why's that?'

'A.1., but under age. Go and draw another cap badge, and titles.'

'You young fool,' my father greeted me. 'You might've got yerself stuck on an overseas draft.'

'Well, you got yerself on one, dad, and you 'ad a family.'

'Not the same. I wasn't fifteen. Now what about yer job? I suppose you got the sack?'

'No. I sacked meself.'

'Why?' he demanded heatedly.

'That bloomin' foreman. Got smothered with ink through 'is own fault. Blamed me an' said I was a clumsy long bastard.'

'Listen. Did you sign for the duration of war?'

'Yes.'

'Right. Don't take on as a regular without asking me first. I'm spendin' the night at 'ome. I'll see your boss tomorrow on the way back. Things'll 'ave to be sorted out.'

'Will they? That's good, they owe me three days' wages.'

'You cheeky young sod! Now listen. Write regularly to yer mother. Try not to start smokin' or drinkin' – it'll eat yer pay. An' watch yer step with girls, or one of 'em might leave yer with a receipt. Oh well, you've done it now, Jesse. Up to you. Good luck.'

'Thanks for what you've done, Dad.' I watched him go, thinking how unwell he looked compared to the day when he'd enlisted; those years in France had taken a heavy toll. Then I glanced at the half-crown in my palm, a sizeable chunk of his pay.

The Middlesex badge – 'Ich Dien' (I serve, they told me. Hey, wasn't that German?) was exchanged for one resembling a flaming grenade. Royal Fusiliers? I'd read about them. Weren't they known as the 'Shiny Seventh?', and one of few regiments allowed to march through the City of London with drums beating, bayonets fixed, and colours flying? Just think . . . if the war lasted long enough I might yet win that V.C.!

Back in the barrack-room I suffered legpulling; the other chaps probably thought me some kind of halfwit. Later, in the evening, I began to feel very uncomfortable inside. Apprehension, and perhaps brown stew, were having effect. I only half heard the chatter going on around me. It was my first night away from home, and as I sat on that narrow, unresilient bed, spitting and polishing, I tried to think myself patriotic while all the time a quiet voice in my ear was insinuating that I'd merely been stupid. Long before a bugle blared 'Lights Out' I was between the blankets, wearing shirt and drawers, which were warm, but around midnight had to get up in a hurry and scramble into my trousers. In the latrine I yanked the latter down and squatted, completely forgetting the long johns.

After endeavouring to clean up under the glimmer from a solitary low-powered bulb, I groped my wretched way back to my far from restful kip.

In a single day I'd twice joined the Army, worn puttees upside down, and shit myself.

CHAPTER TWO

Boy Soldier – Royal Fusiliers

A peculiar trio next morning. Two middle-aged men, one hefty with a huge beard, the other short and stocky, plus myself. Beardy emerged from the Orderly Room, quizzing a railway warrant. 'Where the bloody 'ell's Walton-on-the-Naze?'

'Buggered if I ever 'eard of it,' asserted Shorty.

'Near Clacton,' I said, not long from school.

To retain our strength, we'd been given bully beef sandwiches. Kitbags were weighty, but a lorry took us to the station. I'd never before seen a Tommy with a beard, and on the short walk from Broad Street to Liverpool Street Station everybody turned and stared after the whiskers. One glance from the redcap on the platform and our way was barred. 'Passes?'

Beardy fished out the warrant, and the redcap got a glimpse at him from a flank. 'Fasten that collar.'

'It's bleedin' tight —'

'Fasten it, and don't swear at me!'

Fuming, Beardy held everything up while struggling with hooks. We found an empty compartment at the very front of the train, and Beardy ripped off his tunic and slung it on the rack. 'Cheeky young sod!' Passing through Stratford, I looked in the direction of the West Ham soccer ground – when would I again watch my heroes? The other two were shouting against the roar of the train, cursing something called the 'Derby Scheme'. Apparently men above calling-up age had been invited to join something they thought was a Reserve, and here they were in uniform. If Lord Derby had chanced to enter our compartment I wouldn't have given tuppence for his life.

At one station, seamen invaded, giving Beardy incredulous stares. One muttered to me: 'Is that old geezer a Cossack?' I was looking eagerly for the sea, having seen it only once, on a paddle-steamer from Tower Bridge to Southend. It was George the Fifth's coronation day, with bunting everywhere and fireworks on the way back.

An inspector entered and grinned at our warrant. 'We're not going to Walton. You boarded the wrong part of the train. Didn't they tell you at Liverpool Street?'

'Didn't tell us a bleedin' thing,' Shorty assured him.

'That bloody redcap's fault,' boomed Beardy. 'Where are we then?'

'Running into Harwich.' We were juddering to a stop. 'Join that train over there, and change at Colchester or you'll go back to London.'

The grinning sailors made way, but by the time we'd been cleared by another redcap the whistle was blowing. Arriving at a stumbling canter we were confronted by a packed corridor. Thrusting our way between protesting bodies we forced kitbags to the floor, with one diminutive civilian rescuing his dislodged trilby. 'Mind my hat, you!' he scowled.

Beardy glowered back. 'Mind it yerself – I've got enough to mind!'

The little man's mouth opened, then closed. Sweat ran from us. Eventually, at the elusive Walton-on-the-Naze, no military transport was in sight except for a contraption resembling two dogcarts fastened to a pair of horses. By it was a Tommy. 'Goin' anywhere near the Royal Fusiliers, mate?' queried Beardy.

The man, after focusing on the whiskers, nodded. 'Yer luck's in. Chuck yer stuff in the back, sit in the front, an' for Christ's sake 'old on!'

Anyone who has ridden in a horse-drawn Infantry limber will appreciate the warning. Hurtling along, we bounced about painfully on the wooden bottom, finding it difficult even to speak. Shorty's top denture suddenly rattled loose, and after some trial and error he managed to stuff it into a breast pocket. Beardy made a foolhardy attempt to eat the last of his bully beef and lost it over the side; I saw a dog pounce on it. We alighted stiffly by a field containing tents pitched on what looked like churned mud, and a bugle sounded. Several people arrived, followed more slowly by a man with a big badge on his sleeve. After regarding us in silence for a very long moment he inquired: 'Is the battalion barber in camp?'

'Playing "House",* sir,' someone answered.

---

* Now called 'Bingo'. The only gambling game permitted in the Army.

'Then dig him out.' He looked woodenly at me. 'Boy?'
'Yessir.' And to make a good start I saluted.
'You don't salute Regimental Sergeant-Majors.' As a chap
with a stripe led me away I thought I heard the R.S.M. mutter
something like 'another of the little sods', but may have been
mistaken.

*   *   *

Plum and apple, apple and plum,
Plum and apple, it is always one;
The A.S.C. get strawb'ry jam,
The R.F.A. get eggs and ham,
But the P.B.I.* get plum and apple, apple and plum.

My kit was dumped just inside the entrance to a bell tent. The
occupants were absent, their beds made down on the bare
wooden floor. I was taken to draw my own, plus a groundsheet,
and ventured a naive inquiry that brought a gleeful yell from the
storeman to someone unseen: 'Chap 'ere would like a piller.'
'Okydoke,' came a muffled reply. 'One 'ot waterbottle or
two?'
'No pillers outside officers' quarters,' laughed my lance-
corporal. 'I'll help you with your bed when you've had a
haircut.'
The barber, obviously peeved at being torn from his gaming,
gave me the shortest 'back-and-sides' I'd ever suffered, in about
thirty seconds flat. As I left, Beardy and Shorty arrived, looked
at my coiffure and grimaced. The lance-jack made me a 'pillow'
with various clothing. 'You'll need the great coat over you – gets
chilly at night. The other chaps are out or in the canteen. You've
missed tea, but it was only plum-and-apple as usual. First
parade for you will be band practice – nine a.m.'
Outside, a man was just leaving the barber's. 'My mate lorst
'is whiskers yet?' I asked.
'I *am* your bleedin' mate,' was the literal answer as the
erstwhile Beardy dabbed his chin. 'I asked for the Navy so I
could keep me beard, but o' course the bastards wouldn't listen.
Christ, I could do with a pint!'
We awaited Shorty, who soon emerged, resembling an old lag
just let out of clink, then headed for the canteen marquee. They

* Poor Bloody Infantry.

went into the 'wet' end and I the 'dry', to see a group of boys in one corner. One of them came over to me. 'You the new boy? Welcome. Got any rent to lend?' He added that no meal was served in camp between tea and breakfast. Not being a simpleton as far as pocket and stomach went, I shook my head and he lost interest. All were obviously Cockneys, with the exception of one lad who stayed very quiet. I stood him tea and 'wad' – a kind of rockcake with the accent on the first syllable – when the others departed. His name was Alan and he'd been to High School. Alan was already enlisting, saying that from the tales they told, some of the others had been pretty bright sparks in Civvy Street. 'They actually boast about what they did. Why did *you* join?'

'Well, my dad volunteered. When the Zepps came later on we copped it one night. Ceilin' fell in upstairs – good job no-one was in bed. A bomb went right through a pub nearby and exploded in the cellar – killed everyone in there. I 'ated the Jerries then. Fed up with 'iding under the stairs. I joined up and gave a wrong age. Me old man found out, so I'm 'ere.'

Dog tired, I left and slid into my kip, dozing fitfully between periodic bugle brays, but became fully awake after dark as people arrived; each in turn either kicked or trod on me. Others passing outside tripped over ropes or pegs, emitting sulphuric adjectives that I was fast beginning to accept as the normal vocabulary. When this lurid period stopped, another began as rain battered the canvas.

I slept, to be aroused by a distant bugle; it was daylight. One body stirred, swore, and made for the exit slit. I stared up at a set of male organs dangling over my face. 'Is 'e goin' to pee through the flap?' I thought, aghast, but was astonished when the figure raised a bugle. When it rained, someone blew the repeat call to save the orderly bugler a wet walk to our end of camp. At such close quarters the blaring was fiendish – I was nearly blasted out of my blankets. Luckily it wasn't the excruciatingly extended 'long' version but the short reveille:

> Get out of bed, get out of bed,
> You lazy bastards.
> Get out of bed, that's what I said,
> You lazy bastards.
> One more day to serve the King.

The L.B.'s sat up one by one, cursed, groaned, yawned, stretched, scratched and farted. Apparently all Infantrymen, including the sergeant in charge, slept in dayshirts. The rain ceased, and kits were placed outside in line on groundsheets. Men were detailed to sling everything in if it rained, and to guard against 'scroungers' – the word 'theft' was never heard. One had to be particularly wary when a draft was leaving, a parody on 'When I Lost You' fully illustrating the point:

I lost my rifle and bayonet, I lost my oilbottle too.
I lost my tunic and trousers, I lost my puttees too.
I lost my razor and toothbrush, I lost my cardigan too.
I lost my holdall, now I've got sweet — all . . .
Since I lost you.

Breakfast now, at the noisy table reserved for boys. I noticed Beardy's face was in a mess. 'First time I've ever used a bloody cut-throat razor!' I heard him glooming.

I soon found that boys were the reverse of popular in the drums-and-fifes band. Spares were scarce, and the flautists detested their instruments being used by 'snotty-nosed' kids, as they so delicately phrased it. I was assigned for tuition to a B-Flat Flute who received me with obvious repugnance, but thawed a little on finding that I possessed a handkerchief.

Soon I was 'Titch'. Practice ended at midday, and after brown stew I felt like a look at the sea. No-one should have gone out before four, but I'd already been shown a well-used exit behind the latrines. On the road I met someone, swishing a cane and looking smart, and I stared to the front as a good shoulder should. 'Hey . . . *you*,' I heard. 'Come back here.' The voice, though youthful, was authoritative, so I obeyed. 'You deliberately ignored me,' he said, tapping his shoulder with the cane.

'Know what this is?'
'Yessir. A pip, sir.'
'Why didn't you salute?'
'Sorry sir.'
'How long have you been in the service?'
'Three days, sir.'
'I see. Well, you know now what to do, don't you?'
'Yessir.'
'Very well, you may go.'

I turned away. 'No!' he said sharply. 'Salute first.' As I did, he came to attention and solemnly returned the compliment. We about-turned together and stepped off. It must have looked good – a pity there were no spectators. I'd now ignored an officer and saluted someone not entitled, but I'd learn.

Soon afterwards a new, unpopular order decreed that boys would attend afternoon school, an ex-headmaster having been subpoenaed. Wherever he'd reigned in pre-war days, he could never have taught such recalcitrants. Passers-by would have been justified in thinking something under Queensbury Rules was going on. Once, when rain on the marquee roof was almost drowning his voice, he told us that the east coast was the driest part of the country. A deafening howl of derision ascended. It *might* have helped if they'd given poor old Bandsman Ridgeway a stripe.

I wrote to mother and Jean and, hating 'Boy', promoted myself 'Drummer'. Jean's reply explained that her father had forbidden friendship with a soldier, so all letters must be sent via mother, who would stick them in the window.

There was much rain, and a 'flu epidemic. The unit didn't escape and a military funeral took place. Practice was essential, so the band rehearsed on the road, away from mud. Alan had a cymbal hanging from a strap, while I made up the number with a flute I pretended to play. We slowmarched, my fingers waggling, with Alan banging his cymbal in unison with the bass drum. The 'bonk' of the muffled drum was sharply cut off, but the cymbal gave off a long, reverberating wail, sounding as though it were being struck late. The bass drummer waxed wroth, and poor Alan went to pieces. He and I exchanged instruments, and I larruped good and proper. 'You're worse than the other bloody kid!' exploded the drummer. A furious altercation ensued, not easy when trying to slow march to the dirge of the Dead March in Saul. The irritated drum-major flipped a hand and we straggled to a halt. I was put in the back row and told to watch the drummer's arm. With no chance to protest verbally, the cringing flautists now had their ears violently assailed. Yet, on the day, things were perfect, except I suppose for the chappie in the coffin.

I'd never make Kneller Hall, Mecca of Army musicians, with the B-flat flute. I liked the piano, but the one in the canteen jangled as though half the strings had broken. The first time I sat down to it and tentatively began to 'Keep the Home Fires Burning' there was an instant roar from the other side of the canvas partition: 'Shut that soddin' row!' Housey-housey was about to go into session.

Boys weren't allowed arms and equipment, and did little apart from band practice. On my first church parade (compulsory) I'd just been vaccinated and nearly passed out, to find that owing to the needle I should not have attended. We were never absent from pay parade, of course, and once weekly were marched to the town's slipper baths. One evening I wandered over the fields and saw a schoolgirl blackberrying. When I offered to help she promptly scuttled away to a distant cottage, having obviously been warned against us licentious soldiery.

*   *   *

An overnight training exercise. I was detailed to a ration lorry, and when it parked at dusk I persuaded the driver to lend me his gun to act as sentry. Nor did I slouch about on the job – no sir! I patrolled my self-imposed beat smartly, or stood to attention with the weapon at the slope. ' Oh Gawd!' groaned the driver at last, 'if yer must do that, don't challenge civilians or you'll scare the guts out of 'em. Just watch out for tin 'ats. That's what the enemy's wearin'.'

So, when anyone approached I merely took a pace forward and *looked*. Two women said: 'Oo!' and hurried past. Eventually the driver settled down to sleep inside the truck, while I dozed in the cab, but was out at dawn, raring to go and wishing certain London females could see the performance. No movement for an hour, then footsteps. Blimey, an enemy officer! Stealthily I raised the gun, loaded with blank, silently pushed the safety catch, aimed, then yanked the trigger . . . crack! I sprang into view as a hasty scramble sounded inside the truck, but the officer didn't even pause. Taking advantage of rank, the swine! I'd capture him instead. 'Stop! Put yer 'ands up!'

'What the devil – don't aim that bloody thing at me!' he exclaimed, violently.

'Sorry, sir. You're dead, sir.'

'What?'

'I just shot yer, sir. You're wearin' a tin 'at.'

He indicated a pair of white armbands. 'Can't you see I'm an umpire?'

'A boy, sir,' muttered the driver. 'Ain't been in the Army long.'

'Then what the hell's he doing with a rifle? And *you* get this vehicle away from the road and under cover or I'll put you out of action.' He stalked away.

The driver, thinking of his reception if he missed breakfast rendezvous, obeyed with alacrity before leaping out. 'Gimme that bleedin' thing. When yer git one o' yer own you'll find out what a bloody mess blank makes in a barrel.'

*   *   *

Autumn, with underfoot conditions indescribable, but one day we struck the leaky tents, vacated the queerly-patterned field, and invaded the little town to be ensconced in empty houses, one being filled by the boys. All leave was privileged, and not a 'right', but I received the usual seven days after three months' service. With a week's pay and ration allowance, plus cap at rakish angle, I clumped along our terrace hoping to impress old pals. I saw only one, who waited until I'd passed before yelling: 'Good job we've got a bleedin' Navy!'

'Blind ole Riley!' mother greeted me. 'You're taller than your father.'

'D'they call yer "Sticks"?' asked Esther.

'No – Titch,' I answered, sticking an envelope in the window. Jean knocked later, and we went for a walk and entered a cafe. She'd left the shop, and was now 'on munitions'. Standoffish, she insisted on paying her share and exhibited more cash than I could earn in a year. As we left, she suggested a cinema on Saturday afternoon, and I replied that I'd hoped to watch West Ham. 'We can go to the pictures any night, but I ain't seen the team this season.'

'I'm not standing in the cold for over two hours.'

Glancing at her expression, I gave in, but she remained prickly. 'Jean, have you met anyone else?'

'Of course not. Have you?'

'Only girl I spoke to was a kid pickin' blackberries. She did a bunk.'

'That awful slang. That's the Army. You were silly to join.'

'Maybe.' I began to steam, but when she also included my father I demanded to be told what she meant.

'My father says he was a fool to go with so many younger men —'

I lost my temper. 'Tell *your* old man,' I broke in furiously, 'if it wasn't for fools like mine, 'e'd be workin' for a German —'

She was already on her way, fast, with people staring, and we never met again. Football before girls in future!

End of leave. 'Jean seein' you off?' asked mother.

'She's already seen me off,' I muttered.

'Oh?' She didn't seem very surprised. 'We'll come then, for a blow.'

'Now look 'ere,' I adjured, 'if there's any chaps I know, don't call me "Jesse" or kiss me.'

Mother looked blank, and Esther bridled. 'An' why not?'

'They'll say it' a girl's name. I won't 'ear the last of it.'

Without comment, mother handed me a big parcel, plus an apple; I felt myself flush as I took them. At Liverpool Street, Fusiliers were openly embracing their nearest and dearest, so I gave both mine a hug. The train chuffed away, with Esther yelling: 'Ta-ta, Titch!' Gosh, it seemed only yesterday when dad went off to France in 1914. A band had been playing 'God Be With You 'til We Meet Again', amid loud cheering. And, in the Underground going home, Esther and I had sat close to mother as she cried quietly.

*   *   *

At last! An armistice, and the genteel Walton streets rang with song and dance. Routine relaxed, and 'duration' men had one thought – when do we go? I felt the same, for with the end of Lloyd George's 'war to end all wars' my chance of a V.C. had gone. Boys on our billet top floor bombarded passers-by with missiles, while Alan, myself and others tried to sleep through the racket. However, we woke fast enough when the Orderly Officer entered holding a revolver!

Evidently our Commanding Officer had had his fill of boy soldiers, for we were unexpectedly posted to another Fusiliers unit in Aldershot Command. The escorting lieutenant and sergeant managed to lose two of their charges in London; they turned up several days later, in arrest.

Frith Hill, Blackdown; we filled a large hut. Beds were long planks on trestles, and one could receive a painful nip on the backside when the palliasse grew thin. A middle-aged corporal lived inside an enclosed cubicle, and when he told me at reveille to bring his 'gunfire' from the cookhouse I felt suspicious. No leg-pull, for tea was obtainable if you were early enough. It was called gunfire, we heard, because a bloody-minded cook had once loaded it with laxative. Surprisingly, we got on well with our quiet corporal. If things grew too rowdy he would retire to his cubicle and stay in purdah, until the racket subsided.

Walton had been quiet, but this place was funereal. All around were pines. It was mostly 'fatigue' jobs for us, and when they ended for the day, idle hands got into mischief. One night two chaps raided a civilian-owned canteen and removed its stock of cigarettes. Another fellow, boasting that he could break glass noiselessly, demonstrated on the cook-house. There was a midnight feast, with the corporal snoring through it all. Before reveille the door crashed open to reveal the battalion police, Orderly Officer, cook sergeant, and the man who'd risen early to prepare breakfast. Not a crumb did they find.

No sign of demob, and we grew sick of the everlasting fatigues. Christmas neared, and it was normal to release every spare body, but there was a shock when leave for boys was cancelled – and who could blame the C.O. for this revenge? I was furious, having done little to deserve a ban – Alan was proving a good influence! The corporal, single, wasn't bothered, but we were, and also the handful of personnel left to administer our creature comforts, though they'd get New Year leave. Dad had also been unlucky in his unit's ballot – there were horses to look after – and as Aunt Lizzie had moved, mother and sister would have to console each other on Christmas Day. I 'borrowed' a stamp from the corporal . . . sorry, mum.

On the 25th, Frith Hill Hutments were deadly. Breakfast was served amid acrimonious exchanges with the solitary cook, who with unprintable sarcasm offered to bring dinner to the hut. During these pleasantries most of the Boxing Day sausages disappeared. We took back the corporal's breakfast, then some cooked sausages on the smelly stove while others gambled. Soon I was broke, and then another chap rose. 'That's me skint . . . skint on Christmas Day in a dump like this. For two pins I'd bugger off!'

Pregnant silence for a few seconds, then people began putting on puttees, including myself. Alan came over. 'I'm not being odd man out,' he said surprisingly.

With the corporal still abed, we departed. Somebody started the old Cockney classic, and the last line was yelled at the pinetops: 'We don't want yer Christmas pudden – stick it up yer arse!'

Thirty miles to London. It was cold and dry, but none were marching fit. Despite previous agreement, older chaps forged ahead, and after a time Alan and I were bringing up the rear

with no-one in sight. On we went, with no vehicles in either
direction. Eventually Alan paused at a junction; he lived at
Chertsey. 'This is where I turn off. Only six miles to go.'

'Lucky blighter!'

'Titch, you've hardly started. Come with me, and you'll be
made welcome.'

Sorely tempted, I replied: 'Sorry. No place like yer own 'ome
at Christmas.'

'Let's get it straight. Some said they'll never go back. How
about you?'

'Back tomorrer. If redcaps turned up my mother'd go scatty.'

'Right.' As we parted, he called back: 'Don't forget Staines.'

Not likely. Staines Bridge, notorious, was the only Thames
crossing for miles, and from the way I was feeling, a detour of
yards would be too much. Redcaps guarded the bridge day
and night, but . . . this was Christmas Day. Hours later, it
seemed, I stopped, waiting anxiously until a man appeared.
'Any redcaps on the bridge, mate?'

He laughed. 'Go on, your luck's in!'

Thankfully I clumped over into Middlesex. My home was in
Middlesex, on the far edge of the county. The Underground
was working – they might let me post the fare. A cyclist
wobbled into view, stopping when I spoke. ' 'Ow far to the
toob?'

'Hounslow – seven miles.'

Blimey! If my feet weren't on fire, I must have worn through
the skin and was scraping the bones. It was growing dusk
when I slowly overtook a woman with a pram, and she looked
up. 'Come a long way, haven't you?'

'Blackdown.'

'Good heavens – where are you going?'

'Bow.'

'The Underground's running. Got any money?'

I did not reply, and she took up her bag. 'Stop a minute.'

'No thanks,' I said resolutely, but she continued to offer a
sixpence. 'This will take you a good way.'

I swayed towards her, then away, then back again, all pride
evaporated. 'Thank you very much, missus. Give me your
address an' I'll —'

'Of course not, my husband's in the Army. Someone might
help *him*'

I renewed my thanks, and limped on, one weighty boot after
the other, collar upturned, hands in pockets; good job it was

nearly dark. Here was the station at long last. ' 'Ow much to Bow Road mate?'

'Ninepence.'

' 'Ow far for a tanner?'

'Mansion House.'

No clipper; perhaps there wouldn't be one at Bow. I eased tortured muscles on a cushioned seat in the waiting train, and later sat tight at Mansion House until someone yelled: 'All change.'

In rattled a Barking, again almost empty, and at Bow Road there stood the clipper. 'I didn't 'ave enough, mate,' I said. 'You can 'ave me name and —'

'Off yer go; 'appy Christmas!'

There was still a mile to walk, then, clumping down our basement steps, I heard the door flung open. 'Oh, we thought it was dad. It's only our Jesse, mum.'

'Sorry to disappoint yer,' I grunted.

'Blind ole Riley – French leave!' was my greeting.

'No. Changed their minds. We all got 'ome.'

'Where's yer pass?'

'Pass on Christmas Day? No-one to sign 'em.'

Mother remained suspicious until I revealed toes sticking through ventilated socks. 'Look at all the 'taters,' grinned Esther.

'One o' these days,' I warned her, 'I'll warm yer bum.'

'Enough o' that,' said mother, and treated a blister the size of a florin. 'Did yer walk all the way?' she asked rather unsteadily.

'Not all. Back tomorrer. Hey, any dinner left? I'm starvin'.'

No scurrilous rhymes about the pudding, and afterwards I slept until ten a.m. Then, after obtaining a 'loan' from mother, I was startled when she announced her intention to see me off. 'Eh? Sunday service on the Underground, Mum, an' I don't know what time my train goes.'

'Scared o' the redcaps,' chanted Esther.

'Will you shut up?' I shouted.

'That's enough,' said mother. 'We're comin'.'

Buying a ticket at Waterloo, I found that my train would leave in twenty minutes. Found, too, a redcap waiting, and in trepidation asked mother if she wished to go on the platform. Of course! With Esther gripping two platform tickets, I joined the queue and kept as close as possible to an overgrown Tommy in front. The redcap, seemingly uninterested, suddenly extended a hand . . . towards the big bloke. 'Pass?'

Sweating, I sidestepped and went through. 'I thought 'e'd got yer, Jesse,' giggled Esther, and I nearly said that if she didn't keep her trap shut, someone would get me – I could have throttled her.

'Dad's getting a medical board,' observed mother. 'When are you boys gettin' out?'

'Nobody knows.'

'Let's see yer face when the train goes this time,' remarked Esther. 'Last time there was a bloomin' great apple in front of it.'

In camp was Alan, and our luck was in, with no roll-call on Christmas night. The corporal, who could have pinched us, did well out of our parcels. The remainder straggled in over the next few days, to be confined to camp for a time. Who cared? Precious little attraction around Frith Hill Hutments!

                    *   *   *

Heavy snow. We boys dug various establishments out of drifts. One chap broke a leg tobogganing on a sheet of corrugated iron, and a fathead (guess who?) went through the ice on a pond. Bored to tears, we decided to make a second mass exodus, waiting for payday. Alan remained, having confessed to his parents on the first illegal visit. We were lucky indeed to get a lift on a big van going to Smithfield Market. Having written that I was expecting leave, no-one was surprised. ' 'Ow long 'ave yer got this time?' asked mother.

'Back Tuesday, mum.' (The redcaps usually turned up after five days!)

After the icy camp, the house was cosy, but I was uneasy. Mother seemed *distrait*, worried about my father's health, and to my relief didn't see me off. Gosh – *two* redcaps! A tank to a tintack I wouldn't escape twice. Instead of nonchalantly meeting their gaze I tried to slink past . . . 'Pass?'

'Ain't got one.'

'Where's your unit?'

'Blackdown.'

'You're out of bounds. Are you absent?'

'Yes, but I was on my way back —'

'Come with me,' one ordered.

The booking clerk, having seen it all before, refunded my fare with a grin, but I was feeling only thankfulness that mother wasn't a witness. An officer told that I was in arrest until an escort arrived. Into a truck with my captor, and soon we crossed the Thames and turned right. 'Not the Tower?' I joked.

'Right first time,' he grinned, 'you're highly honoured!' But I couldn't believe it until we went through the gate. I was put in a communal cell with others. One, a big negro, was obviously London born. From the general talk I gathered that some were held for offences far worse than absenteeism, and during the night two were removed by civil police.

Roused, I rose aching from the hard floor, but one young private lingered. The guard sergeant prodded him with his boot, and the negro spoke threateningly; 'Don't do that!'

'*What*?' demanded the astounded sergeant.

'Touch 'im, an' you'll 'ave an accident.' It was obviously meant, and the sergeant, after a long, disbelieving stare, left.

'Desertion, son?' asked a man in civvies.

'No. Absent. I was on me way back.'

'Lousy bastards! I'd been away six months. Got a job too. It'll be glasshouse* for me. Listen, if you push off again, get off somewhere down the line and finish by tube or bus. Reverse it goin' back. Redcaps are bloody uncanny.'

My escort arrived, a Warrant Officer and a private; they were doing me proud. I was shocked when the W.O. produced handcuffs. 'D'yer 'ave to use those, sir?'

'I wouldn't trust you boys an inch.' He fastened me to the private, then picked up my parcel. 'I'm not taking them off before we're in the train.'

'My dad might be on the station, sir,' I exclaimed in trepidation.

'Bit late to think of that now.' I never forgot the walk from the truck to the platform.

In the guardroom at Frith Hill, Alan arrived with my tea and blankets, and next morning it was: 'Escort and accused . . . shun! Cap orf! Quick march left-right-left-right-left-right HALT! Boy Shaw, sir.' I collected seven days C.B., plus loss of pay, but at about sevenpence per diem the State didn't benefit a lot financially. Two return tickets for the escort, a single for me, plus cost of a reserved compartment. Hooray for discipline and the tax-payer!

*   *   *

The remaining waifs and strays were back within a week, scoffing at my story of bed-and-breakfast in the Tower; the

---

* Military prison.

escort had to corroborate. We cleaned, dug, scrubbed, peeled spuds. Several, intent upon discharge, were continually insubordinate, but much was unreported because N.C.O.'s were reluctant to be thought incapable of controlling 'kids'. One chap obtained some live ammunition and was about to toss it into an incinerator if the sanitary man hadn't intervened. A much better use for that incinerator was baking purloined spuds. One night four militants were handcuffed in the guardroom but in the morning were found wearing wide grins but no bracelets; too large. The big grumble was that the war was over – why couldn't they go home?

An unexpectedly pleasant move for us – Shoreham-by-Sea. On top of that the Forces had a rise, with boys' pay up to ten bob weekly – riches indeed. At mother's suggestion I made her a small allowance to be put by for me. We could have enjoyed this congenial Sussex resort until demob, but when the inevitable fatigues started it was boredom again. A hated task was refilling trenches dug along the Adur banks – mud, clay, chalk. We'd be literally plastered. The sergeant in charge was once so exasperated with the behaviour that when asked what we should do with some left-over soil he said, seriously: 'Dig a hole and bury it.'

Browned off in more senses than one, we went for a stroll around instead of digging, to find that the C.O. was also browned off. He shocked us with a regulation that permitted the birching of naughty boy soldiers, and we had to bend over a table while the provost sergeant laid into us, but although it hurt both pride and backside it effected no lasting cure . . . and after Lukey and Broomy it was like being tickled.

Through stupidity, the sojourn by the sea lasted but six weeks before a new unit 'welcomed' us at Clipstone, Nottinghamshire, but this proved vastly different. It was our 1st Battalion, regulars who stood no nonsense. The C.O. at once distributed us among the companies. Soon after arrival there was an accident when a shot was fired and a chap's leg was amputated. On hospital fatigue that day I was told to bury a dog and to get the blanket fumigated afterwards. After digging the hole I shook out the blanket and saw the leg. The 'joke' sickened me.

Next day I lost Alan. Never robust, he was discharged on medical grounds, and I gave him a wedge of cake for the train from my parcel – my sixteenth birthday.

I became a permanent hut orderly, for many units were in this big, open camp. I got on well with most people, mainly because

I spat and polished for them and tickled the ivories in the evenings. I wrote letters for two illiterates and read them the replies, and became especially chummy with one lance-corporal, Joe, a regular. He was a renowned predator; at the moment it was a canteen girl.

My father was out. His health impaired, he was unable to do his former job. No pension and, like many others who'd helped to make it a 'land fit for heroes', he was out of work.

Some older men were now getting away, one after a celebration for becoming a grandad. Having now mastered Tommy Atkins's classics, profane and otherwise, I was accompanist. Two songs only were fit for Puritans – it seemed surprising that 'Sweet Adeline' and 'Nellie Dean' had escaped Army additive, for they were always bawled out after everyone had become well oiled. Others more than made up the deficiency:

'We haven't seen the Kaiser for a hell of a time –
Haven't seen the Kaiser for a hell of a time;
We went to France to see what he was doing,
The old Fusiliers will be his —— ruin.
We haven't seen the Kaiser for a hell of a time,
P'rhaps he's been blown up by a mine – LET'S HOPE SO!
Maybe he's the leader of a German band, but
He's no cousin of mine!*

Another canteen favourite (tune, regrettably, 'The Church's One Foundation):

We are Fred Karno's Army, a useless lot are we;
We cannot march, we cannot fight, what —— use are we?
And when we get to Berlin, the Kaiser he will say:
'Mein Gott! Mein Gott! What a —— fine lot
Are the boys of Company "A".'

*   *   *

Incredible. No boys in trouble since joining the new unit, and now a break in routine. Owing to unrest in the coal pits, the Battalion entrained at short notice. At Leeds, crowds of men greeted us with stony silence but no brickbats. We slept on the

---

* 'He's no cousin of mine' was a phrase used to denote that you detested somebody – always someone in authority!

hard floor of a drillhall, to which we were confined. This caused
frustration both inside and out, for no local girls had shown
hostility.

The cindered parade ground was utilised for soccer, and then,
after no disorder in town, companies were allowed out in turn,
although determined Casanovas had already been waiting for
dusk before climbing a five-foot wall. I didn't hanker for the
outside world, and Joe was curious. 'Why ain't yer goin' out,
Titch?'

'Well, I'd rather play football.'

'Come an' find a bird. Plenty of 'em.'

'No thanks. Only bird I ever found chucked me up.'

'Oh? Didn't like it when you tried yer 'and on, eh?'

'Didn't try anything on.'

'P'raps she wanted yer to.'

'No again. We 'ad a barney an' I insulted 'er old man.'

After a fortnight's fraternisation there was a 'short arm'
inspection (for venereal disease), and while the M.O. was
appraising our company's penises a charlady wandered in with
bucket and broom. Whoosh – the simultaneous dropping of
shirt fronts wouldn't have disgraced the Guards!

The last soccer ball burst on the abrasive surface and I had an
evening out, but with only one-and-fourpence couldn't patronise fleshpots. While looking in a shop window a second
reflection in the glass revealed a young girl. 'Hallo!' she remarked brightly.

'Hallo!' I responded. 'Er . . . nice evenin', ain't it?'

'Nice enough for a walk – have we to go?'

'Not arf!' I exclaimed with alacrity. She was a stunner, with
skin like milk and a golden pigtail. I made to step off but she
tugged my sleeve.

'Not that way, me dad lives up theer. Don't like soldiers.'

'I don't blame 'im.'

'Me mum's not too bad.'

'Good.' I was finding conversation difficult, for although her
accent was delicious she spoke at the top of her voice. Then she
put her arm through mine.

'By the heck, ain't thee tall? Is it cold up theer?'

At that I gave my customary weak grin. Then: 'Have we to go
on tram?'

Help! One and fourpence! ' 'Ow far? I mustn't be late back.'

'Not far. We can get t'moor for threepence each.'

We walked to the bus stop, with my number nine's a bass

accompaniment to her treble two's. I glanced surreptitiously at my companion. Suppose the other boys saw us. In particular, what would Joe do? Suddenly I realised that I'd strenuously resist attempts to dispossess me of this lovely little bit of crackling.

A tram – 'Killingbeck'. It held one long seat on each side, and the girl at once placed an arm around my waist; I had to sit bolt upright to avoid crushing it. Despite the noise, other passengers were taking interest in the prattling. 'Me dad works in pit. Would ya shoot him?'

'I couldn't —'

'Speak *oop*, lad, can't hear a word ya saying,' she shouted.

'No gun,' I half-yelled.

'You all had guns.'

'Not all. I'll get one when I'm eighteen.'

'Tha look eighteen.'

'Sixteen.'

'I'm nobbat sixteen and all.'

'An' never bin kissed!' I exclaimed involuntarily amid the grins.

'Huh? Who ya kidding?' Her name, everybody heard, was 'Jennifer'. Her friends called her 'Jen'. What was mine?

'Jesse. Me friends call me "Titch".'

'Titch! Ee, that's a good 'un!' She screwed sideways for a second. 'Royal Fusiliers. Tha talks like a Cockney.'

'I am.'

The tram squealed to a stop. 'Coom on, frame yersen. We're here.'

We got off to general hilarity that left the girl unmoved, and soon climbed over a padlocked gate; I had more than a fleeting glance at shapely legs. It was a lovely evening full of birdsong as we reached a hedge some fifty yards from the road. 'Sit theesen,' she invited, and we sat for some time talking while I stole fleeting looks at that beautiful face. 'Penny for ya thoughts, Jesse,' and, when I didn't reply, 'Has cat got thy tongue?'

I blurted: 'I'm thinkin' I'd like to kiss yer,' and went hot.

'Who's stopping thee?' she laughed, then pushed off my cap. I'd never imagined that a kiss could be so electrifying. We clung, until she pulled away and murmured so softly that I hardly heard it: 'Are we gonna do?'

My throat went dry and I couldn't reply, and at that very moment was saved by the bell – a tram bell. Every face on the

upper deck seemed to be turned our way. 'We must go,' I
muttered. 'If I'm late I'll get jankers.'

'Tha's nobbat saying that,' she pouted. 'Evening's young yet.
What's jankers?'

'I couldn't come out.'

'Ee, we can't have that.'

We sauntered across the field towards the gate, and there was
a yell: 'Oy! You two!' Above the hedge we'd left a man's head
appeared. 'Coom out of bluddy hayfield!' We increased our
pace, but he and his dog pushed through the hedge and caught
up with us. 'Couldn't tha go round t'field instead of through
middle? Neether on yer seen mowing grass afore?' Though
sounding wrathful, he took a long gander at Jenny's red garters
as I helped her over, then again exploded at me: 'Don't climb
ower fastening – use t'other end. Bluddy townies.' Then the
miserable cuss undid the lock to let out himself and the dog. By
this time I was steaming, but that animal looked as nasty as its
owner as both stood looking belligerently after us.

Jenny suddenly giggled. 'Old devil. He was watching us. Got
mad because we did nowt.'

'Fancy an ex-boy scout gettin' over the wrong end of a gate,' I
muttered to cover my confusion. 'What's "mowin'" grass,
anyway?'

'Never heered of it. Hope it rots.' As we alighted in town after
another verbose ride, Jenny saw a clock. 'Plenty of time. Let's go
on station. Gorra penny?'

'Eh? What for?'

'Don't be gormless, lad. I want to *go*.'

A metaphorical penny dropped and I fished out my remaining coins. 'Why didn't you go in the field?'

'What? With *you* theer?' Blimey, some of that female logic I'd
heard about.

At the drill hall we weren't the only pair standing close
together, and as Jenny plainly expected to be kissed again I
obliged. 'Jenny and Jesse – Jen and Jess,' she murmured. 'Ee, I
like that. Jess, tha's a reet slowcoach, aren't tha?'

'I thought I was doin' all right. Jenny, I think you're the
prettiest girl I've ever met.'

'And tha's a bit of all reet for a Cockney.'

Someone approached, glanced, hesitated, and walked on.
'He'll know thee next time,' observed the girl.

'Name's Joe. Pal o' mine. Now don't forget – Thursday at
five.'

'Can't ya climb owat wall tomorrow?'

'Easy, but not 'till after dark.'

She pouted: 'Me dad wants me in before then.'

Another rib-cracking hug, and we parted. As we expected, I was immediately confronted. 'You bloody dark 'orse. Where did yer pick that up?'

'*That*,' I answered ungallantly, 'picked *me* up.'

'What's that?' Instantly he began probing, and like a B.F. I let out a whit too much. ''Eh? She asked you to and you didn't?'

I nodded reluctantly. 'That's what it sounded like.'

'Well, of all the dumb clucks – I meantersay!' He kept at it until lights out. Next day I mooned about obsessed by the girl's kisses and the scent she'd worn. I *must* have been mistaken – something in the Yorkshire patois I'd not understood. Later, a blow when I tried to borrow two bob from Joe until payday; I fancied a couple of ninepennies in a cinema. 'Sorry, Titch. Bad news for yer. Back to Clipstone on Friday. You're on the advance party – Thursday night.'

'That's all right. I can still see Jenny.'

'No. The A.P. ain't allowed out on Thursday – jobs to do.'

I dashed to the notice board, and Joe was right. His voice sounded quietly from behind me: 'I'll look after 'er for yer.'

I wheeled on him. '*You* fixed this!'

'I did not. Honest. The C.S.M. does the detail.' As I looked towards the wall he warned: 'Don't, Titch.'

On Thursday I gave him a note. 'Give 'er this an' tell 'er to write.'

'D'yer realise what yer doin'?' he demanded, but I insisted. To my fury, the whole unit except the advance party was allowed out that evening, and I watched from the wrong side of the gate. Joe went straight to Jenny, who looked across and blew me a kiss. Off they went, while I spent frustrating hours on various tasks. But I was waiting when Joe walked in swiftly at the last moment, heading for the bed I'd prepared for him. 'All right, all *right*,' he grunted, removing his belt. 'See yer in a jiff. Somethin' to do that won't wait.'

'But I'm off in a minute. Will she write?'

'Didn't give 'er the note.'

'Well, you're a bloody fine pal,' I said hotly, and chaps stared at us.

Joe spoke softly: 'Lucky for you that I am, Titch. Listen, she's just a little pro. Asked me for money afterwards.' I felt as though I'd been slapped in the face as he whispered: 'She'd done it 'eaps of times – told me so. Forget 'er. The way she's going she'll soon be up the spout, and then, if she 'ad *your* name an' address . . . savvy?'

Oh yes. I 'savvied', but although the brutal words were common sense I felt nothing but scorching resentment for Joe, who turned towards the latrines. 'I'm off for a Dreadnought.'

Again I stopped him. '"Dreadnought"? Are yer sayin' now she's got V.D.?'

'Never chance it,' he muttered. 'Remember what yer told me yer dad said about girls givin' a receipt?'

'A baby, o' course.'

'No, yer silly sod . . . the pox. Look, there's the A.P. formin' up.' Away went Joe for his prophylactic, and fury was replaced by misery; the first girl for whom I'd fallen was a prostitute. I tried to sleep on the journey to the siding at Clipstone, but the wheels kept up a rhythmic 'Jenny . . . Jenny . . . Jenny', changing to a snarling 'Jennifer-Jennifer-Jennifer' as they rattled over points.

Joe never again mentioned Jenny, our only arguments being about football. 'West 'am?' he scoffed. 'I meantersay! Spurs'll flatten 'em!'

'Think so? Wait 'til old Syd. Puddefoot starts.'

'Puddefoot? The Lilywhites'll make 'im pick 'is putty feet up!' and so on ad nauseam, until drowned by exasperated profanity from the rest of the hut.

Demob continued slowly, with people bored stiff. There were brawls with other units in nearby Mansfield, and pickets patrolled with entrenching-tool handles for swatting militants. But this Battalion had certainly tamed our gang, and one boy actually earned a stripe!

Motivated by the growing number out of work, a controversial proposal was put – sign on for two extra years and receive £10, or £15 for three years. Boys too. 'What about it?' grinned Joe, who as a regular wasn't affected. 'There's a draft for Egypt soon. Didn't you want to travel?'

'Yes, but I must ask me old man.' His reply was prompt. The decision was mine, and if I remained I'd soon learn the difference between wartime and peacetime soldiering. 'What's 'e mean by that, Joe?' I asked, perplexed.

'You won't 'ave it so cushy. Knows a thing or two, does your dad.'

At an impromptu meeting of the boys, I hung back when the

rest unanimously opted for the lovely lolly. I'd lost much interest since the war ended. They all signed, and turned an empty hut into a gambling hell. Hours later, when the 'casino' closed, everyone but two were broke. The latter stowed away the cash, and for some obscure reason the others cursed *me*. Three years extra without a cent to show for them, but why take it out on me?

While Joe was on embarkation leave, West Ham were away to Barnsley in an evening match. No radio in those days, but in the early hours next morning my returning pal entered the hut and switched on the light. 'Hey, Titch, wake up an' push the pease-pudden out o' yer eyes.' With difficulty I focused on an early edition newspaper – Barnsley 7, West Ham United 0. Hell! It was a wonder I didn't suffer permanent ear damage!

Joe was glad to be going, because his 'bird' was trying to get 'serious'. 'It's a grand chance to get shot of 'er. She won't 'urt. Plenty more chaps around after I've gone. Y'know Titch, I've 'eard there's some lovely birds among the Gyppoes.'

'I can see some sheik stickin' 'is knife in yer ribs!' Although I still liked Joe, I felt spasms whenever remembering Jenny – that little femme fatale was slow in fading.

The night before the draft left there was a booze-up. I shouldn't have been at the 'wet' piano, but now the provosts kept well out of the way. Next day I went along to the siding. 'Cairo, 'ere I come!' grinned Joe, arm round his 'bird's' waist. 'Write an' let me know who takes my wench out when the canteen shuts tonight. Better still, Titch, take 'er out yerself. She'll teach yer a trick or two!'

'Oh Joe,' she giggled. 'Aren't you a one?'

'Pack it up, Joe,' I expostulated.

He got in when the whistle blew and doors slammed. The train jerked, and Joe yelled: 'Up the Spurs, an' a Soldier's Farewell to the lot of yer!'*

*   *   *

The depleted Battalion went on a route march, boys included, though we wore belts instead of full pack. I learned that my own company's favourite song was:

---

* Sorry that I can't explain exactly what that meant, but if you really want to know, ask any soldier who served in the First World War!

Have we got the wind up? No, not likely!
Never let that be said.
With bayonets we still stick 'em,
That's the stuff to give 'em,
Stick 'em where the Jerry sticks his bread – UP HIS
    DIRTBOX –
Do we love the Jerries? I should say so
When we get the word to go.
Now's the time to show yer pluck,
Over the top an' the best o' luck,
Have we got the wind up? NO!

An extraordinary one sounded from the company behind
ours. Tune, again regrettably, 'Holy, holy, holy':

Grousing, grousing, grousing, always bloody-well grousing,
Morning, noon, and evening, our grumbles rise to Thee.

My name was on the next demob list, and again I was abused
by the gang, none of whom had managed to get on the draft.
However, they finally shook hands, and Lance-Corporal Dobbs
promised to arrange a reunion. Where? Wormwood Scrubs?

I could retain my greatcoat or receive a pound in lieu. 'Bring it
home', mother wrote, 'I'll get it dyed and it will last years'.
Nearing London I went to the lavatory, returning to find that
the compartment had emptied except for a smart young civilian.
Blimey, my greatcoat! I looked wildly at the packed corridor,
then glared at the youth. Having now mastered the full Army
vocabulary, I let fly: 'If I 'ad me 'ands on the —— who pinched
my coat I'd strangle the ——!'

He blenched, then said: 'Oh, *demned* bed luck, old boy,' and
made for the corridor as the train stopped.

I was demobbed at the old huge Crystal Palace, and an officer
asked about my coat. At my tale of woe he looked as though he
were about to say: 'Tell me the old, old story!' Instead, to my
amazement, he gave me a brand new one, and not from the
grisly heap on the floor.

Later, I heaved a kitbag, greatcoat, and self through our front
door.

Mother said: 'Cup o' tea, Jesse?' and kissed me.
Esther said: 'No V.C., Jesse?' and kissed me.
Father said: 'Wotto, Jesse,' but didn't kiss me.
And Jesse said: 'No more blo . . . bloomin' Army for me!'

CHAPTER THREE

Cockney in the Welsh Guards

'Letter for you from Egypt,' Esther told me. 'I steamed off the stamp to take to school.'

Thank goodness it hadn't been opened, or the contents might have given mother a seizure; Joe was certainly whooping it up.

I'd been shocked by my father's appearance – he'd grown haggard. 'Look for a job before your leave's up,' he advised. 'There's still a war on.'

True. At the Exchange former comrades-in-arms were now enemies in the battle for work. A clerk told me peremptorily that I couldn't draw benefit while still on paid leave. 'I want a job, not benefit,' I said. Soon it was discovered that I should be at the juvenile department instead of the men's, and my dole dropped to nine bob. 'They ought to come 'ere an' see how a juvenile can eat!' said mother.

A year of purgatory, the exchange an obscene, soul-destroying canker. You signed, waited hopelessly for the clerk's headshake. At the Victory March, Lloyd George said: 'The clouds of war have now dispersed and are being followed by the rainbow of peace.' Blimey, he should have made that speech outside the Stratford Labour Exchange!

I started work, labouring to clear a building site. When the 'brickies' moved in, I moved out. I got another job, sitting on my hunkers in a nursery putting seeds into tiny holes dug with something called a 'dibber', and have hated gardening ever since. It lasted a week until someone returned from illness – I was merely a makeshift. Yet a third job, guiding a blind piano-tuner around and carrying his bag. I was sacked when he engaged a school-leaver at a dollar a week less. Five bob bought a lot in those days. Thoroughly sickened, I chanced to meet my uncle, Bob, a master builder but lacking capital to go big. "Ow's it goin', Jesse?'

'Rotten. Can't get anything permanent.'

'Yus. Proper barstard, ain't it. Tell yer what, I've got a contract to turn a big 'ouse into a shop near 'ome. It'll keep yer goin' for a few months. Pound a week an' yer dinners. Okeydoke?'

'Okeydoke.' Bob was a worker, and I certainly earned my quid. Soon we were augmented by an electrician, and I went on a message to Aunt Flo. A cousin was just leaving, carrying our dinners. 'Hot-Pot,' she announced.

'Good egg! Look 'ere,' added Sir Galahad, 'you don't 'ave to carry that lot. Give 'em 'ere an' take this note to yer mum.' Ten seconds later my rubber heel skidded and three huge helpings of hot-pot cascaded down stone steps, the crash almost louder than Aunt Flo's anguished wail from inside the house.

The job was completed, but I got home to hear mother singing, for the first time for ages; dad had found work. Unskilled, which must have jolted his pride, but permanent, that was what counted. Desperately I visited the printer, prepared to face a dozen bullying foremen, but didn't get past the reception.

An exciting advertisement – men needed for the Spanish Foreign Legion, with hundreds of pesetas offered as bait. With unemployed pals I walked to the Embassy, and an astonishing scene. Dozens were jammed by the entrance, and being admitted in small groups. We got mixed up with reporters, photographers, and police, but gained a word from one chap who emerged. 'You make your own way to Suthampton for a Spanish boat, and there's no cash before you board it.' Later a statement from the Ambassador – he now had sufficient men and was delighted. The police then cleared the street. Next day I showed dad the picture of a fellow up a lamp-post, peering into the Embassy windows. 'Think yerself damn' lucky!' I was told.

*   *   *

Everybody works but Jesse,
Who hangs around all day;
Football on the gravel,
Kicking his boots away.
Mother does some sewing,
So does sister Tess,
Everybody works in our house
But our young Jess.

Well taught by our expert mother, Esther left school and obtained work with a dressmaker. I got a part-time job that petered out, and once again had to state that my benefit had expired, which meant that I was now entirely dependent upon the other three for every bite I took, and I used to bite plenty. My shamefaced confession, as before, was received in silence. Next day I asked a man who'd been out of work longer than myself: 'What 'appened when yer dole ran out?'

'I've got a wife and three kids, Lofty. I went to the R.O.'

'R.O.?'

'Relieving Office.'

I went, and was interviewed by people who reminded me of the school committee, who in quick time established that the other members of my family were earning. 'Sorry, lad,' said the spokesman. 'We're handling public funds. Here's a voucher for five shillings-worth of grocery – many shops accept them.'

Mother went berserk. 'But I'm only tryin' to 'elp,' I howled in despair.

'Don't yer know these R.O. people go visitin'? They went to old Sarfiss the bachelor along the Terrace the other day an' wouldn't give 'im anything because 'e 'ad a pianner – told 'im to sell it first. Blind ole Riley, suppose one o' the neighbours saw yer goin' into that place for parish relief with the riff-raff?'

'They ain't riff-raff, an' I can take it to a shop where they don't know us —'

'Not on yer life!' She ripped it to bits, and I stomped out feeling riled, to glance back through the window; she was crying. And that very afternoon my father, cycling from work, saw me playing soccer on gravel – the grassed fields were reserved for organised matches.

He was ready for me when I came in. 'Football in the park, at our expense.'

'In the afternoon, dad. I'd been lookin' round as usual all mornin'. D'yer think I *like* bein' out o' work?'

'I'll give yer one more week to find somethin',' he promised grimly, and who could blame him?

* * *

Only one thing left now – from one R.O. to another, and in the window of the recruiting office I saw what I wanted. There he stood in all his splendour, with St James's Palace as background.

'I'd like to join the Army, sergeant. I've got previous service.'

He studied my certificate – character 'good' – who'd blundered? 'H'm. Royal Fusiliers. I suppose you'd like your former regiment?'

'Could I join the Guards?'

He looked pleased; would probably collect a bigger fee! 'You could, and for three years instead of seven. There are vacancies in the Welsh. Doesn't matter if you aren't a Welshman. At the moment they're at Chelsea.'

Not the Tower, thank goodness! 'All right, sergeant.'

'You've certainly got the height, but I'd better check the breadth!' He wielded a tape measure while I sucked in deeply and held on. 'Try again,' he urged, and I dragged in a terrific lungful of East End ozone before behaving like a punctured balloon. In vain; I couldn't manage the vital last inch. But that sergeant hadn't got his job for nothing. 'There's another way. If you give your age as seventeen, you'll pass.'

Tickled to death, I tried to sound naive. 'I don't mind, but is it an offence?'

'Technically, but there wouldn't be any trouble if it were discovered.'

Good, but we hadn't yet finished. 'You'll have to forget about your bit of boy's service, and as you'll be officially under age, you'll need parents' consent. I'll post them the form and you can bring it.'

Mother took the news calmly, but not father. 'You're barmy! You'll soon know the difference between wartime Infantry an' peacetime Guards.'

'I s'pose it'll be a little bit 'otter.'

'A *little* bit? Oh well, you'll learn. Up to you.'

'Er . . . no, not quite. I gave a false age.'

He gaped at mother. ''ear that? I'm buggered if this ain't where we came in!'

'No,' I said, 'I 'ad to give a *younger* age this time.'

'For Gawd's sake why?'

'Because in the Guards me chest ain't big enough for eighteen but all right for seventeen,' I blurted lamely, then got mad. 'Nothing for *you* to laugh at, young Esther.'

'Wants to stand outside Buckingham Palace,' she mocked.

'If you'd joined your old mob again there'd 'ave been none of this nonsense,' observed my father. 'I think you're daft. Anyway, get on with it.'

'One more thing. Officially I'll be under age. I need consent.'

'Eh? I'm not backing that lie!'

'Dad . . . you gave me a week. If this falls through it's out o' work permanent.'

He remained adamant when the declaration came next morning, and biked off to work. I put the form before mother, who hesitated. 'You're selfish,' said Esther, pulling on her coat.

'Exactly opposite,' I shouted angrily. 'I don't want to scrounge on you three for ever.'

'I didn't mean that. Mum might be prosecuted.'

That penetrated. 'See yer later, mum.' Soon a post office nib scrawled 'Jesse Hennessey Shaw' and 'Esther Charlotte Shaw' and I headed for Whitechapel.

'Quick work,' said the sergeant jovially after glancing at the forgeries, and made out a warrant for Caterham. I nipped home to tell mother, without disclosing my subterfuge, and at Charing Cross refrained from waving the warrant tauntingly at the redcap . . . we might meet again.

I was about to become a Guardsman, but somehow the eagerness I'd felt before had evaporated. I felt depressed, perhaps because it was February, and cold. At Caterham I slogged up a hill before stopping at a gate – had I come to one of His Majesty's prisons in error? I could see men in whitish suits and stocking caps who were being shrieked at by an invisible somebody who seemed in a fiendish temper, and suddenly felt a griping sensation at my bowels. As I dithered, a sentry watched me expressionlessly. Then I passed through the gate, muttering something I'd heard somewhere about 'abandoning all hope when ye enter here'.

Could I have seen into the future, I'd have about-turned and gone back down that hill a damned sight faster than I'd climbed it.

* * *

The barrack rooms couldn't hold all the recruits for five regiments, and the Welsh, being junior, were accommodated in huts called 'Tintown'. Quite a crowd at the medical exam, where I passed A.1. We drew ill-fitting khaki, and the convict-like garb I'd seen was canvas fatigue dress that became pastry-cook white after repeated scrubbing. We also drew a housewife* apiece. Some clowning started when we got swagger canes, but was stopped by a bark that shook us rigid. Thirty 'Taffs' struggled to

---

* Wallets containing needles and thread, etc.

a hut and grabbed beds. No time was wasted. We donned
canvas, plus stocking caps that had to be folded meticulously
into three layers, and for budding guardians of the Royal
Palaces we looked peculiar. We were chased outside to where
our squad sergeant was waiting, and his corporal aide de camp
got us into order. Carrying a sheet of paper, the sergeant began
interrogation, eventually reaching me. 'Name?'
    'Shaw, sarn't.'
    'Shaw. H'm. Seventeen. Were you issued with a razor?'
    'Yes sarn't.'
    '*Sergeant*, not sarn't. Don't have that bum fluff on your chin
after dinner.' As he left me I unthinkingly banged my heel to the
'stand at ease' position, and he glanced back. 'Served anywhere
before?'
    Startled, I answered: 'Yes, sergeant – South London Cadets.'
    'How long for?'
    'Er . . .'
    'Come on, how *long*?'
    'Two days, sergeant.'
    Guffaws from the squad which were stifled by one look. 'Why
did they chuck you out?'
    I blushed. 'They didn't, sergeant. My mother objected.'
    This time the hilarity was allowed for five seconds. 'All right,
all right. Now we'll forget about the Cadets.'
    We practised foot drill where we were, and at dinner there
was brown stew – the Guards' nosh was dismally similar to the
Infantry's. Then an M.O. lectured us about women and wine,
and someone mentioned the short rations. 'Trouble is,' he
replied, 'You fellows have been stuffing yourselves at home.
Here, you'll get what's necessary for health.' True, but not
much comfort to growing lads.
    After dinner, the sergeant had memorised every name.
'Shaw, bring that chin of yours here – double! Christ, what have
you been up to?'
    'First time I've shaved, sergeant. Cut-throat razor. Cold water
too.'
    'Listen, lad. I've shaved in cold water for the last twenty years.'
    'Liar!' I yelled, silently.
    'Pay attention, everyone,' he went on. 'Badly shaved means
"not shaved", and you'll lose your names.* Buy safety razors.'

---

* You 'lost your name' for minor offences, dealt with by an officer. Being dirty
meant an 'extra parade' in full equipment, and 'idleness' an hour's extra drill.

Next morning, on the parade ground, our squad formed up in the rear, and were soon in a melee. Sometimes our sergeant would be a hundred yards distant, and half of us would wheel left instead of right, to cause scrums when we ran into other squads. Skidding in those awful boots, we swung arms to shoulder level while keeping canes parallel to the ground, and roared out the drill timings. It sounded like the Tower of Babel with hundreds yelling. Backing up his sergeant, our corporal buzzed about like a wasp, and during rare 'stand easy' we were expected to remember everything we'd been told once only.

'Roberts – Regimental March?'

'"Rising of the Lark", sergeant.'

'Curtis – the Slow March?'

'"Men of Harlech", sergeant.'

'Shaw – Commandant of the Guards Depot?'

'Lieutenant-Colonel Leatham —'

'Initials, initials.'

'R . . . R —'

'You've forgotten, and he's in your own regiment! Lieutenant-Colonel R.E.K. Leatham, D.S.O., Welsh Guards, and never forget the D.S.O.' He glanced around. 'Jones – Colonel of the Welsh Guards?'

'Lieutenant-Colonel R.E.K. —'

'No . . . the Colonel. Anybody?'

'Prince o' Wales, sergeant,' called someone.

'I'll give you "Prince o' Wales"! His Royal Highness the Prince of Wales to you lot. Rhodes – Regimental Motto?'

'Cymru am Byth, sergeant.'

'And that means, squad, altogether . . . *now!*'

'WALES FOR EVER!' And away we go again until ready to drop. Mid-winter but we sweated; snowflakes fell unheeded. Curiously, after the initial insane desire to crash a fist into that snarling face, we developed wholesome respect. Much of the harshness was understandable considering the motley bunch they were trying to lick into shape. Both instructors were Welsh, but had no blue-eyed boys, for their fellow countrymen were cursed as luridly as the rest of us. The afternoon ended in shambles when we practised changing step in slow time, our efforts resembling those of learner drivers struggling with crash gears!

*   *   *

Dear Mother, the Guards are a bugger,
Sell the pig, and buy me out.

Dear Son, the pig's dead . . .
Soldier on.

Before leaving the parade ground, the sergeant spoke rather
hoarsely: 'You know by now this is no convalescent home, so if
any weakling feels that he can't stand the strain he can buy
himself out within three months for twenty pounds. Meanwhile
my job is turning you into Guardsmen, and by God I'll do that if
it kills me. I'll be down at the hut at five for shining parade. Take
'em away, corporal.' We poured into the hut, sweating, swearing, and talking big about twenty quid. The corporal grinned,
having heard it all before. We couldn't have raised that amount
between us.

In each hut was a trained soldier, specially selected from the
Battalion. Though technically of no higher rank than ourselves,
we stood at attention and added 'Trained Soldier' when speaking to him. If he ordered you out of the hut at the double you
didn't stroll out yawning, picking your nose or scratching your
backside – you doubled. However, it wasn't unknown for a
disciplinarian to unbend. An N.C.O. renowned as a 'proper
bastard' went around trying to borrow five bob on Derby Day,
and the trained soldier came in late one night and sat on my
bed. While I shared his fish and chips and beery breath he
regaled me with the evening's erotic romp with some 'old tart'.
Officers, too, could become human. In London, I saw a very
senior one slide downstairs on a tray, in front of the waiters too.
Needless to add it was 'Mess Night'.

'Shining Parade' was the evening anathema when everything
was cleaned, with those in charge hovering like vultures. Boots
were brown, and had to be blackened, boned, spat upon,
brushed, velveted and elbow-greased into mirror-like finish;
even the studs on the soles were polished. It took, literally,
months before roughness on buttons was smoothed, but the
horrid dusty 'Soldiers' Friend' had been superseded by liquid.
The T.S. saw to it that the hut wasn't neglected, and the floor
was scrubbed weekly on hands and knees – no slinging a bucket
of water down and sweeping it through the door. Dismissal
time from shining parade was variable, but with roll-call at 9.30
p.m. very few went out of barracks.

Our squad was mixed – Welsh, Provincials and Londoners – and all but two had been unemployed. One worked in a gents' outfitters and on asking about a Christmas Box had been presented with a pair of braces, retailing at a shilling, so the Army gained a recruit. No doubt about the other chap's job, for when all in the hut was peaceful he'd suddenly yell, all in one breath: 'Star-News-Standard-Globe-Pall Mall-Westminster Gazette-three-thirty winner-every football 'arftime.' In those days London had six evening newspapers, each with several editions and extras on Saturday.

There was a shindy in the hut one night when two Lancashire lads argued about a girl and decided to clog-fight with Army boots. We waited hopefully, having heard of these vicious affairs with the genitals primary targets. Then they shook hands and told us that the 'little cow' wasn't worth it.

Thank goodness I hadn't revealed former service, for the solitary fellow who had was soon informed that whatever 'heap' he'd been in before, he was now in THE Brigade – the Brigade of Guards, and Guardsmen never retreated – they merely withdrew for a time before retaking a position. The *crème de la crème* of that Brigade were the Welsh, whose proud boast it was that in the great retreat from Mons not a single man had fallen out. 'But, sergeant,' I said alertly, 'you said just now that Guardsmen never retreated.'

I held my breath as he came slowly towards me with head thrust forward like a tortoise: 'Are . . . you . . . trying-to-be-funny?'

'No, sergeant, 'course not.'

'For your information, Mons is where the whole British Army retreated. Watch it, or you'll be getting bags of spudhole.'

At the hut I asked: 'What's "bags of spudhole", Trained Soldier?'

'Lots of Glasshouse!' he grinned.

*   *   *

Former terms I'd known were verboten here. Tunics were service dress jackets; Guards tunics were scarlet, for public duties. Sentries wore bearskins, not busbies. Guardsmen used rifles, not guns. The Commanding Officer was now the 'C.O.', and orderly officers and sergeants were now Picket Officers and Sergeants in Waiting. You collected Jankers at Company Memoranda instead of Company Orders, and the Parade

Ground was a Square; the canteen was the wet part where
sorrows were drowned – peculiar people known as abstainers
were relegated to the coffee bar. Scrubbing out a hut was
'interior economy', if you please.

A staff kit inspection left us goggle-eyed as the T.S. laid out
his gear. In addition to all the stuff we possessed there were two
scarlet tunics, two pairs of blue trousers with red stripes, two
grey greatcoats and cape, a huge bearskin with brass curb-chain
and a plume, plus a full set of white buff equipment. Also,
something we coveted, a blue forage cap with leek badge. These
were some of the glittering appendages awaiting those of us
who survived the Depot.

March 1st. Reveille for the Taffs sounded half an hour later
than usual, and there seemed a Sabbatical atmosphere when we
awoke – St David's Day. We put artificial leeks in our caps and
ate real ones at dinner, and as hated shining parade was off I
decided to venture out for the first time. Snapping a waist-belt
around the ill-fitting jacket, I appraised myself in the full-length
mirror. Pirouetting, I held a dignified pose and invited the hut's
verdict. I got it in one voice, and Trained Soldier, entering at
that moment, agreed that a 'bag of shit tied round the middle'
wasn't far out.

Passing inspection at the gate, I eventually found a 'Soldier's
Home'.* A notice by a piano read: 'The key to this instrument is
available for those who can PLAY'. It was handed over by a nice
old lady trying to look pleased, but when I returned it and was
invited to call again it made my day.

Several chaps were weeded out, and the squad was improving, though neither instructor had yet been seen to smile. In the
gym one day I slipped against a hot stove, and in hospital heard
from mother – how about a visit home? I got a chap to write that
they'd have to come to *me*. Another letter from Joe was
unusually subdued. He was in some horrible neutral zone
because of a barney between the Greeks and Turks – he was an
'observer'. Nothing but sand and sand, and none of 'the other'.
He wasn't surprised by my joining the Guards because he'd
always known I was daft.

Mother and sister came on Sunday, bringing father's good
wishes. 'What 'ave yer been up to?'

'Fell on a blood— bloomin' stove, mum.'

---

* They were run by civilians who gave their time and services voluntarily, and
these 'homes' were boons to chaps who didn't patronise pubs.

'Wish you wouldn't swear – dad didn't 'til he joined up.'

'All right, mum. When I'm with you I'll be a soldier and a gentleman!'

'Can't yer get a weekend?'

'I'm waitin' for London and fitted uniform. They give us stuff like sacks to discourage us from goin' out before trainin' ends.'

'Better than the Fusiliers,' grinned Esther. 'I'm dyin' to see yer outside Buckingham Palace in yer warpaint!'

'Shut up, Tess. They don't know about the Fusiliers.'

Leaving hospital, I was given weekend leave, and at home broke rules by putting on civvies – sorry, 'plain clothes', and went with dad to Stamford Bridge to see the last Cup Final before Wembley opened.

*　　*　　*

At the halt, on the left, form platoon,
At the halt, on the left, form platoon;
If the odd numbers don't mark time two paces –
How the hell can the rest form platoon?
(Tune – Three cheers for the Red, White, and Blue)

Rejuvenated by my rejoining, the squad passed out at foot drill – now for the rifle. Whatever my other shortcomings, I was determined to shoot straight. Depot rifles were for drill only, with firing pins removed. I lapped up musketry instruction and practised in the hut, ignoring insults and missiles. We soon learned why Guards were slicker than Infantry at arms drill. Take the order to slope arms, for instance. Infantry command: 'Slope . . . arms!' Guards equivalent: 'Slo-o-o-o-o-o-pe . . . HIPE!' The longer pause between the cautionary and the horribly screeched executive exploded taut muscles that little extra, making you smite the weapon with a force that bruised hands.

We sweated into summer, and on the final passing-out parade, nobody would have recognised the fellows who'd shambled into line for the medical inspection. 'Dicky' Leatham, D.S.O., congratulated us before we slo-o-o-o-o-oped hipes and marched away to Tintown. Our two instructors weren't smiling, they were actually laughing, on parade, mind you. We were told the reason – the first Welsh squad to pass out 'with credit' since the war. All the bullying and sarcasm was forgot-

ten, and we bought our erstwhile tormentors the unofficial but
customary parting gifts . . . and now for London!

*   *   *

Not yet. The Battalion was firing the annual musketry course at
Pirbright Camp, not far from Blackdown! Our sergeant handed
us over, then departed for the Mess, doubtless to drink to the
departure of another 'shower'. First to interrogate us was the
Adjutant, together with that magnificent giant, R.S.M.
Stevenson, whose voice could rip through you from a hundred
yards. Questions were asked of each of us in turn, including:
'Do you play Rugby?'
    'I play soccer, sir,' I answered hopefully, and the Adjutant
passed on, poker-faced, probably thinking me daft to have
joined a Welsh regiment. Before dismissal, however, he did
have a word with me. 'You . . . Shaw, isn't it? When I order
"stand easy", don't remain stiff.' From that moment my nickname was 'Stiffy'.
    The regimental tailor now buzzed around with a
tape-measure, preparing us for regalia needed at Chelsea. He
also attended to our service dress – and what a difference fitted
uniform made to our morale.
    The squad was abandoned, with myself put in the tallest
Company, the Prince of Wales's, known affectionately to the
rest of the unit as 'Piss and Wind' and with discipline tougher
even than the Depot. I was the solitary recruit in my platoon,
commanded by a Lieutenant Jefferson. He was something of a
martinet, though quite young, a combination disliked by certain
rank and file. Personally I found him scrupulously fair.
    Having listened to yarns from our Trained Soldier, I wasn't
very surprised at being informed that a 'Shit and Shankers'
court would be convened after tea, and that attendance was
obligatory. N.C.O.'s left the hut as I took my place with the
platoon, seated on the floor in a circle, facing inwards. President
and Chairman, the two oldest soldiers, sat on kitbags. 'Court in
session,' announced the President, and began to question
everybody in turn. Mine were all loaded – I hadn't a hope.
'What is the weight of a pull-through?'*
    I guessed: 'Four ounces.'

_____

* Used when cleaning a rifle barrel.

'Left shitty flipper to the front,' snapped the President, 'address me always as "Sir".'

Gingerly I proffered my left palm, to receive a sharp slap from a belt. 'Tell me again.'

'Four ounces, sir.'

'Wrong. The weight is the piece of brass at the end. Pay a forfeit by removing your left boot.' I did so. 'Now, what is a blank file?'

Ah! I knew what that was, but it was a devil of a job to explain. Finally I said that it was a kind of vacuum in the ranks. 'A good attempt,' conceded the President, 'but actually a blank file is an empty space occupied by a man not on parade. Remove your right boot.' And so on and so on, until I was reduced to just a shirt and beginning to quake. Came the final query: 'If you were up to your neck in cowshit and the enemy lobbed a grenade, would you duck?'

'Yessir!' I blurted despairingly.

'Wrong!' barked the President. 'Guardsmen never duck – remove your shirt.'

Slowly I dragged it over my head. What now? I wasn't kept waiting. 'Double out of that door, round the hut, and in again.'

Eh? The nearby road through the camp was open to the public, and how about the flints? As I hesitated, people began to look stern. 'May I ask a question, sir?'

'What is it?'

'Can I wear boots, sir?'

A vote was taken and the request granted, provided the laces weren't fastened – it would probably add to the fun! And I certainly found it awkward to trot to the door in unlaced Army boots, minus socks. Thank goodness, no civilians – just a couple of chaps who laughed like hell but didn't seem astonished. I tried to dash round, clutching my genitals, and in my haste tripped over the step when re-entering, shedding a boot, with the court losing some of its pseudo solemnity. 'Kneel,' ordered the President. Whack! That was on my buttocks. 'You are hereby accepted into the Noble Order of Shit and Shankers.' Everybody shook hands with me, and according to other members of the former squad I'd got off lightly. One who'd demurred was threatened with a 'severe flumbucking with the bristly end of a dry-scrubber'. Sounded unpleasant. I heard that if I'd answered in the negative to the query concerning 'ducking' I'd have been told that a Guardsman with a faceful of cowshit was better than a dead 'un.

* * *

Here I am at last, with the other recruits, ready to fire the Young
Soldiers' Course. Tingling with anticipation, I load a real rifle
with ball ammunition to 'group' five shots from a hundred
yards. Concentrating upon all that's been drummed into me I
focus the bullseye, hold my breath, get the tip-of-the-foresight-
in-line-with-and-in-the-centre-of-the-U-of-the-backsight . . .
BANG! I receive a blow on the shoulder from the recoil, the
sights jump crazily – surely that bullet must have gone yards
wide?

We finish our five rounds, the targets sink out of view, and
we advance in a wave while markers attend to our efforts.
Targets begin to reappear, together with signals – waving discs,
up-and-down discs, twirling discs, red flags indicating complete
washouts. I wait tensely. My own target appears and my heart
jumps as a white disc is plonked firmly against the bull. A four-
inch group – a 'possible', and the sergeant in charge looks
up from his sunken position. 'Bloody good shooting! You've a
spot-on rifle there, Shaw – look after it.'

You bet I will! Back I go happily to fire 'application' (in my
own time), 'rapid' (against the clock) and later, when the
statistics are exhibited, a red pin is against my name as top
scorer.

In the coffee bar that evening I was served by a most attractive
girl, whose flawless features remained serene no matter how
busy the counter. Everyone called her 'Flo', and I commented
about her to an older man. 'She won't go out with anyone,' he
informed me, 'though some have tried hard enough!' When the
crush ceased I spoke with her. She hailed from Worthing, but
when I said I'd been stationed in nearby Shoreham in 1919 she
seemed surprised – I was still in my rookie's cap.

*   *   *

Chelsea. The old-fashioned barrack rooms held solid iron beds,
behind which was stacked our multitudinous gear. Scarlet
tunics had 32 brass buttons, and white equipment had to be
blancoed, rifles highly polished and bayonets burnished. The
rolling of a cape and folding of a greatcoat needed a table and
several helpers, while bearskins were carefully groomed and
blue trousers slightly dampened before being slept upon – the
crease could cut your throat. Losses of this public clothing
incurred heavy pay deductions.

No wonder it wasn't unknown for a Guardsman to faint on parade, for with all buttons and hooks fastened it was like being garrotted. At first, the hardest job was standing for long periods without moving a muscle – I wouldn't recommend anyone suffering from chorea to join the Guards!

The barracks were shared with the Scots Guards, and people living nearby must have cursed the bugle calls that blared frequently between 6 a.m. and 10.15 p.m. Work began with a pre-breakfast parade where we showed various items in good order, and on Saturdays the square nearly disappeared under a dust-cloud when we shook blankets. At fortnightly intervals we exhibited scrubbed canvas and short hair, and on Sundays had to prove that we'd not only changed our undies but washed our feet; they were certainly concerned for our welfare. At weekends, provided we'd been good boys with no punishment parades to attend, we were allowed out at midday, but it was quite a shock to find that certain N.C.O.'s weren't above taking a bribe. Not all, of course, but we were soon told about those it was safe to 'tap'. In fact, it was possible to dodge an 'extra parade' for a tanner or a 'drill' for a bob, and the very first time I made my disgruntled exit from 'Memoranda' I was asked, sotto voce, whether I'd like to 'pay it off now or on the 3.30'.

We rookies weren't put on public duty at once, but had plenty of practice – three times a day. At last the great moment came when I saw I'd be on 'Buck' next day. Saturday, so I couldn't go to West Ham – business before pleasure. I sent a postcard home, knowing it would be delivered the same evening, and for one old penny. Ah! Those were the days!

* * *

There's pride and pomp on every hand,
And all because of a word of command,
Behold! Behold! The Changing of the Guard!

After I'd been helped to dress and clumped down the stairs like an over-trimmed Christmas tree, things didn't go smoothly at first. Given the order to 'size', tallest on the right, shortest on the left, the usual mild confusion took place as chaps sorted themselves out. To my indignation one an inch shorter than myself slid in on my right, so I instantly stepped back and pushed in on *his*. 'Piss off, Stiffy!' he hissed.

'Piss off yerself!' I hissed back.

'Stop that talking!' shouted a drill-sergeant, darting over to stand in front of us. Glancing up, he tapped my arm with his pace-stick. 'Move down one – your bearskin's against you.' Apparently some were more elongated than others, and I gave ground, seething.

The Adjutant's inspection was more like a search, but I passed. Several 'lost their names', and one, adjudged to be in general 'bad order', had his rifle snatched away and was put in the nick. This meant that a body was detached from a group of three held in reserve for such replacements.

The Colour appeared, and everybody within sight froze. Scots Guards too. Boom-boom-boom-boom-boom! We were off, and to the blood-stirring strains of: 'Have you ever caught your bollocks in a rat-trap?' we headed for Victoria.

With rifle and fixed bayonet at the slope, tunic, folded greatcoat and rolled cape fastened to full equipment, it was a tidy trek to the Palace. Soon the Central London Recruiting Depot Guard peeled off for Whitehall, and then the Magazine Guard for Hyde Park. But, with brass alternating with drums and fifes, the King's Guard didn't swerve an inch. At the Palace I rolled both eyes at ninety degrees without turning my head – quite an achievement – and there they were. Grins showed that I'd been spotted beneath my bearskin, Esther saying afterwards that my retroussé conk had been the clue.

Inside the forecourt we approached the Old Guard in slow time. A ticklish moment, for our Major in charge had been known to give a command on the wrong foot, and did so now. Instead of thumping to a halt and remaining rigid, our impeccable ranks faltered to a stop. From our accompanying drill-sergeant came an agonised: 'Jesus wept!' and well might He be weeping if looking down upon those lines resembling broken red and blue teeth before they shuffled into position at the order to 'right dress'.

Those chosen as first sentries were taken away, together with the two oldest soldiers whose job was to check the guard room inventory, including, we'd been solemnly assured at the Depot, floral piss-pots for the officers. Now a lengthy hiatus before the band finished playing a selection from 'Carmen' and both Guards paid each other compliments. The Scots Guards slow-marched away, leaving the Welsh in possession. Soon I heard the fading music change to the skirl of bagpipes, and, whether you love or hate them, they're grand aids to marching. I'd been surprised at the non-militancy of our own Regimental

March, 'Rising of the Lark', but the Slow March, 'Men of Harlech', was hostile enough!

Inside the guardroom were unsightly sepia photos of Royalty, the only people to whom sentries 'presented' arms. All others, no matter how big the bug, got a butt salute only. I'd been warned not to miss Princess Mary, who would complain, with jankers the result. True or not, when I presented to her in the Gardens some time later, she gave me a very sweet smile. All agreed that the most popular member of the Royal Family was the Prince of Wales, who 'didn't care tuppence if you recognised him or not'.

Today the King was in residence, so double sentries were on the pavement, but when I arrived in the afternoon the family had departed. My partner, Guardsman Baverstock, as senior, had to signal by banging his rifle butt on the stones – once to patrol, twice to salute, and thrice to present. Almost at once I was galvanised by three heavy slams, and in unison we walloped a magnificent present to a bowler-hatted chappie who entered the gate. The bowler was raised by the smiling owner, but I felt puzzled. Foreign Royalty? Definitely not one of ours. "Oo was that, soldier?' demanded a woman sightseer, as I came down and stood at ease.

I shouldn't have spoken, but did automatically: 'I dunno.'

'Huh! Some sentry!' remarked her charming female companion. 'You saluted 'im, didn't yer?'

'First time 'ere, missus. Ask me mate, 'e's in charge,' and back in the guard-room I tackled him, 'who *was* that bloke?'

'No idea, but I always present to bowler hats.'

I was flabbergasted. 'Eh?'

'Listen, Stiffy. No skin off your nose if you recognise a "nobody", but if you miss a "somebody" you'll cop out, so be on the safe side, and for Christ's sake don't talk to the public!'

I subsequently found that the man who'd smilingly acknowledged our compliment was a minor official from the Office of Works. My next bash was in the evening with the double posts split, and Baverstock in the Gardens. Oh, it was lovely, banging my heels and patrolling and looking for bowlers. Now and then I'd study my orders, for 'Visiting Rounds' – subaltern, sergeant, and two men – would be coming along, and my answers to the sub's queries might gain me a 'credit'. Three credits in a calendar month meant a long weekend leave – worthwhile. There were many orders. Extent of patrol. Be smart and soldierly, but quiet at night. I was in charge of all Government property in view from my post. Fancy, Buck and St James's Palaces, Wellington Barracks, Big Ben and other distant odds and sods were my personal responsibility. Finally, the order board told me, with no punctuation, that 'The coachman of any Royal carriage in which His Majesty or any other Royal personage is seated is instructed to raise his whip to his head as a signal for the sentry to pay the customary salute and sentries will be careful to look out for these signals and act accordingly'. Phew! What a bloody mouthful!

I was on top of the world that Saturday evening, until a crowd of teenagers approached. Hurriedly I replaced the board and waited, immobile as a Tussaud waxwork as their leader, with a shock of ginger hair, planted himself in front of me. 'What did I tell yer?' he demanded of the others, "e's stuffed!'

'No 'e ain't,' said another, 'I can see 'im breavin'.' Several passers-by paused and a woman giggled, but I stared straight ahead. Shockhead tried again, this time admiringly: 'Blimey, ain't 'e long? I wonder if that bay'nit's sharp?'

Something snapped. 'You'll find out if I jab it up yer bottle-and-glass!'

Shockhead looked startled, but only for a second. "Oo's gonna 'elp yer?'

Fuming, I stopped the discussion, but as I started patrolling there was a concerted chorus of: 'Left, right, left, right!' I could have cut loose with my rifle butt. Then from the gate came a policeman, and I'd never been so pleased to see a copper. Away went those insufferable kids into the Green Park.

Unknown to me, Visiting Rounds were behind as I regained the box, still steaming. The sergeant handed the order board to the lieutenant, who eyed the fleeing youngsters. 'What's been going on?'

'Those boys were bein' a nuisance, sir.'

'You're new, aren't you?'

'First time on guard, sir.'

'You'll have to ignore such things. Now let me hear your orders.' Still on edge, I did all right until the last, then said something about the coachman raising the carriage to his head. The escort must have thought it funny, but it failed to win a credit.

On again at two a.m., and I thought it very romantic under the huge gaslights, until it began to rain heavily and I entered the box. No pedestrians, just an occasional taxi swishing past. 'Visiting Rounds' didn't stop, my quiet: 'All's well' being acknowledged with a perfunctory nod. Big Ben boomed the quarters, with every interval growing longer – the novelty had worn off!

Rain was still pouring when we dismounted. No band, and the sacred colour was encased, our scarlet hidden by greatcoats, and rifles, minus bayonets, underarm. Water dripped on the floor as we peeled off and, bogeyed, set about renovating the soggy buff. I readjusted the wicker basket inside the offending bearskin until it canted over one eye. No good. I was stuck with the thing.

*   *   *

Guardmounting took place at St James's Palace when the King was not in residence in Buck, which became secondary. I liked St James's with its quiet posts – few people knew that a right-of-way ran through its precincts. I was sentry on York House, the Prince of Wales's residence, in the small hours when a car whizzed in, and the Prince was out and indoors while I was coming to. A few minutes later he took two small dogs into St James's Street, cheerily acknowledging me – small wonder the rank and file adored him. The Queen Mother, Alexandra, living in the adjacent Clarence House, also had a warm smile. She would watch the Guardmounting from her garden wall, and a memorial fountain stands at the spot.

A favourite Guard was the Bank of England Picket, which lasted from late evening until early morning! Guardsmen received a shilling, the sergeant half-a-crown, and the unlucky officer's guinea reward went to charity. A tiny canteen opened for an hour, so our straight-from-the-mint bobs were soon handed back. The Bank was several miles from Chelsea, a long slog in guard order after a night out, but some officers sported thirty Underground fares to Sloane Square. We knew the definite woulds and would nots, but the possibles kept us guessing. The picket would approach Mansion House station wondering 'will-he-won't-he?' Sighs of ecstasy greeted an order to wheel left, but if we kept straight on – unmistakable groans!

Besides public and barrack guards, another chore was 'Inlying Picket', ensuring available personnel for fire-fighting or emergency. On one occasion the whole lot were despatched to arrest *me*. We'll come to that later!

We 'foreigners' fitted in quite amicably with our Welsh confrères, and I made many friends from the Principality. From the small fry viewpoint, our officers were in three groups. The largest spoke loudly and authoritatively, yet were scrupulously fair. The next were as rigid regarding discipline, but softly-spoken, appearing to award punishments with regret. Lastly, a tiny minority had not a word of praise for anything or anybody, and were inevitably referred to as bastards. I once saw one of the best men in the Company come up from the square after twice losing his name. 'I could castrate the bastard!' he hissed, and a corporal, who should have pinched him for such a remark, immediately offered to assist, and without an anaesthetic.

Apart from Quartermasters, always from the lower ranks, there were no 'rankers' among the officers. The social gulf between them and us, be it a humble boy bugler or an exalted Warrant Officer Class I, was wider than the Atlantic.

*   *   *

October, when Guards units usually changed stations, but we were given an unexpected second tour at Chelsea. Most welcome – we'd expected Aldershot. Several distractions helped to relieve rigorous discipline and winter monotony. Naturally there was a choir, with non-Welsh welcome if they hadn't voices of bull-frog range. That choir was magnificent – broadcasting, cutting records, and competing in the National Eisteddfod. In sport, of course, the rugby fifteen were our pride and joy, some playing for London Welsh. My hero was Lieutenant Greenacre, a three-quarter – to see him sprinting for the line was breathtaking. When the team played the Welch Regiment in the Army Cup final the whole Battalion entrained for Aldershot. We won, and there was a riot of waving caps and sticks – decorum for once took a back seat. The soccer eleven were overshadowed, despite my help!

West Ham, unbelievably, reached the first Wembley cup final the same year – the unfashionable little East End club would play mighty Bolton Wanderers of the First Division. Joe, now back in England, challenged me to a five-bob bet. My father, who had been unwell, said that he would go, and, if God, duties, fatigues and punishment parades permitted me, so would I . . . and they did.

After a squash on the Underground we reached the magnificent stadium to find that the gates had just been closed. Hordes were still arriving behind us, not believing that this much-vaunted place was full. 'No good, Jesse,' said father. 'Let's go back.' But we couldn't, for the crush was now so great that it was impossible even to turn. The brass buttons of my jacket were digging into my chest, so also into the back of the man in front of me. I glanced in concern at the now frail figure of my parent, for it was becoming really dangerous. Then suddenly everything gave way and we swept forward, struggling to remain upright, helpless from the rear pressure. The mob bull-dozed through a gap, with police and attendants reeling. I saw my father being swept aside and deposited in a corner oasis – by heck he was lucky!

The crowd stumbled forward and downward, over a barricade, then fanned out on to the pitch like water from the bottom of a dam; it was utter chaos. Two Guards bands were playing, ignoring the invaders, who formed gigantic rings around them. I glanced down at my boots, noting that the mirror-like finish I'd put on the toecaps had gone for ever.

During the uproar the King arrived and asked who was responsible. Blimey, a few thousand frustrated fans could have told him. One band managed the National Anthem, and the police pushed us back to the touchlines. The teams filtered past backslapping supporters and the game began. There was encroaching – tracks had to be cleared for corner kicks to be taken, and Bolton won. The official attendance was just over 120,000 but I reckon another 20,000 didn't pay.

My father had left before the finish. 'Where did you end up?' he asked, when I got home.

'On the pitch. What about you?'

'Found a seat an' the owner didn't turn up.'

'It ain't right,' reproved mother, 'you both ought to send the money.'

'You 'ope mum,' I laughed, 'well, next time West 'Am go to Wembley they'll win.'

'*You* 'ope!' grinned Esther, but they did, 41 long years later. Anyway, they had consolation in promotion, and were now in the First Division with Spurs. And that was the first, and last, non-ticket Final at Wembley.

*   *   *

A military chest seems to suit the ladies best
There's something about a soldier that is fine.

Having kept clear of jankers, I was now permitted to stay out until midnight and wear light boots when off duty. If awarded C.B. the privileges were withdrawn for a period, and they were miserable men indeed in London who had to stand by their beds at 9.30 p.m.

An important order – we would now walk out in red tunics instead of service dress but, thank goodness, without bearskins! The new regulation was greeted with mixed feelings, but by the fair sex with (literally) open arms. On the day of the change- over, R.S.M. Stevenson augmented the gate inspection to ensure that the regiment wasn't let down, and waited to pounce. To his wrath, the first departures wore greatcoats, enabling them to have jackets beneath. This was official, so Stevo was baffled. Not for long. An expressive look, a twist of his moustache, plus caustic comments, showed the miscreants what he thought of them. Word reached the barrack rooms that Stevo was on the warpath, and tunics it became; I must have resembled an elongated pillar box. 'Thin red line!' shouted Esther when I entered, but other females weren't so derogatory, for the scarlet proved magnetic. Our stamping ground was Hyde Park's 'Monkey Parade', where now no-one else got a look in. Under the gleams from the gew gaslamps, every flash of red was accompanied by one of the fair sex, mostly domestic servants. In fact, they grew so plentiful that difficulty could arise when one changed her evening off, leaving you with a double assignment. You either told one you were on duty and met the other, or dodged both and found a third – exceedingly ungallant! We had much fun in Hyde Park, with not a lot of harm done . . . I hope!

My own pal, Jim Walton, was a syncopated music enthusiast, and we spent hours at the piano. He was also a bit of a misogynist. We'd find two girls in the Park and collar chairs, and very soon my girl and I would be kissing. Not Jim. He'd probably start saying disparaging things about his partner, and both girls would depart in high dudgeon. He had a happy knack of managing this just before the 'couple interrupter' arrived to collect the chairs fee. Curiously, Jim was an expert dancer, motivated by the music. If he hadn't decided to sit by the band during a 'ladies' choice', girls scrambled to claim him. The best laugh Jim gave me was after a compulsory cross-country run at Aldershot; he'd stuffed a pound note in a shoe for safety, and afterwards discovered only a shower of shredded quid.

*   *   *

Lucky chaps in certain 'employ' jobs were excused duties, and one man's department had its own rubber stamp. A leave pass enabled one to travel by rail at reduced fare. This fellow covered his department's name with paper – the date, and 'Welsh Guards' were sufficient. 'What about the officer's signature?' I asked blankly, when he explained the ruse one day.

'Oh, anything indecipherable will do. I sign 'em. It's the rubber stamp that matters.' I felt humble admiration. This genius would go far – probably as far as Dartmoor.

On one occasion only was I given an 'employ', after C.S.M. Trott asked me whether I'd ever done housework. On being answered in the negative he said that I had a good chance to learn by taking over 'sergeants mess cook' for a month! I was dazed, but no-one ever argued with Trotty. In Married Quarters, he would be unaffected, but how about the unsuspecting bachelors? I soon found that the mess caterer's misgivings equalled my own. 'What the hell do *you* know about cooking?'

'Sweet Fanny Adams, sergeant.'

'Then God help us!'

'Amen,' I muttered, as the grinning bona fide cook departed on furlough. Next day I was returned to duty. Oh well, my own father had once been put in the Cavalry when he'd never been on a horse!

* * *

We speak of the Vickers 303,
With mingled pride and blasphemy, etc., etc.

I eagerly awaited the next musketry season, and at Pirbright again admired the fair Flo. A few days later I 'casually' rested my arm on the counter, for on my sleeve were the crossed rifles of a 'marksman'; she made no comment. Back at Chelsea a dozen of us were summoned, and stood cooling our heels outside the Company Office. 'What's this for?' wondered Jim, 'been up to anything, Stiffy?'

'Nothing they should 'ave found out.'

The C.S.M. emerged, looking sourly at us; nothing unusual, he often had good reason. 'Headquarters Wing – Machine-gunners,' he announced. 'Hand in rifles and equipment and get over there.' The door banged.

'Thanks, Trotty,' grunted Jim, 'you might've kissed us good-

bye!' But I felt furious, having intended to win all kinds of pots
and medals at Bisley. Blast! Losing my spot-on rifle, I drew
another that fired low-left, having to be aimed at 'two o'clock' in
order to hit the bull – quite a handicap when firing 'rapid'. I was
so disgusted that, as the Gunners fired only a very modified rifle
course, I didn't bother to get it zeroed.

Nevertheless I was soon fascinated by the Vickers, a fiendish
weapon that we grew to both love and hate. The main handicap
was its weight, with a still heavier tripod, and another drawback
was carrying out gun drill by Chelsea Bridge Road, with ribald
spectators lining the railings. After instruction we fired the gun
on Salisbury Plain in conjunction with Artillery, who pumped
shells over our heads. I'd never imagined such targets – point,
lateral, area, traversing, oblique, width with no depth, depth
with no width, indirect. In rearguard actions we defended heroi-
cally before retreating – sorry, *withdrawing*, by slinging guns and
ourselves into those awful horse-drawn limbers and being jolted
across that baking, heat-hazy Plain . . . thank God for London.

Jim did well, and was made machine-gun storeman, excused
duties. I earned another sleeve badge and was promoted Number
One Gunner, and a much less coveted job. This meant carrying a
revolver instead of a rifle, and as I'd also passed out at lobbing
grenades was fully qualified to kill, though at the moment I'd no
desire to eliminate anybody, apart from one particular officer,
one of the 'bastards', but he was in another Company.

Later, the actual 'Trooping the Colour' ceremony on the King's
birthday was not so exciting as one of the rehearsals. The whole
Brigade were in full spate when a sudden rain shower descended
and capes were unrolled – what a sight as foreign bodies used as
packing came to light. Handkerchiefs, gloves, rag, sheets of
sandpaper appeared, and not all could be tucked away out of
sight. Horse Guards Parade resembled Hampstead Heath after
Bank Holiday when we departed. One chap marched to Chelsea
with a sock dangling.

Civilian Bible Punchers were allowed into barracks, and we
didn't mind because they took no collections. One evening a
Royal Army Temperance Association rep. entered my room,
containing only Guardsmen Rhodes, Tozer, Izzitt, and myself,
and only because we were on Picket. As usual, we were
invited to sign the Pledge and join the Assocation, the rep.
adding that the King himself was a patron. 'Don't try to kid us
that the King doesn't drink,' replied Izzitt, 'I know he does.'

'Moderate drinkers are welcome,' we were informed, but no-one was interested until we heard that meetings took place in the afternoon, once weekly.

'What's that?' said Izzitt instantly, 'in the firm's time? That's different!'

Next morning four leave passes were presented, but as it would mean missing afternoon parade we had to go before the Company Commander, Major 'Cushy' Lewis. To our C.S.M.'s fury, Cushy was delighted, but then we were dim enough to appear by the Square while the parade was forming up. 'Come here . . . double!' roared Stevo. 'Where are you lot going?' Spokesman Izzitt explained. 'Oh, so you've joined the Association, have you?' Stevo's tones were deadly quiet. If this turned into an epidemic the whole damn' Battalion would be dodging practice drill. We made a bee-line for the gate, and Stevo another for the Adjutant. Oh, it was lovely, drinking tea and scoffing pastries handed round by genial ladies while the other chaps sweated on the square, but it proved a one-day stand only. It was discovered that meetings also took place in the evening . . . farewell, R.A.T.A.

Autumn. We kissed the girls goodbye, knowing that those who hadn't managed to acquire engagement rings would soon dry their tears and be back on Monkey Parade with a 'Bill Brown' (Grenadier), or 'Coaly' (Coldstream), or a Jock or Mick, any of whom could guarantee adequate consolation. Not so easy for us, now. Aldershot meant drab service dress, and the teeming thousands of other troops a challenge. Finding an unattached girl here and then getting your feet under her parents' table deserved membership of the Magic Circle, though there seemed no lack of the gentle sex. Lots of it turned up on Church Parades, but none of it ever ogled *me*!

In London, two guards and a picket weekly was routine, but duties here were negligible. Though the barracks had no walls, they had been no obstacle at Chelsea; did Stevo never suspect that the most scaleable stretch was quite near to his own Married Quarter?

With Lieutenant Greenacre in the gunners, I decided in a weak moment to try Rugby in a scratch affair. Battalion fans were in two distinct groups – those who didn't care how points were obtained, and a few who cared a lot; the latter worshipped the try, but abhorred the dropped goal.

My skipper, Sergeant Pates, made me a three-quarter, saying I seemed 'built for speed'. Good, Greenacre was a three-quarter. Once or twice I had the ball for a split second before being slammed violently to earth, and in the second half was moved to full-back, and there was this beefy bloke bearing down on me. A chance to shine, and I crouched. He tapped the ball over my head and tried to run around me, but I wasn't going to be fooled by a trick like that – down he came with a smack. As laughter sounded, I was startled by a left hook that whistled past my ear, and the whistle blew – serve the dirty sod right if he were being sent off. But I was the one at fault, having tackled someone not in possession. Later on, I had the ball not far from the enemy line, and with the goal tempting me I attempted a 'drop' that skidded wide. Instantly there was an outraged shout from the touchline: 'Stop that dropping at goal!' Hell, it was my idol himself, and after that I left the playing of Rugby to the native Welsh!

At one international match at Twickenham, our own Guardsman Rees was playing for Wales. Sensation as a Welsh Guardsman appeared on the pitch, climbed a post and hung a leek on the cross-bar. It was a gunner, Davies, and although the exploit was in the evening papers his only punishment was being evicted by the police.

Soon afterwards the Battalion was stunned when Rees bought himself out and departed for Oldham as a professional – a bitter blow.

*   *   *

November. I was guarding a road junction, and nothing approached until a horse clopped along, carrying a female. 'Whoa boy!' she cried, then eyed me expectantly. 'Move this pole, please.' Her imperious tone was cultured, obviously accustomed to giving orders.

I shook my head. 'Sorry, missus. Road's closed.'

'Don't be ridiculous. I ride through to Rushmoor every day.'

'Side road's closed for twenty-four hours. Belongs to the War Department.'

'What's that to do with it?' she demanded impatiently.

'They close it one day yearly to retain legal possession. Only military personnel may use it.'

'I see. You're a Welsh Guardsman, aren't you?'

I agreed, but couldn't see any relevance, and no civilian was going to boss *me*. Like Horatius of old, I'd defend to the last. Suddenly her face dimpled into a smile. 'Well, could I claim to be military? My husband's a Brigadier.'

I raised the pole. Until then I'd imagined the wives of high-ranking officers to be crab apples. That night, on the same post, when not hoof, boot, or wheel had come along the road since I'd arrived, I walked along to the next barricade, manned by 'Taffy' Tozer. "Ow's it goin', mate?'

'Bloody freezing, boy. Isn't this daft?' We talked until two figures approached, then hesitated in the gloom. They were female, certainly not a chance to be missed, a conversation ending with invitations to their home. They were sisters, war widows, living with their parents. This proved a table under which my feet became firmly planted, but Taffy's friendship was shortlived. Surprising, for his 'widow' was much younger than mine. Anyway it was his palaver.

Christmas Eve. I was on Garrison Magazine Guard, dismounting next morning in falling snow, and later the long walk to Widow Maud's home was worth while, her people having made me welcome.

*   *   *

On my twenty-first birthday, with three other unfortunates, I was on cookhouse fatigue . . . what a way to celebrate one's majority! Peeling spuds for 600 with blunt table knives, and washing 1200 plates in lukewarm, soapless water. That evening, at Maud's house, I was toasted in soft drinks, and we all sat round a table wearing headphones – a new-fangled wireless set had been installed. One hardly dared to breath for fear of disturbing the 'cat's whisker' on its crystal. The outside aerial, fifty feet long, was fixed to a high pole.

Around this period I was happy, free from trouble, and getting along so cosily with the widow that people commented, probably envying my feet under the table. Jim was particularly pungent, but for another reason – he was missing our evenings at the piano. 'Old enough to be yer mother.'

'Cheese it, Jim!'

'Got a kid at school, ain't she?'

"E's twelve. That doesn't make 'er ancient.'

'Not far off it. You're goin' to be 'ooked, Stiffy.'

'I could do worse.'

'You want yer brains tested,' etc., etc.

*   *   *

That season at Pirbright I avoided Flo, or someone would have
called out:

'How's the merry widow, Stiffy? Watch him, Flo!'

On a training scheme my gun was mounted by an orchard.
'Look at that lot,' exclaimed Dusty Rhodes, indicating enticing
fruit.

'That's all we can do!' grunted Taffy, as a woman came from
the farmhouse and watched. That night three Guardsmen crept
out for a spot of scrumping, not bargaining on Sergeant 'Tubby'
Hake returning from the Mess late. In the vernacular, we
'dropped a bollock', and at reveille were marched to the drill-
sergeant in waiting, Freestone, nicknamed 'Windy' but universally liked. 'These three,' Tubby told him, 'were absent from
their hut after lights out.'

Two days before, other chaps had been charged with the
same offence, and stated that they had been with girls, but
within bounds, and were awarded extra drills only. 'Where
were you?' queried Windy, and waited expectantly.

'Out of camp, sir,' answered Dusty promptly, echoed by Taffy
and myself.

Windy tried again, his voice almost pleading: '*Right* out?' To
no avail, for three George Washingtons insisted upon the truth.
Tubby stood listening, doubtless wondering how three such
idiots could exist, and Windy's verdict was obviously regretted:
'Close arrest.'

Detention, or anything over seven days C.B., stayed on
conduct sheets for all time, but lesser awards were erased after a
period. The C.O., Dicky Leatham, now returned from the
Depot, grew annoyed because we wouldn't say why we'd been
out. How could we tell him about a kitbag full of apples in our
hut? Three clean sheets were soiled – detention instead of drills.
'Who said honesty was the best policy?' grunted Dusty. Anyway, we paid it off in camp instead of the Glasshouse, enabling
us to fire our courses, but directly shooting ended we were
doubled back into the nick and stayed incommunicado until
next day. On Saturday we scrubbed out the Sergeants Mess.
Carrying buckets, we were taken along by the police corporal,
who ordered 'Double' and 'Mark Time' alternately. To my
horror, Flo appeared, en route for the coffee bar – she'd been
told about me. 'Mark time!' bawled the corporal, thirty yards
behind, but I couldn't – not in front of *her*. Nipping round the
corner of a hut I waited, trading grapes before the angry copper

arrived, crashing into me. 'What the hell are you supposed to be doing?'

'Didn't you say "right wheel", corporal?' I panted.

'How long has "mark time" sounded like "right wheel"?' he demanded, but after an accusing glare, let it ride.

After it was over, we found the apples untouched, for they were sour. We had gained nothing from the stupid escapade, but had lost much. Spudhole also removed privileges for a time. At Aldershot, I had a tiff with Maud after church parade, then borrowed a bike, aiming to reach London and return by 9.30 p.m. Arriving home dead tired, I felt incapable of riding back that evening and said I had a pass. My father looked sceptical, but made no comment. "Ow are yer goin' along these days?' asked mother. Naturally I hadn't mentioned the spudhole, and at the moment was about to become an absentee.

'Fine,' I answered.

'That's good. Come 'ome for Christmas Day. Our silver wedding.'

I felt horrible. 'Er . . . I dunno, mum. We'll be at Windsor. Lots of Guards and things. Tell yer what,' I joked, 'you write to our old man.'

'What old man?'

'The C.O. – Commanding Officer.'

'Eh? You mean that bloke who mucked things up at Buckingham Palace?'

'No, not 'im.'

'Gertcha! *You* tell yer old man we only get one silver wedding.'

Less than 24 hours' absence brought a Company entry only and I left early, but halfway back a damned pedal broke and I arrived after midnight. Regimental entry. It didn't rain without pouring, for Maud turned up, prepared to kiss and make up. I was told to inform her that janker wallahs weren't allowed visitors. 'Meet me on the side road,' I whispered, and she did, seconds before the suspecting police corporal appeared. Five more days, consecutive. I was doing very well!

One loathsome jankers chore at Aldershot was the emptying of piss tubs. These large, attractive objets d'art were placed on landings overnight and removed at reveille. It was the devil of a job to avoid spillage on the stairs, especially on the Saturday morning after the paynight before.

The Vickers platoon competed for the Smith Dorrien Cup, open to the whole Command. We won it, and as Number One I did my share. Soon after that we changed station. Maud and I agreed to correspond, but I didn't expect to see her again.

*   *   *

Victoria Barracks, Windsor, was unique. Long corridors, one-man cubicles and, amazingly, running hot water! Jim and I got together again. The coffee bar was now N.A.A.F.I. (Navy, Army and Air Force Institute) instead of N.A.C.B. (Navy and Army Canteen Board – or to us Never any Cakes or Buns or yet again – Notice. All Crumpet Buckshee). Very quickly an alternative to N.A.A.F.I. was invented. Sorry, unprintable!

Windsor livened up considerably when His Majesty resided in the Castle for a month, with our band up from town. They hated it, for Guards bandsmen live out of barracks in London. In Windsor I once found myself standing by Queen Mary in a shop, but her private detective protected her.

Jim and I and the usual gang were at the piano one evening, howling out some chorus, when the guardroom picket shoved through and brought the racket to a stop. 'Stiffy, your widder's at the gate.'

Bellows of mirth from the tables and indignation from the vocalists: 'What a nerve!'

'Bloody cheek!'

'Tell 'er to piss off back to Aldershot, Stiffy!'

I rose. One had to obey these summonses. Males could be invited into the canteen, and females to the coffee bar or library. Naturally I chose the last-named. 'You haven't written for weeks,' she remonstrated.

'Sorry, Maud. It's a lot busier than Aldershot.'

'Can you come out?'

'Yes. Riverside? Pictures? What time does yer train leave?'

'It doesn't.'

'Eh?'

'I've somewhere to take *you*.' She'd actually rented a bed-sitter, but any funny ideas I might have had were quashed when I met the owners. The husband was a retired bo'sun, and his wife a real battleaxe who said I was welcome, so long as I didn't stray above the ground floor.

Jim was disgusted. 'Weddin' bells next?'

'On twenty-five bob a week? The C.O.'d never give permission.'

'I can see you *'aving* to get married.'

'Stand by, then, mate, for best man!'

Almost at once Maud entered hospital – quinsy. Curiously, I was also under medical attention with a badly cut hand, and not allowed out, but the thought of Maud without a visitor was too much. Bad hand or not, the wall was no harder to climb than Chelsea. Next morning I was sent for, wondering dejectedly who'd spotted me. Said 'Cushy' Lewis: 'Shaw, the Commanding Officer has passed this letter to me. It's from your mother.' Oh blimey, my jest had been taken seriously. What now? 'You've been doing better lately,' went on Cushy, 'keep out of trouble and I'll see you aren't on duty at Christmas.'

'Thank you, sir.' I was marched out, dazed. Sentiment in the Guards? I'd be as good as gold! Writing home, I said I'd bring a lady friend, but was surprised to learn that the lady was very unwilling. 'No!'

'Yes!'

'They'll say I'm too old for you.'

'Let 'em. Anyway, I've told 'em you're comin'.'

Well, the family and all the clan seemed friendly enough, but when I took Maud to Waterloo next morning – she was spending Boxing Day at Aldershot – she was silent until the train was about to move, then said: 'They thought I was too old.' Imagination, I told her, but she shook her head resolutely. 'I could tell.'

Outside the station I met a former Taff who was in the police. It gave me an idea, for my colour service was nearing its end. He was doubtful. 'I guess you'd pass all except the medical.'

'Nothing wrong with me,' I asserted.

'You can be as fit as a fart, Stiffy, but you must have weight. Go and see the doctor who passed me.'

At home, those who hadn't yet departed took pains to show me that Maud was persona non grata, although they liked her. The age differential was too great. Annoyed, I had a bang at the piano, and the neighbours must have groaned. Next day I obtained an interview with the doctor, but it was time wasted. 'I shouldn't pursue it,' he advised, and went on conversationally: 'You know – your legs are out of proportion. Too long. Ever tried high-jumping, or hurdles? I'm afraid we need coppers, not jockeys!' And after all these pleasantries, and without even a testicle test, he charged me five bob.

Back at Windsor, Jim at once confronted me. 'Well, 'ow'd it go?'

'Jim,' I implored, 'lay off Maud, if yer don't mind!' He
grinned, and I changed the subject. 'Tried to join the "Met".'
'Oh? What 'appened?' he asked curiously, and I was daft
enough to tell. For the next few days, whenever we met, he'd go
through the motions of whipping and bawl: 'come on, Steve!'*
Jim had already extended service, but after those two regimental
entries it was by no means certain I'd be allowed to do so, but
my application was granted. 'You're lucky,' observed Jim. 'I
reckon old Cushy was rememberin' the Smith Dorrien Cup.'
Maybe, but anyway, I was in for a further four years . . . or so I
thought!

*   *   *

I was now playing in goal for the Battalion second eleven, and
during an away match the dressing-room was burgled and we
were all left skint. This put me into the clutches of a couple of
the Battalion leeches who loaned cash at fifty per cent a week
interest; heaven help you if you didn't extricate yourself quickly.
I was helping Maud with her expenses and it was some time
before I was again solvent. Only one of these sharks was caught,
when a C.S.M. pounced on a payday. The 'accounts' book bore
dozens of names, including some N.C.O.'s

We were friendly with Eton College, and boats were at our
disposal. Once I nearly took Maud over the weir, struggling
clear just in time. In the Battalion regatta I came second in the
single sculls. I should have been third, but the chap in front of
me hit a moored craft and took a header. Only swimmers were
allowed to compete.

Great excitement when Cardiff City reached Wembley, playing Arsenal. We crowded round the radios. Lewis, the Arsenal
goalkeeper, was Welsh, but received scant sympathy from his
fellow-countrymen when accidently helping the ball into his
own net, and a yell of delight went up from the barrack rooms as
the F.A. Cup left England for the first time.

The next momentous event shook not only myself, but all my
pals. Vickers sergeant Dai Roberts took me in front of Cushy
Lewis, who told me that as I'd stayed on the straight and narrow
for some time, he considered that a little extra responsibility
might cement the reformation. 'I agree,' remarked Dai as I
emerged, rather dazed.

---

* Steve Donoghue, champion jockey in those days.

Before the shock wore off I sought Jim. 'I'm gettin' tapes.'
'What? Get off! I'll believe that when they're on yer arm!'
The last time I'd been marched before Dicky Leatham hadn't
been pleasant, and Stevo's expression was sardonic. Dicky
remained poker-faced. 'You've been recommended for promotion,' he informed me, adding sonorously, 'you will always
remember that you were a non-commissioned officer in the
Brigade of Guards.' I was marched out, now an acting lance-
corporal, unpaid, and, as the grinning gunners soon told me,
unwanted. Nevertheless, the tailor sewed on my stripes – two
instead of the Infantry's one. In the guards the difference
between a full corporal and a lance-jack was an extra brass strip
on the cap of the former.

I bounced into the store, and Jim regarded my exhibits sourly.
'I'll give yer three months before you're busted, and anyway,
I'm employed, so yer can't stick *me* on a sentry-box!' Just then
the C.S.M. entered, and Jim, still speaking to me, had to spring
to attention, even if I were unpaid and unwanted. I further
annoyed him by grimacing from behind the C.S.M.'s back, then
my ego was deflated as the latter told me I'd no right in the
stores unless on business. Jim himself had declined promotion
some time before, preferring the independence of his job.
Unfortunately, our fun at the piano now had to cease, for I had
to patronise the 'rat pit', or Corporals Room.

I also sported a bayonet and 'frog'* when walking out, and
soon the weapon was displayed to the family. 'Good toothpick,'
was Esther's verdict.

Lance-jacks had to practise drill orders on the square, facing
one another a hundred yards apart. Until one learned to yell
'from the chest' it felt as though your thrapple were being torn
out. Eventually I reached the quota who were paid for the stripe
(the mortality rate among lance-jacks was horrendous). One and
ninepence a day extra.

*   *   *

A soldier's life is full of changes;
Today he's here, tomorrow there. (Welsh Guards Choir)

Whither from congenial Windsor? Wellington? The Tower? No,
Chelsea again. We were delighted, but not Maud, who detested

---

* Equipment holding the bayonet and suspended by the left buttock.

London. 'I'm going home for a while,' she said. 'People will be calling me a camp follower!'

Back to scarlet and blue for walking out, but the novelty had grown thin, and many chaps, against regulations, bought plain clothes to wear when on leave. One firm was advertising fifty-bob suits, and I started saving towards a double-breaster.

I now posted sentries instead of being posted, and to my glee, and Jim's disgust, his assertion that I'd never 'stick him on' was wrong. During one difficult period the employ were pressed into service – once only, unfortunately. All kinds of sacrosanct hidey-holes were flushed out. Some, like orderly room staff and officers' servants, hadn't worn 'Christmas Tree Order' for years, and the indignant Jim found himself with me on St James's.

Later the beloved Queen Mother Alexandra died, and we lined the funeral route, the silence enhanced by muffled drums. Snowflakes were falling, and with rifles reversed and bowed heads we peered below our bearskins at the poignant figure of King George, under the avid stare of thousands, a lonely figure trudging behind his departing mother.

A happier event at Cardiff, where the Prince of Wales presented us with new colours. My first visit to Wales, but with no chance to see its grandeur, though the march to Llandaff Cathedral was unforgettable – all the populace had turned out. The local paper carried a banner headline – CROESO i'r TYWY-SOG – and with no Welshman in our compartment an argument began on the return trip. Sergeant Roberts came ambling along the corridor, ensuring that his gunners were behaving, and took one look: 'Welcome to the Prince.'

Train trips were always enlivened by choir members singing, and Londoners joined in renderings (various) of 'Mae Hen wlad fy Nhadau' and 'Sospan Fach',* although there were occasional Cockney classics such as 'Any Old Iron' and 'You won't find many pimples on a pound o' pickled pork'.

*   *   *

I met Mary Jones, whose sister Kathleen was friendly with Corporal Sandford, one of our employ. Both were in domestic service, and a piano was available when the owners were away. Letters between Maud and myself had ceased, and I accepted Sandy's invitation to go along. Mary was a petite brunette, a

---

* 'Land of my Fathers' and 'Little Saucepan'.

typical Welsh lass with a soft voice and ready smile – in one word, sweet. I showed her a little of London, and she asked whether I'd seen Wales. 'Only a trip to Cardiff. On parade all the time.'

'I've mentioned you. How about a weekend?'

'Won't your folks look sideways at a foreigner?'

'You'd be welcomed. By the way, our home isn't posh.'

'Ours isn't, either. Wonder if I could scrounge a *long* weekend?'

But privileges, girl friends, and all other off-duty delights were suddenly blown sky-high when we were all confined to barracks. Industrial unrest had erupted and the General Strike was on. Unemployed, workers, and militants of all creeds were itching for confrontation.

We'd never imagined anything so frustrating as this incarceration. All kinds of odds and sods from other units invaded the barracks, with bedding put down anywhere. Our post office telephone had a permanent queue, and the 'Naffy' was run off its feet and then out of supplies. Gambling started in odd corners, and one horrible Infantryman produced a Crown and Anchor board, attracting innocents like moths to a flame. Before his confounded dice had been shaken a dozen times, my double-breaster had gone west, blast him!

After two days the gunners were detailed to obtain meat for hospitals from a cold storage. Wear lots of clothing, we were told, and all wriggled into two shirts, two pairs of socks and a woollen cardigan, making sure by adding greatcoats, of all things. When the maintenance men at the plant saw what we were wearing they laughed like hell.

Now a task that was vastly different – a party were to escort lorries to obtain food from the docks for distribution among shops. Major 'Bobby' Auld, in charge, gave terse advice. 'Don't invite trouble. When we move, you'll be responsible for your own vehicle, so pray that it doesn't break down. This job could be tricky.' Each of us was given a paper, signed by Prime Minister Baldwin, promising that the Government would support any action taken to safeguard the supplies. Lorries, high and closed-in, were in Hyde Park, and the drivers were holding a noisy meeting with, apparently, everyone talking and no-one listening. 'If you're the gaffer, guv'ner,' said one, 'we ain't leavin' without an escort on each lorry.'

'That's why we're here,' replied Bobby patiently.

We were detailed, and I got into a cab, but when Dusty Rhodes climbed into the back he found a number of students, and these were now harangued by the driver: 'Listen, you blokes. Don't move that tarpaulin, and not a cheep out o' yer 'til we're through the dock gates, or you'll all be bleedin'-well slaughtered; me too. They would pick *my* truck,' he muttered to me. With difficulty I got the rifle between my knees, for the bayonet was fixed. He glanced at it. 'Got one up the spout, corp?'

'Yes,' I answered untruthfully, for ammunition was in pouches, but his query made me realise that I was no longer playing at soldiers. Guards discipline being what it was, each of us would comply with any order given by Bobby. But, if we broke down and were attacked, could I bring myself to shoot or bayonet a fellow-countryman? True, I had 'Honest Stan's' guarantee, but it was a frightening thought. God, don't let it happen!

We left via Marble Arch, the convoy moving so slowly that a cyclist was able to overtake each vehicle in turn, yelling: 'Don't shoot workers!' After the City, we now had to traverse the toughest East End streets, where I'd been born. Shouts, boos, plus missiles thrown by kids too young to know what it was all about. When nearing the dock gates we slowed to a crawl, and there were the police and the inevitable pickets. 'Strike-breaking bastards!' was the most complimentary thing I heard as they reluctantly gave way, and I hope never again to see such malevolent faces. The youngsters inside must be holding their breath, for had they been discovered the pickets would have wanted to tear them to pieces. Then we were through, and my grip on the rifle loosened. Dusty and the students emerged, half smothered. The escort weren't involved in loading, but hung about in that poignant world of lifeless ships, with not a wisp of smoke from any funnel. Departing, the East End crowds were even thicker, but again it was mostly verbal brickbats.

*   *   *

Unexpectedly the strike collapsed. Employers and employed licked their wounds, but we in the Army, at any rate, knew where the next meal was coming from, and our jobs were secure. And, soon afterwards, when the pay of newcomers was slashed and there was still no shortage of recruits, it spoke eloquently of conditions outside.

Celebrating freedom, the corporals held a dance. Mary and Kathleen were unavoidably late, but as they tripped across the floor to Sandy and me, every male eye watched them – a prettier sight couldn't have been seen. My first dance, and my dainty partner's tootsies suffered, but she was most encouraging, saying that I might be a 'natural'. 'A natural what?' scoffed Jim next day, but kindly made marks on the floor. 'Let yer hoofs land on those,' he said, 'practise with a kitbag.' I'd long before passed his 'life' span of three months, and managed the long weekend.

Mary was again delayed, but knew a train that would allow us to catch the last bus to Cross Keys, where her family lived. She was mistaken, for we by-passed the Severn Tunnel and arrived in Newport around two a.m. It would have to be the *first* bus. I was looking around for a cup of tea when a chap approached. 'Taxi?'

'They'll have been abed for hours,' murmured Mary, then asked: 'Will you take us to Pont y Mister?'

He nodded, and we got in. 'Why Pontymister?' I asked.

'It's halfway. My married sister. They're both sports and won't mind.'

I wasn't so sure. Arriving, our jehu demanded a fare that made me blink; double after midnight. Mary knocked softly, then louder, and an upstairs window opened. Mary's brother-in-law was indeed a sport, continuing to smile after being directed into a cold bed alongside me.

'What are they thinking at home, I wonder?' said Mary, on the bus.

'I could give a bloody good guess!' I thought, remembering who were waiting – dad, mum, another sister, plus three brothers I hoped weren't the type who hit first and asked questions afterwards. At the house, I saw two chaps of my own age looking through the window, and very courteously allowed Mary to take the lead. She had no need to knock, for the door opened and a female typhoon whirled out, and as it whirled it talked. With some difficulty Mary managed to convince her mother that she hadn't spent a dirty night, and was clasped to the bosom. We entered, and everyone proved friendly on hearing the explanation. This was indeed an unfortunate household, for father and sons were all unemployed miners, and typical of the area. Yet there was banter, laughter and song. I was made to feel very welcome, although I did hear someone ask Mary what the hell a Cockney was doing in the Welsh Guards.

Later, Mary and I climbed a hill rising almost sheer from the backyards, and sat listening to muted voices and barking dogs. Familiar and nostalgic, zinc baths hung on the walls of tiny terraced houses below. A woman scolded a child – it sounded just like my own mother. 'I told you it wasn't much to look at,' remarked Mary quietly.

'On the contrary, it's well worth looking at. We've only got a railway.'

The two house floors were connected by a staircase-cum-ladder, and the upper rooms partitioned with curtains. I shared with two brothers and slept at once; Mary and I had had about three hours since six a.m. the previous morning. I never took her to my own home. After Maud, I didn't feel much like it.

*   *   *

Another musketry season, and I wondered whether Flo would mention apples as she saw me through the ratpit's serving hatch. 'Hallo, Stiffy. I see we've to congratulate you.'

'Same to you. I 'ear they've made you chargehand.'

At that moment, of course, Jim's phiz appeared at the main counter behind her.

'Er . . . what about a serenade?' he drawled, and I felt myself go red.

'Why not?' smiled Flo. 'Play my mother's favourite – "Love's Old Sweet Song".'

I saw Jim grin broadly, but buttonholed him later. 'Say, did you 'ear Flo tell me that she'd never 'eard "Just a Song at Twilight" played better?'

'She said,' corrected Jim, 'that she'd never 'eard that *piano* played better. 'That piano,' he added crushingly, 'was put in the ratpit only yesterday. I was on the advance party – remember?'

'She didn't mean it the way you're twistin' it,' I replied warmly, and next day Flo showed me a photo of her mother, our heads close together at the hatch. As I looked for the hundredth time at those lovely features, Mary, Maud, Jean, and distant Jenny were forgotten, yet I couldn't rev up enough courage until the afternoon before we left, when I saw her out of uniform – she'd two hours off. I knew that this would be her last stint at Pirbright, for she was being sent permanently to Aldershot. It must be now . . . or never. 'Who,' I asked cheekily, 'are you spending these two hours with?'

'No-one.'

'I've heard,' I went on carefully, 'that you've never been out with anybody.'

'That's right.'

'Well, you don't wear a ring, so you must have been asked.'
She laughed. 'Yes, a few times.'
'Are you a man-hater, then, or don't you trust Guardsmen?'
'I've never met anyone I fancied, that's all.'
'Oh. Er . . . 'ow about a stroll?'
She laughed again. 'Stiffy, I thought you'd never ask!'
'Eh?' I was quite startled. 'D'yer mean it?'
'Yes. But first, how about the merry widow?'
'So you know,' I muttered. 'Jim, of course.'
'No,' she contradicted flatly, 'he's said nothing, but others
have.'
'Well, I've not heard from her for months.'

As we left camp, our departure wasn't unnoticed, and we
walked along a canal bank and sat on a lock gate. A schoolboy
angler was into a shoal of small roach, and every time he jerked
one out he grinned at us, and we grinned back. Peace and
tranquillity, apart from the occasional bugle bray and fish
struggling in the keep net. The kid packed up and left, but I
made no attempt to kiss Flo. Back in camp I was intercepted by
Corporal Edwards. 'You're getting expert, Stiffy, catching a bird
nobody else could trap. But why does she have to pick a mug
like yours?' So I told him, and a few others, at the piano that
evening:

> The best-looking girls get the worst-looking men,
> The others get nothing at all.
> Don't you worry, fellows, if you're ugly like me,
> You're sure to pick a pretty peach right off the tree.
> If you happen to go to a fancy dress show,
> See the prettiest girl in the hall;
> Hear the people whisper: 'What a sweet little thing,'
> But when they see her old man they say: 'God Save the King!'
> The best-looking girls get the worst-looking men,
> The others get nothing at all.

Soon Flo wrote to say that her transfer was through, and at the
next corporals' dance Mary also had news. 'Kath and Sandy are
engaged.'
'Yes. Sandy's lucky. In line for sergeant, with tradesman's
pay on top of it.'
Mary went rather tight-lipped; she had probably heard about
a certain stroll along a canal bank. And then came an envelope
from Maud. No letter – merely a cutting from her local paper. A

list of the autumn posting to Aldershot, with Welsh Guards underlined . . . oh crikey!

*   *   *

Meeting Flo after our move, she announced that it was her half-day and she'd like to see a film, but we hadn't walked a hundred yards before there was a tug at my bayonet from behind and a voice remarked that it wanted to speak to me privately. Flo walked on, and I waited for it. 'So *that's* why you didn't write. Somebody younger, I see.'

'Maud —'

'I might have known it was time wasted,' she broke in, then went swiftly after Flo. After saying something, she walked away.

'It had to come, I suppose,' sighed Flo as I rejoined.

'What did she say?'

'That she'd been let down and I'd be the same.'

'Oh no.'

'Shall we go for a bus ride instead?' We decided on Pirbright, with myself feeling thoroughly ashamed for having treated both Maud and Mary shabbily. Had it not been for changes of station I might have married the former despite opposition. Mary, however, was herself married soon afterwards. Meanwhile, at the lock gate, we were silent until I lobbed a pebble at a dabchick bobbling in the reeds. 'You might have hit it,' protested Flo.

'Sorry about Maud,' I muttered at length.

She smiled. 'That's over. Tell me about Mary Jones.'

'Blimey!' I blurted. 'Someone's been doin' overtime.'

'Never mind that. How about her?'

'She was very nice, but I wasn't serious like this. You're the last.'

'How often have you said that?'

'Never until now.' And I did something I'd longed to do for five years – kissed her.

On the return bus she said: 'I'm not calling you "Stiffy" any more.'

'Right. You'll be "Florrie", and I'll start saving.'

*   *   *

For me there began austerity that wouldn't have disgraced a Trappist monk. I salted away most of my pay, with Florrie and I spending our off duty walking; much hiking country lay around. I was now well up the lance-jack seniority list and Dicky Leatham would certainly give me permission to marry – I fancied the Guards Chapel in London! We'd rent a room until I qualified for married quarters in due course, with everything set fair for a military career. Learning that a town licensee was in need of a weekend pianist, I went down and got the job. Against regulations, of course, to take paid employment outside the service. I'd soon have enough cash for a double-breaster *and* a ring – in fact I had everything worked out like a 'TEWT' – Tactical Exercise Without Troops. And then, in the midst of those roseate dreams of Nirvana, came disaster.

One pay-night, with the bar packed, two people peered through the window of the pub, and next morning Lance-Corporals Cannon and Shaw were summoned to the Presence. Quoth Stevo: 'Last night the police-sergeant and I saw you pair in the Wellington public house with private soldiers. You're in open arrest.'

Soon we were in front of Dicky Leatham. Cannon had nothing to say, but I, for a change, had plenty, assuring the old man that I was merely at the piano and had never had a drink in my life. Dicky heard me out, then spoke quietly: 'You are not here for drinking with privates, but being in their company on licensed premises. It's written plainly enough in Regimental Standing Orders. You are both deprived of lance-stripe.' Outside, I ripped off the tapes, was posted back to the Prince of Wales's Company, and soon Guardsmen Cannon and Shaw were in canvas, scrubbing a floor on hands and knees.

'What a soppy way to get busted,' grinned Jim at dinnertime, 'and you a T.T.'

'That's what everyone keeps sayin',' I replied savagely. 'Today's Saturday, and when I think of all the N.C.O.'s who'll be drinking with privates tonight I could spit!' I then rang Florrie. 'Can I see you tonight? I'm not at the pub. Got to be in by nine-thirty.'

'Oh. Trouble?'

'I'm afraid so.'

'Come along. I've news for you too.'

The Dorset Regiment was in Malplacquet Barracks, and the corporals had been astounded when their ratpit had been entered by a 'stinking Guardsman', as we were affectionately known to the Infantry. But now every ratpit in the Army was forbidden me, and I fetched up at a deserted main counter –

most people went to town on Saturday. My sweetheart glanced
at bare sleeves. 'What happened?'

'Pinched for bein' in the pub.'

'I didn't know that was a crime.'

'Privates in there – that was the crime, an' I'm busted.'

Unseen by me, a chap had arrived behind, and got restive.
'Hey, you're holding up the Army.'

Normally I'd have grinned, but now needed only a crack like
that. 'Are yer callin' the Dorsets "Army"?'

He clenched his fists, and Florrie's even tones sounded: 'Now
then, you two.'

I made way. 'Sorry, mate.'

'O.K.,' he laughed.

'Wait on the road, Jess. I'll come out,' said Florrie, and we
strolled slowly towards Farnborough. 'What's *your* news?' I
asked suddenly.

'I'm being promoted Manageress.'

'What? . . . Congratulations!' I stuttered. 'You're promoted
an' I'm *demoted*.'

'Cheer up. It isn't the end of the world.

'End of *my* world. Back to square one.'

'You might regain your stripes. It happens.'

'Odds against that.' I was intent upon a masochistic orgy.
'Goodbye, I s'pose?'

'Well, we *are* in a mood! Come and see me tomorrow. You
may feel better after church!'

Following promotion, she continued to serve behind the
counter during pressure, and was very popular with the
Dorsets. Meanwhile, back to the pub piano. They'd have to
prove that I was a 'professional'! After some time I went home
for a weekend, minus certain ornaments. They knew I'd been
broken, and demanded to know why. 'I was in a pub with
privates.'

'But you don't drink,' exclaimed three voices in chorus.

'If anyone else says that I'll break the pledge,' I fumed. 'I was
just playin' the pianner. See yer later. I'm goin' to see the
'ammers.' Passing the Clarnico sweets factory, screeching: 'Yoo-
hoos!' sounded from an upper window. I looked up to see girls
waving. Something descended and I caught it, then acknowledged and walked on quickly. Warm chocolate wouldn't look
good on a red tunic.

Before returning to Aldershot I had more news for the family.
'I've met a girl.' Silence, so I persisted. 'I'm getting engaged,'

and at that they sat up. 'I'm sure you'll like her. She's in the Naffy, and a manageress,' I ended impressively, producing a photograph.

Mother glanced at it. 'Well, if she's as nice as she looks, bring 'er 'ome.' A month later I did. 'We must 'ave an engagement party!' beamed mother.

*   *   *

Back on the mat. During a field exercise I was taking a message to Battalion H.Q. when Bobby Auld shouted that I was under fire, and I loped into some gorse. Usually affable, something must have upset Bobby, for he said that wasn't the way to double when under fire and bagged me for idleness. Hardly had I paid off the jankers when the Company was ordered to show boots in good condition. Mine were minus a few studs, so I borrowed a pair, something that most people did at some time or other. My unlucky day, for there was a spot check and the real owner's number was revealed. Eight days, for 'being in possession'. Here we go again.

I wasn't alone in trouble. A deserter named Jimmy Steel, disenchanted with the outside world, gave himself up, prepared to do a spell in the Glasshouse before soldiering on. He got his spudhole all right, but was told that his services were no longer required . . . he'd awarded himself six months in clink for nothing. Jimmy didn't like it, and on hearing the sentence bolted from the escort. I had grand janker's eye view of the hunt as they reached the road with a rapidly increasing gap between hounds and hare. Alas! Jimmy made the cardinal error of keeping to the highway, and when the escort comandeered a car he'd had it.

A few weeks later Cannon and I were called to the Company Office. He entered first, to emerge grinning. 'Getting my tapes back. You too, I bet!' No such luck, for Cannon was alone in his joy – I was being returned to the Gunners. Most unwelcome, for although Dai Roberts was still there, Captain Greenacre was now Adjutant, and Cushy Lewis had been replaced by Major Fox-Pitt, who for some time had made no secret of his dislike for myself. It was reciprocated, but with the difference that he could call me anything he wished while I had no such advantage. Added to this was my feeling of frustration at recognising a damned good soldier. I wasn't surprised to learn later that he rose to a distinguished position commanding the Guards

Armoured Division during the Second World War. Goodness knows why he took such a jaundiced view of everything I did – was it because he hated my Cockney accent? Other Londoners in H.Q. Wing progressed happily enough . . . why single out me?

Tragedy occurred while practising for the Smith-Dorrien Cup. An Irish Guards marker in the butts dashed up the bank to right a fallen plate as we opened fire; he died. It so affected us that the shooting for the actual trophy was abysmal – no repeat victory. An 'accident' of different calibre happened during rifle firing when Lieutenant Jefferson parked his car to the flank of the 300 yards point. After we moved back to 500 someone put a round through it. The bullet pierced the boot, ricocheted from the steering wheel and smashed the windscreen. A vicious deed, for although the officer was a martinet (he eventually rose to Brigadier) he was always fair. The moron responsible for the act was lucky, for had a line been taken from the chip on the wheel over the hole in the boot, it would have pin-pointed the firer's position. Before that was realised, Jeff had moved the vehicle.

Drawn against the Dorsets in a soccer cup, they beat us, with Florrie there supporting 'her boys'. After the game she seemed distrait. 'You're very quiet, considering your chaps won,' I observed.

'I was talking with Taffs I knew at Pirbright. They said there's a certain officer they called "Foxy" who's after your blood.'

I laughed. 'Major Fox-Pitt. That's no news to me!'

'Jess, it isn't a joke, you know. Remember you've only eighteen months to go.'

*   *   *

Sandy married his Kath, but I wasn't invited to the ceremony! Unhappy when her sister departed, Mary returned to Wales, and for the Taffs it was Wellington Barracks. From there the King's Guard had no long, exhilarating march, the First Division arriving at Buck gates only seconds before the odds and sods in the rear had cleared barracks. We shared Wellington with the Grenadiers, and bugling must have re-echoed in both Palaces. Did they ever cuss us, I wonder?

On picket, I was told to liven up the guardroom fire, and set the chimney alight. Ripping off bayonet and jacket, I fought bravely as the place filled with soot and fumes. In dashed the boy bugler, itching to create uproar. 'Three foot o' flames coming out o' the chimney,' he shouted gleefully. 'I'll sound fire call.'

'Not yet you bloody don't!' coughed the sergeant. 'Get on with it, Shaw.' Soon came a loud clanging outside, then in ran a man with a big brass helmet. 'Who the hell sent for you?' demanded the sergeant.

'*Somebody*, or we wouldn't bloody well be here. D'yer want any help or not?'

'I think we can manage now, thanks.' The appliances left, having been called by the Bill Brown's guard, with a grandstand view from the other end of the square. I paid for new boots and puttees.

Next a rumpus in my barrackroom. In charge of the latter was a young lance-corporal named Wyman, who stood no nonsense. Youth and discipline were resented by some older people, one of whom entered with a skinful of beer after lights out. On being told to keep quiet he became quite abusive, then threatening, and as the oldest soldier there I had to go to Wyman's assistance, then give evidence at the resultant court-martial.

On St David's Day we were inspected by the Prince, who had only to cross the Mall from St James's. We'd spent hours brushing, burnishing, blancoing, and now blinding rain was being accompanied by blinding language. A message arrived – the Prince would look at us under cover. Furniture in the huge messroom was pushed against the walls, and as H.R.H. left, our three cheers nearly raised the roof. Detractors of Edward, both before and after his Abdication, were many, but none were among the 'small fry' of the Welsh Guards.

The Thames now overflowed an embankment one night, with people trapped in basements and drowned. We went along to Millbank military hospital, groping around to salvage medical supplies.

A visit by King Amanullah of Afghanistan saw us lining the route along Constitution Hill. Awaiting the cavalcade, I heard the raucous tones of 'Prince' (I've gotta horse) Monolulu behind me. This racing tipster, with his huge, befeathered headgear, turned up at all these functions and was no respecter of personages. After cursing my bearskin that was partly obscuring his view, he yelled an insult at a mounted police inspector. The crowd roared, the copper went red, and I laughed – couldn't help it. Unfortunately, C.S.M. Wilce wasn't amused. 'Stand fast Shaw,' he called, when we dismissed in barracks.

Shaw stood fast, was given a stern warning, and was on the point of being let off when Stevo came bristling along, stopping for an explanation. 'Laughing on ceremonial parade, sir,' said Wilce.

'Oh, was he? Then bag him,' and I was bagged. Incredibly, Fox-Pitt must have had an off day, for I was awarded extra drills instead of jankers. Years later I saw Monolulu on Birmingham racecourse, and asked whether he remembered King Amanullah.

'Oh yes. I was there, near the Palace.'

'So was I – in the Guards. They did me for laughing at you.'

'The bastards! Never mind. *I'll* give you a winner for nothing' . . . it lost.

*   *   *

I became miserly, buying an old pushbike to avoid fares home. A cycle permit enabled one to wear service dress – trouser clips weren't compatible with red tunics. Traffic was now thick, and if a policeman's hand was raised, a bike could filter through to the front. Buses were restricted to 12 m.p.h., and nifty passengers hopped on or off at 'speed'. One N.C.O. purchased a motorbike. He also had access to certain supplies, and one evening a search of his sidecar revealed a lot more than his 'unexpired portion of the day's rations'.

There were now rumours of a surprise move to Palestine later that year. If true, what would Florrie say? Meanwhile, manoeuvres, in Berkshire. After pitching our wigwams, we saw some hostilities before the actual battles began. The Church Army erected a marquee, doing a roaring trade with hungry warriors before the Naffy's big top rolled up. And the manager knew his rights – yessir! Delicious repartee. I'd never dreamed that the Church Army even knew such naughty words. They had to move out, and did business in the evenings.

One gunner, a bemedalled 'old sweat', was an accomplished scrounger on exercises. After dark, he'd creep away to the nearest house, to knock and ask plaintively if there was any bread to spare, at the same time proffering a pound note to show that he wasn't begging. His money would be waived away and something tasty added to the bread, but on one occasion he met his Waterloo when a hard-hearted householder produced a loaf and added nothing to it except nineteen shillings and sixpence change. Our con man returned, seething.

The manoeuvres dragged on as always. Long, hot days. Long, cold nights. Rain, or icy dew. Lying in stubbly fields with a plane droning overhead, and everyone impatient for the 'Disperse'. But on this particular night I was feeling happy, for I'd soon be off for my engagement party; a weekend pass had been granted . . . but 'the best laid schemes'.

Returning to camp, the rifle companies dismissed, but the Gunners, as usual, had to clean the grimy Vickers, and as a Number One I was also responsible for the tripod. Later, heading for my tent, I saw my bête noir approaching. Because of the pegs there was barely room to salute, and after I squeezed past there was a peremptory: 'Come back here!' I did so, and stamped to attention. 'The Battalion's been in over an hour and you haven't shaved. Disgusting!'

'I've been guncleaning, sir —'

'Stop talking!' Calling the nearest N.C.O., he put me on a fizzer. I'd never yet been guilty of insubordination, but came perilously near it at that moment. I managed to keep my mouth shut, or it would have meant a shout of: 'Fall in two men!' and an escort to the nick.

An hour later he awarded three drills, which meant that I couldn't leave for the party until four o'clock. Bad enough, but when I heard that my pass was cancelled I felt homicidal. 'Punished twice for a non-offence!' I raged to Jim. 'What kind of party will it be without the fiancé? Flo's already there, and about twenty relatives have been invited.'

'Tough,' admitted Jim.

'Look,' I said. 'I'm goin'. To hell with Fox-Pitt!'

'I've always said you were daft, Stiffy,' he replied quietly, 'but this time I can sympathise.'

'Thanks, mate – you can bring my blankets to the nick tomorrow night.'

When 'cookhouse' sounded and the tents emptied I pushed through a hedge, yanked the stick from my sleeve and belt from beneath my jacket and stepped off smartly. Soon a car approached, and I glanced casually at the driver. Crikey . . . Fox-Pitt! He braked, then changed his mind and accelerated fiercely towards the guard tent, turning in. Remembering Jimmy Steel's mistake, I vaulted a gate and peered back. If anything like Greenacre's Buick came after me I'd be caught in seconds on the road. A bugle blared for the picket 'at the double', and soon they ran out in a body. Unseen, I loped across the field. They were wearing clodhoppers and dangling bayonets, and I heard later that they sweated for three miles after being torn from their dinners. Had they succeeded in running me to earth that afternoon, I reckon that I, too, might have been torn.

Across country now. There would certainly be redcaps at Didcot, and I made for the next station down the line. 'Weekend to London, please. What time's the train?'

'Another half-hour. Change at Didcot.'

'Eh?'

'You won't have long to wait there. The "fast" to London doesn't stop here. All right?'

'All right' my Aunt Fanny! The slow chuffed in, then out, and at Didcot I dived into the gents'. As the express arrived, I peeped out to see the redcap looking the other way, and entered a compartment like a rat up a drainpipe. Good. I now had only to alight near town and use the Tube as the chap in the Tower had advised years before. When the inspector left us I followed him into the corridor. 'What's the last stop before Paddington?'

'No stop,' he grinned, far more amused than myself, for as he hadn't kept my ticket we must be arriving at a closed platform. At Paddington I could see two hated red glints by the gate. Plenty of troops were surging towards them, but in London a Guardsman in service dress and webbing belt would stick out like a sore thumb. Withdrawing, I saw a heaven-sent escape route via an empty train alongside, and soon stepped on to another platform, deserted except for a porter sweeping. He spotted me immediately, and was obviously interested in my manoeuvre. 'What are *you* supposed to be doin'?'

'Dodgin' the redcaps. No pass.'

'Or d'yer mean "no ticket"?' he remarked sceptically.

'What? No, 'ere it is. I must get 'ome. Urgent.'

'Come on.' Leading the way to the gate, he glanced along and winked. 'Gorn.'

'Get yerself a pint, mate.' I offered a bob that would have bought two. He refused it, and I made for the Edgware Road and a number 8 bus.

                    *   *   *

'I'm not going back until Monday,' observed Florrie. 'How about you?'

'Me too.'

'Good,' said my sister. 'No organist for tomorrow's services. I told the vicar you'd oblige.'

'Told 'im *what*?'

'You can, can't yer? The times I've 'eard yer messin' about on Aunt Lizzie's 'armonium.'

'That's nothing like a church organ, you chump!'

'Only wants yer to do the 'ymns.'

'That's all 'e'll get – providin' I can choose 'em – *and* the keys.'

The vicar agreed, and I practised, with Esther pumping. By the organ was a note from the real musician – 'Don't have everything out', referring to the numerous stops.

Later the party was great. Florrie looked stunning, and if my many girl cousins were broken-hearted at losing such an eligible bachelor, they showed commendable fortitude. The racket ended with an old favourite that probably dated from when the Militia was first formed. Guests seized fire-irons, umbrellas, walking-sticks and other odd weapons and crocodiled round the room and into the street, yelling:

> Brave men, bold men,
> Second-best Militiamen;
> Pawn our shoes, all for booze,
> Life it is so charming.
> Break of day, march away,
> People stare – what can they say?
> Always fight, never run away,
> Bold Militiamen.

At Matins next day my sister sat with me for moral support. There were muffled thuds and thumps as the congregation began to enter, then a horrible series of squeaks and groans as someone began pumping. With dithering fingers I began my voluntary – 'O Rest in the Lord'. 'Hi! Ain't that for a funeral?' hissed Esther.

'Shurrup!' I was trying to look in the mirror. 'The choir's comin'!' They knew there'd be no accompaniment to chants and psalms, and after the first hymn verse, during which I noted several white-robed figures glancing at one another, things weren't too bad. The flock then beseeched the Lord to forgive their 'erring and straying like lost sheep', but I knew that whatever the Lord decided about my own deviations, there would be precious little forgiveness from the regimental shepherd when I returned to the fold.

Eventually vicar and retinue began to depart, and I gave the congregation a treat with Handel's 'Largo'. Reaching the fortis-

simo finale I forgot orders and 'had everything out'. A hideous
cacophony began percolating, and on raising my hands from the
manuals a dozen discordant notes continued to roar into the
roof until expiring in doleful gurgles as the air ran out.

Tuesday. After the Lord Mayor's Show came the dustcart. At
'Cap off' time I was elated at hearing myself being charged with
absence only, but Fox-Pitt instantly rectified that. 'March him
out again. I want that charge rewritten.' Through the tent wall I
heard the voice going on: 'I checked with the guard, and he
didn't use the gate, so must have broken out of camp. The
man's no good, and never will be any good.' Up now in front of
Dicky Leatham. Fourteen days jankers. Back to London. No
pisstubs on Birdcage Walk, thank goodness!

*   *   *

> The Moving Finger writes; and having writ,
> Moves on; nor all thy Piety nor Wit
> Shall lure it back to cancel half a line,
> Nor all thy Tears wash out a word of it.
>   (Omar Khayyam)

Soon it was confirmed that the Battalion would visit the
Middle East, but alas, without myself. I was called to the
Orderly Room, where a clerk showed me a memorandum . . . I
had a fortnight left before being sacked. Stunned, I turned away
with everyone looking at me, and in Stevo's eyes was unmistakable sympathy. Though not entirely unexpected, it was still a
numbing blow, and the Gunners offered advice: 'Write to your
M.P.' Oh no. The last thing I wanted was publicity – if it lay with
me only my nearest and dearest would know. At Jim's suggestion that the padre might help I shook my head. 'No good, Jim,
it's already a *fait accompli*.'

'I feared things were going this way,' said Sergeant Roberts,
'I'm sorry.'

'So am I! But thanks, Dai – you've been one of the best.'

My most dreaded task awaited at home. 'Discharged?' repeated my surprised mother. 'You've still got nine months to go.'

'Not long enough to go to Palestine,' I lied, but my father
wasn't fooled. Grimfaced, he remained silent.

Unwilling to wear the repellent suit I'd receive if I failed to
buy one, I ordered a made-to-measure – in those days you could
collect within 72 hours. I also treated myelf to a rakish trilby

and, on impulse, a walking-stick with silverplated knob. 'I ain't leavin' lookin' like a tramp,' I told the Gunners. 'Anyone wanna buy a bike – cheap?'

My last public duty, like the first, was on Buck, and the drill-sergeant, unaware of my near future, chose me as Colour Escort, the first time I'd received that honour. A quiet word from Stevo saw me replaced. Two days later I was on picket, and then, with time running out, Barrack Guard – they were certainly exacting their pound of flesh. With no urge to leave barracks, I concentrated upon my turnout for this swansong, and again the inspecting officer knew nothing of my fate. 'Give this man a credit,' he ordered, with everyone trying to keep a straight face; I bet it never appeared in Orders!

Both guard N.C.O.'s were old pals of mine, and soon I was posted by the Birdcage Walk gate, rolling jaundiced eyes around. Along came a comely girl, pushing a pram. 'Hallo, Kath,' I said lugubriously from beneath my bearskin.

She peered. 'Stiffy! I say, you shouldn't be speaking to me, you know.'

'What the 'ell do *I* care?'

'Look *out* – he's *watching* you!' But the sergeant, after giving Kath a grin of recognition, turned his back.

'A lovely baby,' I said.

'Yes, Stiffy. You know, we were thinking you and Mary would hit it off. You didn't treat her very nicely, did you?'

'No,' I admitted, adding bitterly, 'but she's lucky. How about *my* business?'

'Yes. It's a shame. Sandy says there are others with worse records.'

'How is Mary, anyway? I 'eard she's married. Is she happy?'

'Yes, she is married, and expecting. She's happy enough.'

'I'm glad someone is,' I muttered.

'Well, I must be off, or Sandy'll get no dinner. Good luck, Stiffy.'

Watching her trip away, I suddenly felt like weeping.

*　　　*　　　*

　　　Wrap me up in my old canvas jacket,
　　　And say an ex-Guardsman lies low;
　　　Six stalwart Gunners shall carry me,
　　　With steps that are mournful and slow.

Last day. Handing in public equipment and clothing, it was noted that some other items that should have accompanied them were missing. No action by C.Q.M.S. Wenban, for the chaps to whom they'd been given would have instantly erased my Regimental number from them! All the Army gear I had now was canvas suit and eating irons. 'Doing anything tonight?' asked Jim.

I tried to grin, though feeling like death itself. 'No pressing engagements.'

'Don't suppose you feel like a tune?'

'You suppose correctly, but why not? If Foxy's expecting me to go around with a little bell and shouting "Unclean" he can think again! By the way, 'ave you a copy of the "Brigade Mag"?'

'In the store. Why?'

'I want the editor's address. Written a few verses.'

'About bein' chucked out? You bloody cheeky —'

'No. "Ode to a Naffy Girl". I wrote them long ago.'

'Cheeky'? Anything but, and it was mere bravado at the piano that evening. Among other classics, I remember we sang 'Ain't we got Fun?' and 'Ain't it Grand to be bloomin' well Dead?' I was continually asked about my future plans, and at length said that I intended to follow the only trade in which I had experience.

'What's that?'

'D'you really expect me to put that into words?'

There was an incredulous chorus: 'You silly bastard, Stiffy!'

'You'll never get away with it,' asserted Jim.

Don't suppose I will, but there's two million unemployed, y'know.'

'Well, best of luck to you, Stiffy. Christ, you're going to need it, boyo!'

True. A foolhardy project, but there it was . . . I was built that way.

*   *   *

Next morning the condemned man ate anything but heartily, then shook hands with all who wished to shake, a temporarily heart-warming panacea. As I reached the square the Adjutant's parade was forming up. The drum tapped, and I halted; I was still a Guardsman. 'Your discharge book will be posted today,' said the Orderly Room. 'Do you need a railway warrant?'

'No thanks, it's only a bus ride.'

The guard-room opened my small case, ensuring that I wasn't nicking any Government property, then I passed through the gate for the last time. Through the railings I saw the parade being inspected. Men would be 'losing names', but I'd swop places with any. Under the blue caps were faces I knew, and at least a dozen had conduct sheets worse than mine – some recording drunkenness. And there went the owner of the supercilious face I hated, en route for the Company Office, doubtless feeling satisfaction at ridding himself of Guardsman Shaw. What a pity 'drumming out' had been abolished – how he could have gloated at my humiliation in front of that grand Regiment. My sudden, flaring resentment quickly faded. After all, I'd asked for a lot of it.

Should I raise my trilby mockingly, or blow a raspberry? No. I continued tapping my walking-stick, trying to look jaunty but with a heart as heavy as lead. Behind those wooden expressions, what were they all thinking? In an hour's time they'd be in the Naffy – 'Did you see old Stiffy go off?' Then the few bits and pieces I'd left behind would be auctioned in aid of 'Company Funds', whatever they were suppsed to be.

I glanced behind for a final look, but a building was beginning to obscure them . . . the Guards Chapel, where I'd hoped to be married. His Majesty's First Battalion, The Welsh Guards, Ffarwel am Byth (Goodbye for Ever).

CHAPTER FOUR

Infantryman, Royal Sussex Regiment

At home, I told a silent audience that they wouldn't be burdened a day longer than necessary. Next morning my father and sister left for work, the former with a face like a thundercloud, and I waited for the postman. 'Hallo, there 'e is.'

Army characters were graded Exemplary, Excellent, Very Good, Good, Bad, and Very Bad. The first thing I saw astonished me, until I read on. 'Well?' demanded mother expectantly.

I placed the book on the table. 'Look.'

'"Clean and Sober",' she exclaimed animatedly, then I pointed to the assessment of character. '"Bad",' she whispered, 'your father was right.'

'Yes,' I muttered hopelessly.

She looked again. '"Clean and Sober"? Then why "Bad"?'

'Nothing criminal. Mostly absence, plus the efforts of one particular swine who hated me.'

'Well, what now?'

'No dole. Same as the sack. I've got an idea. Tell you about it later.' I got pen and paper.

'Who are yer writin' to?' she asked after a time.

'Florrie. She don't know yet.'

'If you ain't the limit! What a shock for 'er.'

'No. She warned me last year.'

'What are yer sayin'?'

'Goodbye, o' course. What else can I say?'

'Now you listen to me. Go an' see 'er.'

'Eh? I ain't got the guts.'

'*See* 'er. Can't make things worse, and leave that book for yer father to look at. Might think o' something.'

'Plenty for 'im to think about already! No-one else'll ever see it. Leave the key 'andy in case I'm late.' At the canal bridge I ripped the book to bits and dropped them into the cut. At Waterloo a redcap was obviously appraising my short-back-and-sides. Absentee? Possibly no plain clothes' pass? 'Say just one word, mate!' I thought viciously.

The Naffy was closed, and I knocked. 'Come into the office, Jess,' invited Florrie. Sick at heart and convinced that it would be goodbye, I explained. 'Let's leave it until the morning,' she said. The barman of the 'wet' section had a spare bed in his room, but though exhausted mentally I lay awake for several hours. In the morning Florrie not only said she'd stay with me, but asked for no promises.

'I'll earn this,' I assured her, feeling choked.

'Well, what's your next move?'

'I'll join up again.'

'*Jess!*'

'Before you say how daft I am, remember – no dole, trade, or reference. Two million out o' work.'

Gradually she saw it from my viewpoint. 'Jess, you're going to need an awful lot of luck.' And now, which unsuspecting unit? 'Join the Sussex,' she suggested.

'Depends on where they're stationed!'

In a barber's being shaved, I felt more cheerful than I'd thought possible. Given that luck, I swore to myself, things would be vastly different.

*   *   *

Bright, alluring posters. 'If you play soccer, the Royal Scots for You'. 'Let Professor Tank Teach You a Trade' – referring I presumed to boy soldiers! Hallo! 'Join the Welsh Guards'. The artist had got it plumb correct, from the number of buttons to St James's in the background. I could see nothing about the Sussex, so went inside. Asked my fourth recruiting sergeant: 'What can I do for you, sir?' (Sir? What would he call me if he knew?)

'I'd like to join the Army, sergeant.'

He seemed perplexed, and I realised that I was head up, chin in, chest out, stomach in, toes at an angle of forty-five degrees, arms at the side, fingers slightly clenched, thumbs in line with the seams of the trousers . . . the lot as per Manual of Military Foot Drill. Once a Guardsman . . . I relaxed, trying to appear slovenly, but of course there was also my semi-convict hair-do. 'Have you served before?' he inquired.

'Yes, sergeant. During the war.' I handed him my certificate.

'Ah! I thought so. Infantry. Boy. Any trade?'

'Warehouse labourer.'

He stared. New suit. Spotless shirt, mirror-like shoes. Hands that obviously hadn't laboured for years. I hastened to add that I had no skilled trade and he wrote 'Labourer'. Then I saw a glint appear in his eyes, something I'd been expecting. Help! Here it comes: 'Would you consider joining the Guards?'

'Er . . . somehow I don't fancy them. I prefer the Sussex.'

'The *Royal* Sussex,' he corrected gently. 'You know, the Guards are nearly always in town, and you sound like a Londoner.'

'I'm sorry, sergeant. A friend of mine in the Guards put me off them.' I made it sound final.

'Well, why the Royal Sussex?'

'My fiancee's idea. She comes from Worthing.' It sounded rather lame.

'I'm afraid they're closed for recruitment – up to strength.'

'That's a blow,' I muttered.

'It may be possible with a special enlistment application – with former service you'll probably be accepted. You'll hear within a few days.'

'Where are they, sergeant?'

'First Battalion's at Bordon, the other in India.'

I nipped back to Florrie. 'Bordon, only ten miles away, an' the Taffs won't be in Aldershot for a long time.'

'I'll pray for you, Jess. Write soon.'

Back home, mother was so delighted by Florrie's decision that she didn't bother about anything else, but my disturbed father beckoned me outside. 'For Gawd's sake! S'pose you get rumbled?'

'I know, dad. Court-martial. Glasshouse. Slung out again. But I must risk it or it's unemployment. Permanent. I'd rather kill myself!' He gestured helplessly and walked away. Welcome visitors were former pals, one bringing an envelope containing ten bob – my verses had been accepted and were later printed in the Household Brigade Magazine. It was like a comic opera, though I could see little comedy!

The Royal Sussex agreed, subject to an unexpected proviso – evidently the Army were now selective. Two questionnaires had to be filled in by non-relatives, and one query fairly yelled at me

– 'Has he to your knowledge ever served in H.M. Forces'? I set to work with a pen, inwardly quaking, and two neighbours supposedly supplied the information. I waited in some trepidation in case confirmation was sought, and it wasn't. Came my summons, and I was in again. For how long?

*   *   *

You can tell them all
That we stand or fall
For Sussex by the Sea.

The Depot was at Chichester, and as at the moment no new squads were being formed, I was placed in the one almost due to pass out. Without exception they were teen-aged Sussex lads and I was a head taller than any. Plagued by guilt I suffered extreme nervous tension, sweating whenever my name was called. Keeping very much to myself, I overheard a reference to a 'surly long bastard', but concentrated on my equipment, especially on some blackened leather, which I treated with acid to bring back the original colour. Next day an inspecting officer wanted to know why mine was a different hue from the rest of the squad. 'He's restored it, sir, that's all,' explained bemedalled Pat Daly, a squad sergeant, who afterwards got me alone. 'I don't know about a boy in the Fusiliers,' he grinned, 'I think you're a bit of a dark horse.' I'd been stupid, so drew in my horns, especially when the lads began leg-pulling about 'old sweats'.

I was drawing the new lower rate of pay, but was lucky to be getting any kind of cash. Pat said that the Second Battalion was always kept up to strength, adding the advice that the more useful you proved at home, the less likelihood of being sent abroad. Had it not been for Florrie I'd have welcomed India, but as things were . . . che sera sera!

The rifle drill timings were faster, and the marching, too, was ten paces a minute more than the Guards'. As the tallest, I was automatically right-hand-man of the squad. Important, for in the fixing and unfixing of bayonets all movements stem from him, and a false one ruins the whole thing. All went well, the squad passed out, and was granted the customary long weekend. Still very apprehensive, I daren't risk Aldershot or London in uniform so remained in barracks.

*   *   *

Bordon Camp had gained notoriety shortly before when a
private had shot the bank manager; the former was hanged.
We halted at the guard-room and I heard a voice say: 'Hey –
look at that long sod!' The 'long sod' was posted to 'C'
Company, and compared to what he'd just left, life was
heavenly. Though discipline was certainly not lacking, it
wasn't the nasty, snarling kind. Everyone was more relaxed,
yet as full of esprit de corps as any Guardsman. But I had an
unexpected jolt on the first night, when a provost asked why I
was wearing canvas. In this unit it mustn't be used after the
sounding of evening 'Retreat'. My 'rookie' excuse was accepted, but with the promise of a 'fizzer' next time. Ugh! The very
word made me wince.

Plenty of drill and field training, but no guard duties, which
were carried out by the unit police. After London's multitudinous tasks it was like being on holiday. My immediate nickname
was 'Jasper' which puzzled me. I understood why my C.S.M.
Warters, was 'Pawny', that sounded like an Indian name for
'water'. I also saw plainly why one of the senior members was
known, even to his brother officers, as 'Coffin Dodger', but
never discovered why, in this Battalion, any Shaw was a
'Jasper'.

On my first route march I was surprised when the youngsters
started an old wartime ditty, 'Here's to the good old beer', with
all its unprintable verses. My own platoon had their own pet
effort. No rhyme, and a most peculiar dialect, but the metre was
perfect, and that's what counts when marching:

> 'Whur be ee gooin' tew, Jake?'
> 'Oi be gooin' darn hayfield.
> Oi knaw whur thur's a blackburd's nest.'
> 'Well, I'm boogered if Oi doan goo wid yer!
> Now whur be that blackburd tew?'
> 'I knaw whur ee be.
> Ee be in yander blackberry boosh,
> And Oi'll be arter ee'
> 'Oi doan believe ee, Jake,
> Ee be a boogerin' liar!'

Another one new to me was, again regrettably, to the tune of
'Through the Night of Doubt and Sorrow':

Feed a cold, but starve a fever,
That is what the old wives cry;
Starve a cold and it won't leave yer,
Feed a fever and you'll die.

A letter from Joe, via the Welsh Guards, which my mother had carefully put into another envelope. This correspondence could be dangerous, and I didn't reply.

I soon had new pals, including Charles Bellis, an officer's servant at present looking after a Captain awaiting return to India. One night Charlie sprained his ankle badly, and when I took his 'small kit' to the medical hut he was in a quandary. 'Jasper – the Captain.'

'What about 'im?'

'Someone'll have to look after him and his missus 'til this clears up.' He touched the bandage gingerly. 'It's a mess night tomorrow too.'

'All right. I'll tell Pawny.'

'*You* do it.'

'Me? I'm only a rookie.'

'It'll just be a day or two. See Pawny.'

I approached the C.S.M. diffidently. 'Take over then,' he agreed, 'if it's only for a short while.'

Back to the M.H. 'O.K. What now?'

'Get to their bungalow at 7 a.m., and the old man'll let you in and go back to bed. Take 'em in a pot of char, then return here for breakfast. Go back, wash up, clear up, do a few odd jobs —'

'Arf a mo,' I interrupted suspiciously. 'What kind o' jobs? Any cooking?'

'Of course not. *She* does that. Clear up and clear off. Anyone can do it.'

Having performed enough chores in the Guards to qualify for a diploma in domestic science, I'd no doubt that I could do it, but I wasn't yet satisfied.

'Is there a pisspot? Do I 'ave to empty that with a woman there?'

'I've never seen one. After tidying up, go and hide yourself, but not in *our* part of the camp. Brigade canteen's best. Go back after lunch. Wash up, then see to the mess dress. It'll all be laid out.'

'I can see to *that* all right!' I found Captain and Mrs Beatham a very pleasant couple, obviously happily married, and after the early morning cuppas, things went as Charlie had advised, and

I nipped in to see him during dinner break. 'Ain't you lucky, mate,' I told him. 'Your job's a donkey doddle.'

'Not if your boss is single and living in camp,' grunted Charlie.

That afternoon there was a notice – 'Mrs Beatham Out', but I got in and found the mess uniform. It received a real 'shining parade' digout, but I had much trouble with the high boots, the uppers being inside very tight-legged trousers which were fastened under the boot arches by stiff buckles. It was still early afternoon, so I decided to liven up the red tiling on the hall and passage floors. Carrying scrubbing gear, I thrust open a door that hit something with a crash. To my horror, the Captain's wife, *en déshabillé*, was lying on the bed reading. Stuttering, I shut the door with another bang and had the tiles done in next to no time. Luckily for me the lady of the house had a sense of humour, laughingly accepting my apology when she emerged. 'But, madam,' I protested, ' 'ow about that notice on your gate?'

'Oh, everyone does that in India. It only meant that I didn't wish to be disturbed.'

'Blimey, missus,' I thought, 'you were "disturbed" all right just now!' and reported to Charlie, who had managed to hobble to his hut.

'Done the mess dress?' he asked, and I nodded.

'What?' he exclaimed after a time. 'You didn't yank those boots out of the trousers?'

'I did too – bitt of a job, ain't it?'

'Not such a bloody job as he'll have shoving them back in,' howled Charlie, 'they never get taken out, you silly sod.'

'Eh? Then 'ow d'yer clean the uppers?'

'You don't. They never get dirty.'

'Well, what a scruffy way to treat boots,' I retorted loftily. 'Those buckles underneath are red rust,' and mentioned another matter.

'But why go into the bedroom?' demanded Charlie. 'I never do.'

'All I wanted was a bit o' light so I could scrub the passage.'

Charlie nearly exploded: 'Scrub the tiles, you crafty long bastard? You're after my job!'

'I certainly am *not*! Anyway, they're leaving.'

'Could be weeks waiting for the boat.' Next day Mrs Beatham, after commenting on the excellent polishing of the boots, smilingly suggested that in future they should not be removed, and then highly suspicious Charlie rolled up. 'You can hop it.

I'm "M and D" (medicine and duty). Pawny wants to see you at once. The Captain might have mentioned the bedroom business.'

'Oh hell!'

Did I detect regret on the lady's face as I left? Those tiles really gleamed! Nearing camp I felt growing fear. Was I wanted for simply barging into a bedroom or for something far more serious? This was the first of a series of disquieting moments, though this time I needn't have worried; I was being offered promotion. I hesitated, staring at the row of ribbons on Pawny's chest. I'd been promoted before, with unfortunate results. 'Don't you fancy it, Shaw?' he asked, surprised.

'Yessir, thank you.' I'd be useless to Florrie as a private on lower rate. I felt quite unexcited, but my fiancée and the family would be delighted. So here was I, wearing stripes only weeks after being chucked out of the Army. How long could it last?

*　　　*　　　*

Soon I was company orderly corporal for a week, and after checking one hut at roll call, a voice called after me: 'Hey, mush – you come from Yapton?' My sergeant explained that Yapton was a trusting little Sussex village where doors were left open all night! I went back and closed this one, thinking of what would have happened to a Guardsman calling an N.C.O. 'Mush'.

Days passed, and fear of exposure lessened. I was putting on weight, and took over centre-half in the soccer eleven, but to my dismay the keen edge of shooting had gone; undoubtedly nerves. I could fill only an occasional vacancy in the unit musketry team. Led by R.S.M. Hanlon, these 'Dead Eye Dicks' were really mustard.

It seemed strange to lead a rifle section, and to handle a Lewis gun, but I soon learned. I must do well and stay in England. When an Indian draft left, the Battalion was decimated for a time. Our Second was having scraps with hill tribesmen, and I'd been told of what happened to certain component parts of any British soldier captured; it didn't sound nice! However, I did look longingly at Colonial Office invitations to tour West Africa. Nigeria, Gold Coast, Sierra Leone and The Gambia were names that had always fascinated me, but now the name 'Florrie' was even more alluring – these tours were for single men only!

Another anxious moment. After manoeuvres on the South Downs, I stayed with the rear party, clearing up our field – the farmer had a written assurance that no razor-blades would be left to endanger his prize herd, and every square foot had to be scrutinised. Our officer appeared. 'Corporal, a Guards unit is taking a meal in here around midday. I hope they won't leave us another mess.'

Being Guards, they would certainly leave the place as clean as they found it, but my great worry was to keep hidden – the Taffs had not yet left for Palestine. Later, in our one remaining tent, I heard a voice outside: 'Here they come. All piss and wind!' That remark, to my guilty mind, means 'Prince of Wales's Company'! Fearfully I peered out . . . thank God, those cap badges were too large to be leeks. They were Grenadiers. As I relaxed and emerged, there was another outburst from our former speaker: 'Buggered if there's anything special about *them*!'

Wrong. A most difficult drill for any large party is to keep step on grass without the aid of drum-beats, and the Bill Browns were doing it perfectly after a lengthy march. I called my group to attention, and as their C.O. returned my salute, the knowledgable one slapped at a wasp. 'STAND STILL THAT MAN!' roared the marching R.S.M., and the offender, never having heard such volume, froze in sheer horror, and moaned about it for weeks afterwards.

*   *   *

I was granted a plain clothes' pass, visiting Florrie at weekends. The Royal Sussex were for Dover in the autumn, and I again reminded her of what she was already aware – the Sword of Damocles could fall at any moment, but her reply was that she was ready for the worst. That girl certainly had spunk – what had I done to deserve it? We would marry, and she'd carry on working until the Dover move materialised.

In the Battalion sports I won the high jump – length of leg, of course, and a few days later an officer told me that I'd been entered for the Hampshire County Championship. 'I won't stand a dog's chance, sir!' I protested in consternation.

'You never know. Practise. Anyway, the Committee's booked a charabanc for a day's outing.' The looming event, at Eastleigh, kept me awake at night, and on the day no-one was more flabbergasted than myself when I won without once dislodging the lathe; maybe the others had an off day! I received a gold medal, a badge for my blazer, and the congratulations of the C.O. Then it was painted on the Battalion honours board.

Hampshire now chose me to represent them in the Inter-County contest at Stamford Bridge, and I rubbed shoulders with international athletes like Lord Burghley (now the Marquis of Salisbury) and Jack Lovelock, then quickly learned that I was no budding Olympic star. The winner of my event was still jumping in a track suit after I'd been eliminated, so I slunk away to join my father and grandfather in the stand; the latter had been a crack sprinter in Victorian days. 'You did yer best,' he said. Some best! I was given another badge, and never had the cheek to wear it. I did get into the unit relay team, running the 220 yards. Led by the skipper, Lieutenant le Mesurier, we went pothunting, winning every relay we entered, starting with a big silver cup apiece from Kent Constabulary. I was now collecting a sizeable number of trophies.

Talkies hadn't yet reached the local cinema, but plenty of troops went; Bordon was a miniature Aldershot. The projector often broke down, and the resourceful manager filled gaps with solos. One night there were so many stops that the pianist got fed up and left. Egged on, I groped forward when the film resumed, and gave a spirited rendering of 'Fire! Fire!' during a harrowing death scene. Nobody shot me, and when a tremendous groan greeted yet another break, the manager and I had a quick confab and gave the lads a couple of choruses:

> Never mind what the doctors say,
> Cuddle your girl three times a day,
> Oh! Oh! Oh! You can feel it doing you good.
> If you feel a nervous wreck
> Chuck your arms around her neck,
> Oh! Oh! Oh! You can feel it doing you good.
> Though your face is not like Valentino's,
> She's too wise to let you know that she knows.
> So never mind what the doctors say,
> Cuddle your girl three times a day,
> Oh! Oh! Oh! You can feel it doing you good.

The second, as intended, brought down the house and produced good humour:

> I've got the guy who used to be my Captain
> Working for me;
> He wanted work, so I made him a clerk
> In my father's factory.

And by and by, I'm going to have him working
Right up to his brow;
He opens the office every morning at eight,
Then I roll up about four hours late,
Everything comes to those who wait,
I've got my Captain working for me now.

    I got a complimentary ticket, and the pianist didn't go absent
again.

*   *   *

When the C.O. sanctioned my marriage, the hut had a whip
round, a surprising gesture, since most privates look upon
N.C.O.'s as anathema. And so Florrie and I were hitched for
better or worse. Before entering the vestry, the cheeky ex-Forces
vicar regaled everyone with warnings against Army drinking
and gambling. If he'd touched on absenteeism I would certainly
have blushed.

    Dover. The Battalion slogged up a hill, entering the barracks
from the rear. Access from the front was by a huge shaft cut into
a cliff. Inside were three sets of spiral steps, one for Officers and
Families, another for Warrant Officers and Sergeants, the third
for the common herd. It meant a climb of about a hundred steps,
and it wasn't unknown for a chap who'd had 'one over the
eight' to be found asleep halfway up the shaft. I disappeared
into its depths almost as soon as I'd discarded my pack, and
rented a nearby bedsitter.

    Florrie arrived within a week and took over. I was the only
married man in the unit on lower rate, drawing thirty shillings
weekly, with our rent of ten bob the first consideration. I was
also given a piece of meat with two loaves every week, plus a
bob a day in lieu of all the other luxuries I would have consumed
in barracks. My wife proved an excellent economist – she had to
be – and on this sub-standard level she managed, and we were
happy. If my wife ever regretted leaving her secure and pensionable manageress position for something extremely hazardous, it never showed.

    In Grand Shaft Barracks, a job for the orderly corporal was to
climb around various steps and switch on electric lights in
dangerous spots, then get up before reveille to put 'em all out.
But Dover, with its Straits and teeming harbour, fascinated me,
apart from one unpleasant task when I helped in the disembar-

kation of the last of the Army of Occupation on the Rhine. It was
during a heavy gale, and some families were literally carried
ashore. In those days, Dover quayside was wretchedly exposed
to the weather.

*   *   *

One evening an orderly came from barracks – the Adjutant
wished to see me immediately. Florrie and I glanced at each
other . . . was this it? My echoing footsteps sounded like a
deathknell, but again fears were groundless. The Garrison
Commander, Sir Hereward Wake, and his household staff were
going away for nine weeks. He needed a childless couple, of
impeccable character, to caretake. I made a precipitate descent
of the steps, thinking: '"Impeccable"? It *is* a comic opera!'

At Constable's Tower, Dover Castle, a charming Lady Wake
showed us around – a female duologue with myself two paces
behind, and we were left in possession. The winds howled
around, but Florrie and I were warm enough. This unexpected
idyll meant no parades except for pay, and I didn't mind
climbing the shaft and Castle Hill for that.

The Brigadier having discovered that as Constable of Dover
he was entitled to a certain amount of armour from the (ugh!)
Tower of London, this load of old iron was delivered. Struggling
into one of the outfits, I shouted to my wife, and her scream on
seeing me in the gloom of the staircase was equalled by my own
on finding that the stuff was smothered inside by preservative –
my things had to go to the cleaner's.

Brigadier and retinue returned, her Ladyship expressing
herself delighted by the cleanliness. Sir Hereward told me to let
him know if I ever needed help. 'By gum, mate,' I thought, 'I
won't forget that!'

It was now our turn to go on leave, as though I hadn't just
finished one! It was clouded, however, by my granddad's
death. The funeral was delayed when my Uncle Bob, struggling
into new black trousers, accidentally sat down on a frying pan
containing bacon fat. The cortege had to wait, with everybody
reeking of mothballs, while Aunt Flo scraped him into respecta-
bility. If there is indeed life after earthly death, granddad was
probably looking on, cackling himself silly.

Back at Dover I attended another funeral, of an ex-serviceman
who'd won a decoration entitling him to a modified military
ceremony. I was in charge of the bearer party, a most depressing

experience. The widow and family were unable to hide their poverty, and the flowers carried by one child looked as though they'd been gleaned from hedgerows. Her late father, having won a medal for bravery, had been rewarded with unemployment and something not far removed from a pauper's grave.

*   *   *

I was made full corporal, a substantive rank gained less than two years after that ghastly exit that still gave me the shivers. Off now to Chichester Depot for a spell, where I was given a small hut for a married quarter; Florrie soon had it shipshape. I wasn't too happy at my interview, the C.O. remarked that it seemed 'only the other day that I'd been there as a recruit'. It sounded as though in his opinion I'd been promoted too quickly – maybe my imagination. I was also disheartened by being denied a squad of my own – I was of course subordinate to the sergeants. I got many odd jobs, including the supervising of church fatigue one Saturday morning. While the lads did the cleaning I was giving them a jerky rendition of 'Alexander's Ragtime Band' when the padre entered. 'That's a peculiar tune for a harmonium,' he remarked, and then informed me that I could perform at the Sunday service as the usual musician couldn't come.

'May I choose the hymns, sir, please? I don't read music.' He agreed, and as I'd always thought that most hymns seemed pitched too high for average male voices, I brought them down a tone or two, and I think the padre was surprised by the volume of singing. Next I had to deputise for the school teacher when he went on leave, but why me, for Pete's sake? I'd attended a council school, and he was a Warrant Officer in the Education Corps. It didn't prove a case of the blind leading the blind, for several of the lads knew a sight more than I did; I was often very happy to let the class work on its own. 'Imagine,' I said, 'that your mother has written to ask what you think of the Army. Reply, and don't pull yer punches.'

'What will happen to the letters, corporal?' asked a suspicious bright boy.

'No-one else will see them, I promise.' Well, I'd asked for it and certainly got it . . . wasn't I glad when the real teacher returned.

Another scare, a nasty one this time, when Florrie returned in a hurry from shopping to say there were Welsh Guards in the barracks. 'What?' I said in panic. 'I didn't know they were back from Palestine. Are you sure?'

'Certain. They're waiting by the pay-table. I didn't let them see me.'

'Know any of them?'

'I only saw their backs. Be careful, Jess.'

'You bet. I'll reconnoitre.' Pay parade was informal. People just gathered, and names were called in alphabetical order. You march up, halt, salute, grab, salute again, about turn and hop it. Well, they were Taffs all right, and I tucked myself into the background. I recognised only two – Sergeant Catchpole, a good fellow, and another N.C.O. who would certainly denounce me for any possible kudos. If we were paid first I would go missing, and think of some excuse later. The officer appeared with the bag of lolly, to be greeted with a roar of: 'Shun!' from the sergeant I feared. The heels of the Guardsmen banged together as one, and the startled Captain Prince decided to get rid of the noisy lot quickly. They marched off, and I cooled off. How easy to come a cropper! The party were doing a job somewhere and were attached to us for pay and rations – luckily their grub was taken out to them.

To my disgust I had no chance to train a squad of my own, and back at Dover I was at once sent off again, to Woolwich Arsenal, learning how to keep Lewis guns in good order. Again my luck was in, for the one Taff on the course didn't know me. Returning, I was in time to deputise for our goalkeeper, Alf Beer, who'd been injured. We played the Seaforth Highlanders, and nothing went wrong . . . for them. It became a nightmare, and as I picked the ball out of my net for the tenth time, the Scots massed behind my goal counted me out. That wasn't all the misery, for at the post mortem our manager, Quartermaster Jack Steer, told me none too politely that I should have saved at least six.

* * *

Instead of the usual Trooping on the King's birthday, we held a *feu de joie*. This 'fire of joy' was carried out by 600 of us, in one long line along a cliff top, facing France. Rifles, containing blank, were aimed at the sky. The joy began with the right-hand man blowing off his blank, to be followed instantly by the second and third and so on along the line, the effect being exactly like a terrific, long drawn out raspberry. Not easy, and at

rehearsals some people blew off prematurely or after the raspberry had swept past; but perfect on the day.

Suddenly, through my own daftness, the spectre of discovery
again reared its ugly head. I was passing the Vickers Company
(the weapon had now been promoted from mere platoon
strength) and saw a gun being cleaned. I paused for a moment,
just as their C.S.M. arrived. 'Bullock' Oakley was the biggest
man in the unit, a fine athlete, all bone and muscle. 'Interested?'
he asked.

Instead of disappearing at speed, I answered that the Vickers
appeared to be a bit of all right. 'You wouldn't say that if you
had to carry it, corporal,' one of the cleaners observed. 'It
weighs 38 lbs, and the tripod goes 52.'

Again with lamentable lack of acumen I remarked: 'All the
same, I'd say it's a lot better than the Lewis.'

'You think so?' smiled the C.S.M., and next day Pawny sent
for me, and seemed annoyed, saying that I was being sent to 'B'
Company.

'Blast!' I exclaimed involuntarily. 'I'm quite happy here, sir.'

'What "B" want they usually get,' replied Pawny. 'I've an idea
that Bullock fixed this.'

I climbed the steps slowly, finding my wife laying the tea table
(we were now in official married quarters). 'I'm posted to "B",' I
said heavily.

'The machine-gunners?'

'Yep.'

'Well, cheer up. You ought to do well there – they might make
you sergeant,' she joked brightly.

I groaned inwardly – obviously she didn't realise the full
implications. I'd certainly be on the next course at the Vickers
school at Netheravon, with students from the Welsh Guards
who would assuredly know me. This would be infinitely more
dangerous than a few Taffs on pay parade. Despite Florrie's
protests I began a moustache, and inevitably I learned of my
departure for an eight weeks course that would terminate just
before Christmas. Meanwhile I was to undergo tuition under
Sergeant Ted Brand – the 'comedy' was continuing. Being *au fait*
with all he said and demonstrated, I found it extremely difficult
to feign ignorance. Ted, puzzled, showed it one day when our
O.C. came by during a lesson. 'Don't get up,' said Captain
Head. 'How is he doing, Sergeant Brand?'

'Sir,' answered Ted slowly, 'I never have to tell him anything
twice.'

The Captain laughed. 'In that case, Corporal Shaw, I shall certainly expect you to bring back a Q.1.' (Qualified First Class).

I insisted upon Florrie visiting her people for the two months, not wanting her in barracks if the worst happened. On parting, I wondered whether I'd be in civvies when we again met. At Netheravon my allotted hut was deserted. Being evening, everyone would be in the Naffy. I glanced around, to be transfixed by a small brass plate over one of the beds. 'Which regiment?' I wondered, and went over to see a leek embossed upon it, and the name 'Wyman'! The very chap in charge of my room at Wellington. This youngster had my fate in his hands. 'Let's get it over,' I thought wretchedly, and made for the Naffy.

Directly I entered, the fatuousness of my moustache 'disguise' was apparent. Wyman rose from a table, looking incredulous. 'What the hell are *you* here for?'

I managed to mumble that it was for the same reason as himself – to qualify as an instructor. I saw that he now had two stripes. After a cup of tea, he asked me to play the piano. The last thing I felt like doing, but I obliged. We spent the evening together, and once laughed about the barrack-room ruckus when I'd assisted him, but never did he touch upon the crucial subject of my being 'seen off'. At last I was forced to ask: 'Anyone else with you?'

'I'll say . . . Greenacre.'

I went icy – was my former hero to bring about my downfall? I knew that after his term as Adjutant he'd been appointed Equerry to the Prince of Wales, so must now be back with the gunners; this course must be a refresher. Captain Greenacre (he won a D.S.O. in 1945), scrupulously fair but a strict disciplinarian – I remembered an incident when he caught a limber driver neglecting the horses. Although I'd collected an average share of minor punishment from him, as far as I knew he had no reason to bear me any dislike. Nevertheless, he surely must denounce me? My desperate hope was some gossip I'd overheard from two officers' servants, when it appeared that the Captain had no great love for Major Fox-Pitt. During the weekend I once saw Greenacre and Wyman in deep conversation, but dare not quiz the latter, dreading what he might have to tell me.

The course began, and at first my instructor must have thought me dense. Well, it had to come, and during a break it did. Approaching me were several officers, including Greenacre. I had no chance to dodge. Oh God, if you love me, now's Your chance!

Some of them were talking, but Greenacre was not. He just looked fixedly at me. Fascinated, I was unable to glance away, but subconsciously noticed the senior of the group acknowledge my salute. At that moment Greenacre looked at the ground – deliberately I felt sure. Seconds later they'd passed, with no recall . . . I could hardly believe it.

That was the nearest I got to him, for officers were in a separate class. The school played a local fifteen at rugby and I watched from a safe distance. The Captain must have been bored stiff, for most of his team were novices.

I tried to unwind, but spent the longest two months of my life. Whatever my knowledge of the Vickers, it was useless to me as an instructor unless I could teach – that was what this long and intensive course was all about. I'd hate to miss the Q.1 after Captain Head's friendly admonition, and managed to win it, but it wasn't until Wyman got into the passenger seat of Greenacre's Buick and it roared away that I finally came out of purdah.

Florrie was already re-installed in our quarter. 'Merry Christmas – give us a kiss!' I demanded, with a hug.

'You haven't scraped that awful 'tash off!' she said despairingly.

'Any minute now.' I sniffed appreciatively at something cooking.

'I've been wondering,' she said later. 'Any Taffs on the course?'

'Two. Wyman, you remember him. And, you'll never guess – Greenacre.'

'Captain Greenacre! Good heavens! Did he see *you*?'

'He saw me all right, and I'll always be in his debt – Wyman's too. I only wish I could thank them.'

She was silent for a moment, then: 'Jess, you said nothing about it when you wrote. You must have had a rough time.'

'Pretty grim at first. Now you know why I grew this thing.'

An Indian draft left, and to bring the gunners up to strength I was given men to train. All passed, so everything that had been rammed into me hadn't fallen on stony ground. Life outside grew worse, and in the 1931 slump everyone in State employ suffered – even the unemployed lost some of their dole. With dismay I heard that Army pay would be cut, then learned that

only those on the old rate would be affected by coming down to
the new level. Of course, we new 'uns laughed at all the fury,
but later the differentials were restored and it was back to the
status quo.

*　　　*　　　*

Soon I heard an incredible rumour, and immediately tackled an
important pal – Corporal 'Fuzz' Marshall of the Orderly Room;
such V.I.P.'s were handy to know. He laughed. 'It'll be in
Battalion Orders tonight, anyway. We're off to London, relieving a Guards unit for a fortnight. They're off on manoeuvres.'

What a shock! Slowly I walked to my quarter. 'Oh Jess,'
murmured Florrie. 'All these regiments and they had to pick
yours!'

'One bloody thing after another!' I muttered. 'Chelsea! Would
you believe it?'

'Swearing won't help, Jess.'

'Sorry.' I knew something had to be done to lessen her
anxiety. 'Don't worry. The Taffs aren't in town, and it won't be
nearly so dangerous as Netheravon. I won't even grow a
moustache!' I felt better when she smiled, but grew uneasy
again on learning that a Guards drill-sergeant was coming to
teach us the ropes, then finally relaxed; he'd be from the Irish. I
then lugged all my equipment home, for whatever happened I'd
show 'em how to turn out on public duties.

On arrival the 'Micks' drill-sergeant suggested that the privates and corporals he selected should remain unchanged
throughout the tour – officers and sergeants to take turns. It was
agreed, and now the big moment when we all paraded in full
marching order. The D.S. came along, picking out a body here
and there. After inspecting my front and rear, he grabbed my
rifle. I'd used french polish, forbidden in the Welsh Guards.
Without comment he wrote down my name. Next to me was
Corporal 'Tiny' Mills,* only an inch shorter than myself. The
D.S. stepped back, appraising us. 'You pair,' he announced,
'will escort the colour.' Well, that just about crowned everything. I'd be right out in front with no bearskin for camouflage!
In for a penny . . .

Whatever his private feelings, that drill-sergeant never lost
patience. His word of command could never have been equalled

---

* Commissioned in 1942, afterwards killed in action.

before in Dover, and our tiny square sounded like the Caterham
Depot. Meanwhile C.S.M. Oakley gave me a hint, about as
subtle as an elephant's backside, that I should polish the rifles of
the seven selected gunners, but I simply hadn't enough time
left. I compromised by attending to his, and giving the lads the
rest of the stuff. It is traditional for Infantry to pour scorn on the
bullshit of the Guards, but now their own was cheerfully
accepted. Our packs, which should have contained only regulation items, concealed nothing but thin wooden boxes, cunningly
constructed by our Pioneers to fit snugly.

The sweating came to an end and our instructor departed. We
entrained, and I left my equipment to join Florrie in another
compartment – she'd be staying with my family in London.

At Victoria, as our regimental band led us along the road
where I'd marched so many times, I began to feel strangely
carefree. Tiny, alongside me, wondered whether we'd be
allowed out of barracks that night – he wanted to send a
telegram.

'Don't worry. There's a post office in the barracks.'

'How d'you know?'

'Er . . . bound to be with two units stationed there.'

'Two? Anyone would think you've been here before, Jasper.'

Blimey, I thought, I'd better simmer down! 'Well, I should
know, Tiny, I'm a Cockney, ain't I?' Just then we had to march
to attention as the band struck up 'The Royal Sussex', and I
found that Chelsea hadn't altered a scrap except that no leeks
were to be seen. And I'm damned if I wasn't put into my same
old barrack-room – a room that seemed full of the ghosts of
former comrades with whom I could never share quarters again.

*   *   *

They're changing Guard at Buckingham Palace,
Boomp, boomp, boomp, boomp!
Christopher Robin went down with Alice,
Boomp, boomp, boomp, boomp!
. . . 'A Soldier's life is awfully hard,'
Boomp, boomp, boomp, boomp!
Says Alice.

Saturday. History was repeating itself, with the family
augmented by my wife. Crowds were there to see how the 'Line
Regiment' performed, and there was the same old chappie, with

bowler hat and rolled umbrella, who had been ever-present if it wasn't raining. How many times had he seen me in very different attire?

No commands were given on the wrong foot, but those weary Grenadiers sentries must have been surprised when I recited the orders without referring to the board I held, and probably inwardly cussed me for my punctiliousness – with relatives watching I was most officious. 'Any queries?' I asked Private Glaysher. 'No? Well, ignore all these people, and if any kids get cheeky the copper'll see 'em off.' Glaysher, six feet tall and two stones heavier than myself, hardly needed this gratuitous advice.

Off went the Bill Browns, leaving King George and Family in our loving care. In the guard-room, Bullock Oakley examined the waiting guard reports with loathing, for they had to be made out in triplicate. A tricky job. The men's turn on 'visiting rounds' must be dovetailed with sentry periods to avoid clashing, with added complication when double posts were split at night. At my tentative suggestion he cheerfully handed the task to me. I made out an extra copy, and next day persuaded the Coldstreams to sign it, then donated it to our Regimental Museum!

Time passed swiftly, and our last Guard dismounted and neared the barrack gates. At the command: 'Fall in the Escorts,' Tiny and I marked time, then rejoined the First Division. Everyone inside froze, as usual, at sight of the Colour, and Pawny bore it away to the Officers Mess with his escorts sticking like leeches; it was all over. For a short, unforgettable time I'd returned to the past, and after all these years still look at the photos and wonder how I escaped. There must have been cinema-going Taffs who saw me in close-up on Pathé News, posting a sentry. I'm possibly the only man to have mounted public duties as a Guardsman and an Infantryman, but you won't find it in the Guiness Book . . . neither is it a precedent to be emulated!

*   *   *

Back to Dover, with manoeuvres this year on the Arundel estate of the Duke of Norfolk. In the hope of attracting recruits after the London publicity we marched the 127 miles. Rye gave us lunch, also Bexhill and Shoreham (shades of the birch!) We nearly had to push through the crowds at Brighton, and at

Worthing, with my wife also waving the flag, the Mayor led three cheers from the town hall steps as we began the last lap. It had been a week's heat wave, but not a man fell out.

Entering the estate, the band scared a deer, which hit a wall and broke its neck; the Duke gave us the venison. We also collected thousands of deer ticks, which pestered us with irritating red blobs.

During our stay we Trooped the Colour, and the invited public rewarded us by leaving behind a rubbish dump. I was in charge of the cursing clearing-up party, hoping that a few million of our deer-bugs had attached themselves to the litter-bugs. One gunner, Tom Jones, wasn't upset, for Florrie had brought along a young niece, and she and Tom became engaged. He was our cross-country champion.

Back to Dover by train, where tongue-in-the-cheek Jack Steer stated that the solitary recruit secured had been rejected on medical grounds. We now prepared to change station, again by the sea, this time in Devonshire.

We arrived at Devonport just as a Brigade sports meeting was being arranged, and Tom's reputation had preceded him. As it happened, he was pressed into the mile, quite unsuitable, and as he was beaten by our biggest rivals, the Norfolk Regiment, there were jeers and shouts of: 'Who said Jones could run?' He took it very quietly, but in the three miles next day he lapped most of the field and knocked no fewer than twelve seconds off the Brigade record. Not a squawk from the Norfolks, and to rub it in Tom later broke record time for the last lap of the Exeter–Devonport road relay, so it looked very much as though Lance Corporal Jones *could* run!

Soon after that I was attacked by a ghastly pain – pleurisy – and was later given sick leave. I was shocked by the way my father's health was deteriorating, and there was a nasty scare on our return train journey, an encounter with an ex-Welsh Guardsman now wearing a red cap. Before I could dodge he recognised me. 'Why . . . Stiffy! How are you, boyo?'

'Fine, thanks,' I answered, shaking his hand with simulated heartiness.

'You're looking swell, Flo. I heard you two were married. Got him under control?'

'Oh yes,' she smiled, but had changed colour.

'What are you doing these days, Stiffy?'

'Oh, I managed to find a job.'

'Good. Well, I won't detain you. So long, Stiffy.'

'Nice to see you again, Trebor.' I felt him looking after us, and it wasn't until we were seated in the train that either spoke. 'Suppose you had been in uniform, Jess?' whispered Florrie.

*　　*　　*

I was now senior duty corporal, and had already qualified for promotion as far as Warrant Officer, but always lurking in the back of my mind was unease; I'd had more than a fair share of good fortune. Despite the number of unemployed I was hesitant of going on. Extensions after seven years were severely rationed, for they enabled one to continue for an eventual pension. If I turned the offer down it would be snapped up immediately by someone. The moment came when I was approached by the C.S.M. Did I want the next vacancy?

'I'll have to ask the missus.'

'Eh? She's bound to say yes. You've one foot in the Sergeants Mess already, but you won't get in if you don't sign on. Orderly room must be told today.'

The only thing I cared about was my wife's opinion, for I hadn't forgotten her reaction on the station, and to my other spasms. After she informed me that the decision must be my own, I took it, feeling that she would be secretly relieved. 'I shan't be taking the vacancy, sir,' I told Bullock Oakley.

'Why?' asked Captain Head next day. 'As I see it, you've everything to gain by extending, unless there's a job waiting.'

'There isn't, sir. It's personal. Extremely personal.'

'Oh. Can I help?'

'No sir, but thank you.' (My God, mate, if only you could!)

The O.C. didn't pursue it further, but my pals did on learning that no job was lined up, and now a sad event brought another premature departure. 'B' were at Tregantle, in Cornwall, firing the annual course, and I was actually behind the gun when a despatch rider arrived with a telegram for me. I rode pillion, via the old chain-driven ferry at Torpoint, then Florrie and I caught the London express.

At the hospital, in a curtained-off bed, my father was being given oxygen. 'Who sent for *you*?' he asked weakly.

'Nobody. Got a few days leave.'

'You've just had some.'

'Yes, but that was sick leave. 'Ow are yer, dad?'

'Done for, mate.'

The ward sister overheard, and the curtain moved aside. 'Mr Shaw! Why, you'll be going home soon.'

'I know, sister . . . feet first!' he replied. Now how can a man joke when he knows he's dying? Then he smiled at mother and said: 'You ain't been a bad old stick.' They were almost his last words. So, goodbye dad, one of the unsung, comparatively young in years, but prematurely aged by that 'war to end wars'. What a farce! Hardly a corner of the world without trouble, and that wonderful and expensive 'League of Nations' apparently unable to stop even a dogfight.

A wreath from my father's workmates caused me to write to the London County Council, his former employer, and to my joy they offered me a job as park attendant, subject to my Army character being satisfactory. 'How about Sir Hereward Wake?' suggested Florrie, and I wrote, saying that I was aiming to leave the service prematurely. His reply was as expected – surely I could be of more assistance to my widowed mother by staying in the Army. In short, implying that I was a B.F. However, he coughed up a reference. I spoke to the park-keeper, who said that although the job was secure and pensionable, the wages were very low. However, he added, the Labour Party had just gained control of the L.C.C. for the first time, and a wage claim had been submitted. To date I'd never been interested in Socialism or any other -ism, but if the new form of -ism at County Hall brought higher wages I was all for that!

*   *   *

At Devonport I applied for compassionate release, and the Brigadier compromised by granting an early transfer to the Reserve instead of a final discharge. This meant a welcome bob a day, but was also instrumental in clawing me back on the outbreak of the '39 war. Had I known that, forty years later, no less a personage than Her Majesty Queen Elizabeth would be pardoning me for my fraudulent enlistment, I would, of course, have remained with the Colours and probably progressed a little further than corporal. Unfortunately, I wasn't possessed of second sight.

One of the worst things in the Army is that you are often saying goodbye to good friends; Florrie and I had made many in this fine unit. But what a different leave-taking this time! Fuzz Marshall ushered me in front of the C.O., with everything so relaxed and informal as he read out my character. 'Is there anything else I could add?'

'No sir, thank you. It's most generous.'

'I'm sorry you're going, Corporal. Good luck.'

And good luck to you, Colonel Foster, and to the Royal Sussex Regiment. You little knew the viper you nursed in your bosoms!

We would live with my mother and sister until finding a place of our own, and arrived with our few chattels. Catching sight of my red discharge book, my mother looked at me questioningly, and without speaking I handed it to her.

'Exemplary!' she exclaimed after a moment, and continued reading aloud. 'Clean, smart, and thoroughly trustworthy. Intelligent and hardworking —' suddenly her voice broke on adding the very words that were in my own mind: 'If only your father could have lived long enough to read this.'

It was a wretched moment.

CHAPTER FIVE

'Hi, Parky – They're pinchin' yer flowers!'

On my way to County Hall for my interview, I went through a 'No Entry' and emerged from a 'No Exit'. This is quite normal for knowledgeables on London's Underground – it saves time, especially in the peak hours. Back into the sunlight. Surely that face was familiar? Yes, by gum! The man held a suitcase by one hand and a toddler by the other, and walking alongside was a sulky-looking woman with a babe in arms. The predatory 'Love-'em-and-leave'em', the confirmed bachelor, had been hooked. 'Joe!' I exclaimed. 'Must be fifteen years!'

'Wotto, Titch,' he grunted. 'I wrote last, yer know.'

'Yes. Sorry. Still servin'?'

'Yes. 'Ow's the Guards?'

'I'm out. A park attendant,' I answered, with the woman regarding me woodenly.

'*Park-keeper*? You poor son! We're off on leave —'

'And we look like missing the train,' put in his better half impatiently.

'Won't keep you then, Joe.' I stuffed the envelope from County Hall in his pocket. 'Get in touch again. Good luck.'

'And to you – you're goin' to need it. So long.'

'Goin' to need it, am I?' I thought, watching them out of sight. 'And "poor sod", eh? The same to you, mate, with knobs on!' He never wrote.

*　　*　　*

I started near home in Victoria Park, armed with steel pricker to impale rubbish, and sporting a numbered, ten-gallon hat, plus

frock coat, Victorian style. My four p.m. finishes and all
weekends off had ended. As the youngest keeper I fell in for jobs
like chasing youths with soccer balls from the sacred turf to
gravel, getting cussed in the same language I'd used against
keepers myself years before. One day their ball hadn't arrived, so
they had fun by entering a plantation and starting a sod fight.
When I went after them they gained the adjacent canal bank and
pelted *me*. On an impulse I started whanging turves back at them,
and after that relations improved somewhat. I got into arguments
with irate parents after stopping kids riding cycles on footpaths if
the wheels were more than fifteen inches across, and preventing
them from banging miniature cricket stumps into that holy grass.
Sometimes you'd see fisticuffs begin, in which case you turned
your back until someone panted up to inform you. You then
walked very slowly, and one or both antagonists would be glad of
your intervention. Flower-pinchers were a nuisance, but by far
the biggest bugbear was litter, and those fields on Monday morn-
ings beggared description. Later I was transferred to London
Fields, another East End spot in Hackney, and soon found that
Victoria Park was a palace by comparison. I'd long ago discovered
why the wages were so poor – almost all my colleagues were
service pensioners. Oh why the hell had *I* left the Army?

Florrie and I rented rooms, obtaining furniture on the
never-never – there was no other way. She took a part-time job
to help. Never a grumble from her, though I moaned. 'Think
yerself lucky to 'ave a job at all,' reproved my mother. 'What
about those 'unger marchers, and the unemployed lyin' in the
road stoppin' traffic?'

'Well, they got publicity, but nothin' else. I know I'm lucky to
be in work, but that's no reason why I shouldn't look out for
something better. I don't want Florrie workin' permanently.'

That year the BBC ran an anti-litter campaign called 'Beauty
Blots', and on impulse I wrote offering to contribute, sitting up
all night working on my masterpiece. To my excitement it was
accepted. 'You cheeky monkey!' said mother.

'Is everyone who broadcasts cheeky, then?'

'No, but they do it for a livin'.'

'Tomorrow night, after the news.'

The BBC had left my effort entirely unedited, enabling me to
hit out viciously. 'Oh yes, my boy,' I was told later, 'we 'ad it on.
I've never 'eard people more insulted!'

'The truth ain't insultin', mum, an' they're payin' me five
guineas.'

'For five minutes? Get on with yer!'

'Fact. I'll buy yer a new bonnet.'

Next morning an elderly chappie with whom I'd sometimes chatted bore down upon me looking wrathful, so I took a tighter grip on my pricker. 'Is your name "Shaw"?' he demanded.

'Yessir.'

'What the devil d'you mean by referring to us as apes?'

'*Not* you, sir. A very small minority.' I took him on a conducted tour, from broken bottles in the kids' paddling pond to unspeakable items lying in secluded corners, and it ended with his agreement with everything I'd said. My mother, now proud as Punch, showed neighbours extracts printed in the 'Listener', and then the BBC invited me to take part in a sketch that closed the show, which was another thrill for me. The pianist was Ernest Lush, who was still going strong many years later. I was now returned to Victoria Park – was the Council worried about my life? Winter arrived, and I was taken off patrol and appointed mate to the blacksmith. Very soon my awkward hands were suffering.

Meanwhile our wage claim was being considered, though 'claim' was a misnomer. In those days it was a begging-bowl. We didn't get a penny. A Parliamentary election was at hand, and Herbert Morrison, Council leader and head of the committee that had turned down our union, was a candidate, so some of us went along to one of his meetings. At question time Morrison had the nerve to tell us to 'consult our union'. Uproar. Morrison left, but that didn't stop the racket continuing on the floor. 'Why the bloody hell should *you* get a rise?' yelled a fellow at me. 'You only pick up bits o' paper.'

I showed my hands. 'D'yer think these burns come from litter? I'm a bleedin' blacksmith!'

'Who paid yer to come and smash up this meeting?' demanded someone else.

'Who d'yer mean by "who"?' bawled Alf Bartell, a real militant.

'Why *them*, o' course. The Tories.'

'You stoopid git!' snarled Alf. 'I'm no Tory. I'm for Lansbury. Worth a dozen of yer Morrisons!'

At that, I felt as Alice did when the whole pack descended upon her, and as Bartell and I were chucked out, a former vague idea that politics was a dirty game became a conviction. 'Where's your collar?' inquired Florrie, when I stomped indoors.

'In me pocket – the stud's bust,' I fumed. 'My first and last political meeting!' We'd had nothing from Conservatives, ditto from Labour, and the Liberals appeared to be dying ducks. 'All tarred with the same brush,' asserted Bartell next day. 'I'd like to ship the bloody lot to sea and pull out the bung!' I disagreed. Guy Fawkes had a better idea.

*   *   *

Summer, and back on patrol. My most entertaining job was on Bank Holiday, when six lost kids were suddenly thrust upon me to escort to a woman lavatory attendant. Three kids on each side, everyone holding hands. The girls howled incessantly, and the two outside boys had not only shit themselves but wanted to fight. I was forced to rearrange formation, with the two smelly antagonists next to me. Held up every few yards by sympathetic women, this hideous crawl took nearly an hour. Thirty-five more years of this? I would undoubtedly go scatty. Then, unexpectedly, fortune smiled on my day off, when Florrie noticed some lettering on a door. 'S.S.A.F.A.,' she remarked. 'What's that, I wonder?'

'Soldiers, Sailors, and Airmen's Families Association,' I explained. 'Now, *I* wonder?'

The ex-officer inside, after recovering from the shock of someone trying to get rid of a job, was sympathetic, saying that as I'd served during the war, I could fill a vacancy now if willing to do night work occasionally. I accepted at once, went to County Hall and gave notice after visiting my new employer. Goodbye sacred grass and litterbugs. 'Part nights,' I told Florrie, 'but it's a quid a week more. Now hand in *your* notice – it's time you were put in the family way!'

The new job was congenial, sometimes entailing trips to places like Covent Garden and Billingsgate, which seemed more romantic in the small hours! My day shifts were mainly clerical. Within a few weeks I had a six-bob rise, well worthwhile in the Thirties. If things went on like this we might get a car on the never-never, although, of the many men at my firm, only one of the 'lower orders' had such a luxury. He was single, and sour-grapes colleagues alleged that he lived on bread and jam in order to keep his banger on the road.

Only one snag – my wife disliked London. However, my employer was represented in other towns and soon I'd apply for a transfer. If only the other problems could be so easily resolved. As though Italy's bombing of Abyssinia hadn't been enough, a ghastly civil war was raging in Spain and a fanatic named Hitler was beginning to rampage in Germany. And now, trouble on our own doorstep as newsbills yelled: 'The King. Constitutional Crisis'. I'd never heard such arguments as raged over Edward's abdication, and wondered about their reaction in the Welsh Guards.

*   *   *

My wife's mother was dying, and Florrie in her haste took with her our savings book. The monthly instalment on the furniture was due, and if a payment were delayed things could easily turn nasty. I couldn't worry her in the circumstances, and remembered a notice I'd seen – 'Gold and Silver Bought'. That big silver cup? Florrie would miss it instantly from its pride of place. The gold medal would have to go. Taking it from its case I read aloud: 'Hampshire County Amateur Athletic Championships – 1929 – High Jump – J.J. Shaw.' Happy days, but there were things even more important than sport. I felt ill at ease entering the pawnshop. 'I want to sell this,' I lied. The proprietor took it away, to test it I presumed, and returned looking dubious. 'Anything wrong?' I asked.

'No, it's gold all right. Yours?'

'Of course.'

'Pity. With this inscription it'll be melted. 'Pity,' he repeated. Great Scott – a pawnbroker with a heart?

'Emergency,' I muttered, 'I need a bit of cash quickly.'

'If I might ask – how much?'

'Thirty bob would see me through.'

'Well, why not pledge it for that? You can redeem it any time within a year. Cost you a little bit of interest, that's all.' I gratefully agreed.

'O Ye of Little Faith'. Next morning a letter came from Florrie, enclosing the payment due. I really should have known better.

And now, great excitement when the suspected pregnancy was confirmed. My wife was now forty, and in hospital things became very protracted. I divided my time between work, snatched sleep, and dashes to the nearest call box. Finally John Brian arrived, all nine pounds of him, and as we'd waited ten years for this, those cheeky Sussex lads who'd hinted that there would be 'three of us in front of the altar' had been way off beam!

*   *   *

One afternoon after night work, my usual cup of tea in bed was brought in by Florrie on returning from a bus ride with the baby. 'Jess, they're building air raid shelters in Hyde Park.'

'Been going on some time.'

'What do you think will really happen?'

'Only needs a spark.'

'Well, if there's a war, I'd hate being alone when you're on nights.'

'I won't be. I'm not yet off the Reserve. If the balloon goes up before May I'll be called up.'

'Well, that's even worse. How about Brian here in London?'

We made a snap decision. She would take the baby to Worthing now and be out of town should I have to go. If I didn't, my transfer would materialise shortly. We stored the furniture (now paid for) and I took a room near my job.

Troubles continued, with the submarine *Thetis* and a hundred of her crew lost by accident. Things were also fast worsening on the Continent, but a trial air alert was a farce – people wouldn't take it seriously. Lights were left blazing, with bellowing, banging and cursing from exasperated officials, and with one incident in my street. Two steel-helmeted wardens rounded a corner at speed from opposite directions and knocked each other out. Most amusing.

And then came the most incredible happening of all while I was shaving, when the news of a German-Russian non-aggression pact came over the radio. 'Blimey,' I said to my soapy reflection, 'that's it!'

Inevitably, I came in one morning to find my calling-up on the mat, and also a note from my landlord. He and his family had departed for Scotland overnight, leaving the four-storey house and contents – just like that. No mention of my rent, but left a stamped envelope for me to forward the key. I'd just come off night shift, but my case was already packed and I didn't go to bed. I did pay a quick call on my mother, who was undoubtedly remembering 1914.

There was something like chaos at the terminus, with hundreds of mothers and children being evacuated. All youngsters were labelled, with one group of four tied to one another with string. They carried gas masks, small cases or bundles, packets of grub and bottles of pop. Some had never been away from the millions of chimney pots, so the sea and countryside would be an innovation. The quiet rural areas upon which these Cockney hordes were about to be released would need plenty of stamina!

What a scene. Tears, glum silence, excitement, laughter. To lots of these kids it was a glorious adventure, but to those of us with memories of the First World War Zeppelins and Gothas it was the first of many horrors to come.

My train was packed. I stood all the way in a baggage compartment, and decided to spend the night at Worthing. Eventually I found my precious pair on the beach. 'Shouldn't you have reported straight to Chichester?' Florrie asked.

'Yes, but I'm about flaked out. One more day without me won't lose us the war.'

'Where are the First Battalion now?'

'Suez, but I bet they won't stay there much longer!'

We sat in the sunshine, watching our nipper with his little bucket of pebbles. Was my wife wondering, like myself, whether this peaceful expanse would soon be a tangle of barbed wire? To me, everything began to appear unreal – like some horrible dream.

CHAPTER SIX

Seconded, Royal West African Frontier Force

Old pal Marshall, now Orderly Room Kingpin, was so haggard that I hardly recognised him. 'Where the hell have you been?'

'Sorry, Fuzz. A bit awkward when you're on nightwork.'

'*I've* not slept for days. I was just going to give away the job I've saved you.'

'What is it?'

'Officer Cadet Training Unit.'

'Me – *officer*? Well I'm blowed —'

'Don't kid yourself. You're an instructor.'

'Here, arf a mo. I've been away five years.'

'You'll pick it up, like everyone else. It's at Bulford.'

'Good old Salisbury Plain. Gosh, Fuzz, you've shot up. Congrats.'

'And to you. Full sergeant as from today.'

'Full?' I gasped. 'That's quick.'

'You can go off tomorrow.'

Soon I made for the sergeants mess, seeking auld acquaintance. Chaps who'd been subordinate to me were now senior, having remained with the colours, and I was suddenly slapped down by a company sergeant major for using his old nickname. No familiarity. 'You mean in here too?' I asked disbelievingly.

'In here too.' Why, years before when a raw-arsed recruit he'd been glad to clean my buttons. Now he was pulling rank, in the mess of all places! At that I grabbed my parcel of civvies and made for Worthing.

'Is it France?' murmured Florrie, as I entered.

'Not yet, anyway,' I answered, keeping a wary eye on my son and heir and his handful of bread and treacle. Sure enough, as I unlaced my clodhoppers, he grabbed my trousers. After he'd been duly scolded, I inquired above his bawls whether anything had been noticed, having left my jacket hanging with sleeves prominent.

'Oh Brian, look – daddy's a sergeant!'

'Gurgle-glop!' remarked the unimpressed one-year-old.

Next morning the station was crowded, and a couple with several kids settled by us. 'We're in, then, sergeant,' said the man. 'Have you heard?'

'No.'

'The Prime Minister announced it not long ago.'

Florrie and I glanced at each other despairingly, as many couples must have done on that day. Suddenly everyone was galvanised as a siren blew, then most people scattered as though the sky were already raining explosives. The family ran for a tunnel under the platforms, leaving everything behind, while other deserted luggage was scattered around. 'Do you want to take Brian under cover?' I asked.

'Not unless bangs start.'

No gunfire, and when the train and the 'all clear' almost deadheated, the guard waited for no stragglers, with many left cursing. I had a last glimpse of my wife, hull-down among abandoned baggage, holding up Brian and waving.

At Bulford the training staff were mainly of Grenadier Guards, with a few odds and sods like myself. Several married quarters were unoccupied and I was lucky; Brian and Florrie were soon installed. On a 'refresher' at Netheravon I found that Vickers tuition hadn't altered, except that the former eight weeks course was now a break-neck seven days. I pitied those students who were new to the weapon!

The first intake of cadets were from the Honourable Artillery Company, top-rate Territorials and Britain's oldest regiment – excellent officer potential. Training began, and continued throughout a hideous winter. Bad enough for staff, but hell itself for the cadets, who nevertheless proved a grand lot. Neither inches of rain nor feet of snow were allowed to interfere with schedule, and Infantry instructors now discovered just what Guards discipline meant. Any preconceived ideas of 'chocolate soldiers' soon vanished. 'Fancy going into action with these bastards in charge!' moaned one fellow.

Very few cadets failed to qualify, but one in particular did. As the son of a very high-ranking officer he could easily have obtained a commission, but elected to do it the hard way, and now he was sunk. 'What the hell can I tell him?' he asked me, and I could only say that I'd once read a book – *Rough Road* – where a man similarly situated had finally won through. He nodded despairingly: 'Yes, I read that too – but it was fiction.'

Those who had passed had a glorious beery binge before departing for their new units and subaltern pips. Many went to France, and some didn't return.

*   *   *

> 'Tis joy to him who toils, when toil is o'er,
> To find Home waiting, full of happy things.
> (Euripides)

With the war at stalemate, those instructors not in married quarters were extremely bored, but after each day's slogging I was happy enough. Then, most disappointingly for me, it was goodbye to my cosy home with its mod cons, for the Vickers wing was disbanded.

Where now? At Chichester I wasn't sent to join my old Battalion, now in France. Why not? I was A.1. Fuzz informed me that volunteers for West Africa were again required, with the veto on married men now lifted. I applied, waited, and forgot about it. I was now sent all over the country, bringing back absentees, and in one hectic period paid four visits to Belfast. While sitting on a lavatory in Larne I noticed graffiti scratched on the door – 'It's no use standing on the seat, the bugs in here can jump six feet'. Well, he might have put that warning outside!

A Chamberlain speech stated that by delaying invasion Hitler had 'missed the bus', and Germany's prospects had vanished overnight. He should have touched wood, for almost at once the phony war ended and Jerry was at the French ports. At the mess piano I ceased hanging out the washing on the Siegfried Line and wondered whether nephew Tom would get out of Dunkirk. In the midst of that hazardous operation I was again sent to Belfast to fetch a deserter I'd been warned was a 'slippery customer'. At Stranraer the boat waited for a special train, full of tired Dunkirk chaps going on leave in their beloved Emerald Isle. Compartment doors bore loving chalked messages like – 'We'll be back, Hitler, you square-headed bastard'. Somehow, at Larne, my escort and I got mixed up with them, but none objected when all were ushered into a place where a gargantuan feast was laid out. The Irish had stained equipment and torn clothing, while we wore pressed uniform and polished brassware – battle-dress hadn't yet been universally issued at home.

The lad next to me spoke of an incident on the beach when a man, after being warned, again jumped the queue and was shot dead by an officer. I suppose I must have looked sceptical, for the narrator asked his pal for corroboration. Yes, he agreed, it was true. 'Poor bastard!' they said in unison.

The idea of a lengthy journey with a slippery customer wasn't relished, but to my surprise he was quite young and wearing a decoration. I signed, then hand-cuffed him to the escort, his expression reminding me forcibly of what I'd gone through at the Tower. I took off the 'cuffs on the boat and chatted with him, taking a chance by not securing him again, neither did I ask for our reserved train compartment to be locked. The escort and I, dead tired, dozed right off, and when the train stopped in a big, echoing station – Rugby I think – I shot an affrighted glance sideways, to see the 'slippery customer' also asleep.

*   *   *

Churchill took over, and we prepared for invasion, with Sussex fields littered with old junk to hamper landing aircraft. A new Battalion was formed at Seaford, and I joined them, to be given a platoon of young National Service men. I took them to the stores, where we glanced up at a doubtful plane which dropped a bomb. An engine crew on the adjacent railway line were killed, but there was no panic among these lads who so shortly before had been civilians. Bold enemy airmen encroached at high altitude, unloaded inland, and returned at hedgetop height to strafe with cannon. One afternoon the platoon were on the prom, doing physical jerks, when a homeward-bound Heinkel let fly a long burst. No-one was hit, and in shirts and shorts the lads hunted for the empty shells as souvenirs. All personnel with a rifle (there weren't enough yet for recruits) fired at any enemy plane within range, but of course all war aircraft now had their vital statistics protected by armour. One once roared towards us from the west and I gave it three rounds rapid before recognising a Blenheim, and I wasn't alone. It was shot up all along the coast, and a furious message with a sarcastic P.S. arrived from the R.A.F. – despite the intense barrage their plane hadn't been scratched!

At length alerts were ignored unless danger came near. Dogfights took place high overhead, and sometimes a speck

would trail smoke and plummet to destruction. Although taut-
ness persisted, I somehow couldn't imagine being invaded.
Occasionally, as the platoon took a breather, I might see a
small coastal vessel labouring into Newhaven Harbour, but
could not visualise that wet expanse black with landing-craft.

I was now given a beach pillbox to man at night, armed with
a Bren, and tried not to think of the effect from a German naval
shell hitting direct. Never having handled a Bren, I had to ask
my corporal for a crash course.

By the Seaford front there was a cafe that did business
during the whole of the invasion scare period. Very few
civilian customers, but the cafe was hugely appreciated by the
troops. The owner, widow Jessie Dwyer, vowed that she
wouldn't close it until the first wave of coalscuttle helmets
swept over the prom. Quite a crowd in there one afternoon
when there was an enormous explosion, and we dashed out to
see a pall of smoke not far out at sea, and nothing else. A tiny
potato boat had been struck by a magnetic mine. All the crew
died, and spuds by the thousand were washed ashore.

*   *   *

Manning the pill-box at night, I was excused morning parades,
until a summons from the Colonial Office got me out of bed.
West Africa! My wife took the news calmly, for she was
another who didn't expect an invasion. Halfway through a
week's embarkation leave I was disgusted at receiving a telegram ordering me to be at the Grand Central Hotel, Maryle-
bone (then a transit camp) next day. I got there at eight p.m.,
and inside sat a military clerk. 'Sergeant Shaw, Royal Sussex,' I
said.

'You're in for the high jump, sarge.'

'For Pete's sake why?' I demanded.

'The draft left an hour ago.'

'Left? I was told to report by ten p.m.'

He grinned. 'Ten *a.m.*, sarge.'

'Eh?' I fished out the wire, then relaxed. 'Look.'

'Plain enough. Your unit's error.' He went out, to return and
say that I'd be on the next draft, and meanwhile return to
Seaford. 'Want a bed for tonight, sarge?'

I declined and, still cluttered with full gear, walked through
an air raid to Victoria, arriving late at Worthing; they'd thought
me on my way to the high seas. Next day at Seaford the

Orderly Room blamed the post office. 'Excuse me,' I said, 'what about the leave I've lost?'

'Embarkation leave, and you didn't embark,' I was crisply told, 'and what about the extra ration allowance you were paid?' At that, I pushed off, back to the pill-box, sirens and dogfights until the second summons arrived, with another week's leave we arranged to spend in London.

'Come and see what they've put in our garden,' invited my mother, and showed me an air raid shelter resembling a bald hedgehog. 'D'yer reckon that little thing's safe?'

'Yes, except for a direct hit, which ain't likely.'

'Good job there's no munition factory near,' she went on, and I looked surreptitiously at the railway track, only ten yards from the shelter and a legitimate target. 'Where are yer supposed to be goin'?' mother added.

'West Africa. I'd like to see some o' those witch doctors.'

'But ain't there cannibals in that place?'

'Don't worry, mum,' chirruped Esther, who had long since been married to a neighbour's son. 'Cooked or raw, our Jess's much too tough for any cannibal!'

It was Saturday, and I went to the Hammers, probably the last chance for ages, but during play an alert sounded and the teams ran off, leaving behind thousands of disgruntled Cockneys. A real raid on this luverly sunny afternoon? Rubbish, bleedin' rubbish! They just wouldn't disperse.

Then there was sudden agitation at the barking of guns and roar of multiple aero engines. Most fans swarmed for the exits, but I waited. The Boleyn ground was never easy to leave in a hurry – I'd had some. From behind the bank upon which I stood, loud explosions sounded. They continued, and I climbed to the top, followed by a young girl who'd been standing near. We peered over the wall to see the whole of southern West Ham – the docks area, a mass of billowing black smoke. The girl showed no fear – just bewilderment. 'In broad daylight!' she exclaimed blankly.

'I was in the first day raid of the last war,' I replied. 'That was Saturday too.'

The explosions stopped and the engines faded; the raid had lasted but a few minutes. Flames were jetting redly through the black smoke. 'Horrible,' said the girl. 'Is it the beginning of the invasion?'

'I thought there wouldn't be one – now I'm not so sure.'

The people jammed by the Underground entrance made me

walk home via a path by the Northern Outfall sewer – I'd used it
years before when not having the railway fare. I'd never before
seen the gate padlocked – now who the heck would want to
sabotage a sewer? I climbed over, doing the same at the other
end. 'Where on earth 'ave yer been?' demanded mother.

'Walking. Any tea left in that pot?'

'Now listen. You take Florrie and Brian to Worthing out o'
this.' She was uncompromisingly insistent.

'All right, mum. Tomorrow. P'raps they'll give us a rest after
this lot.' They didn't. From the top floor we could see the docks
fire still raging, and the Luftwaffe took full advantage later. We
piled into the hedgehog – mother, sister, brother-in-law Bert,
we three, cat, and grub. The raid went on in waves, until there
was a lull and we ate. Well into the picnic, another lot started
and bombs fell not far away before there was a heavy thud and
the shelter shuddered. Everyone stopped chewing, and we
heard a distant ticking – a terrifying moment. 'If that's a time-
bomb we must get out if it's close,' I said urgently. 'Gimme the
torch, Bert.'

'Careful, Jesse,' implored mother, as I scrambled out.

'You bet!' Shielding the rays from above, I promptly fell face
first into left-over soil, and got up spitting out dirt. 'Blast! Bulb's
bust. Can't see a thing.'

'Come back in,' shouted Esther suddenly. 'It's the thermos
flask.' Steam was escaping from around the cork. It was a
moment none of us ever forgot.

'I hate this thing,' remarked mother, scrambling out after the
all-clear. 'I think we'll use the public shelter an' talk with the
neighbours!'

*   *   *

Next day amazing rumours were circulating concerning an
invasion that had been beaten off; people were discussing it on
bus and train. The south coast, we heard, was red with blood
and covered with corpses. We learned the truth at Worthing,
where the sea was just a huge cerulean expanse, holding
nothing more threatening than a coal boat making leisurely for
Shoreham.

The London blitz now began in earnest, and one nasty Nazi
dropped a bomb on Buckingham Palace; Royalty weren't
immune. Churchill ordered a continuous barrage during raids
so that people wouldn't be forced to endure explosions caused

only by the enemy. Then, all too soon, I was back at Maryle-bone. 'Got news for you, sarge.'

'Tell me.'

'The boat you missed was sunk. Forty chaps lost. It's an ill wind. You leave tomorrow night.'

'Any restrictions now? I'd like to go out.'

'All right if you're in by reveille.'

I dumped my gear on an Army bed, and from the look of the erstwhile hotel, the owners would present quite a claim after the war. On the centre-sunken roof lay jagged bits of A.A. shells that were schoolboy prizes in the first world war. The sirens sounded, and with public transport stopped I started the trek to say farewell. Soon the raid was in full swing, but the psychological effect of the barrage was magical – the more it banged the safer I felt. A warden intercepted me and was satisfied with my explanation, and near the Bank of England I heard an engine coming from behind, and a lorry stopped when I waved. 'Goin' anywhere near Bow, mate?'

'Stratford. Hop in. Thought you was a copper with that tin hat. I've already had the gloves on twice but I'm sleeping in me own bed tonight, raid or no raid. What part of Bow?'

'Victoria Park actually. Cadogan Terrace.'

'I'll drop you right there an go on through Carpenter's Road,' said the Good Samaritan. 'On leave?'

'Just finished one. Goin' to West Africa.'

'Are you by Christ? Well,' he remarked, as unmistakable whistles and crunches sounded from the rear, 'I reckon you're going at just the right time!' A statement that did little to cheer me.

The house was locked, and I reached an empty hedgehog via the canal bank and the railway, hoping that no trigger-happy chappie of Dad's Army would put a bullet up my backside. Finally I ran my quarry to earth (literally) in a huge covered trench by the park. It was packed, and the air could have been cut with a knife. 'Off tomorrow night,' I announced, 'to one of the most peaceful places on earth. I feel that I'm running away.'

Hearing that they were leaving London for good, I said goodbye in the small hours with a lighter heart, and had a shock when reaching the spot where I'd stopped the lorry. Both Bank and Royal Exchange had suffered, with chunks of masonry in the road. At the hotel I crawled into bed and, like many others, missed breakfast.

Later some kit was withdrawn, but tropical gear more than replaced it. We marched to the station wearing topees and a few people cheered and clapped; I felt important. Soon after leaving Euston the train stopped, and didn't move for several hours, during which bombs dropped and the barrage raged and shell splinters tinkled around us.

Broad daylight before we reached Scotland, and on Gourock quayside dockers indicated the *Empress of India* – that would take us, via Canada! Naively we swallowed this, but of course the lighter took us nowhere near the Empress, if that was indeed the ship. Instead, we boarded a P & O vessel, the *Canton*. Almost new, she was officially an 'armed merchant cruiser', carrying naval guns and plenty of A.A. weapons. No convoy. We'd be on our own, with our small draft of about fifty officers and sergeants outnumbering the crew. A whole liner to ourselves – we must indeed be V.I.P.'s!

Gannets wheeled and shrieked, plummeting into the sea for fish. Never having been further from England than the end of Southend Pier, I noted the strengthening gusts with misgiving. Imagination, or was I already feeling queasy? It was dusk as we headed into the Irish Sea, and at once we had to grip the rail when the *Canton*, empty of cargo, began to roll. It became freezing on deck and, miserable, I went inside. What was that song my mother used to sing while slaving at the sewing machine?

> No-one to say goodbye,
> No-one to grip my hand;
> No-one to bid me a last farewell,
> Leaving the dear Homeland;
> Here, on a crowded quay,
> Sad and alone am I;
> No mother's tears, no dear wife's kiss,
> No-one to say goodbye.

Blimey! Ain't it harrowing?

CHAPTER SEVEN

The Nigeria Regiment

One the floor were mattresses, and I lay on one for two days, leaving it only to vomit. The ship, when not standing on its bows, tried to sit up and beg. The crew said they'd never experienced a worse gale. Those stretched helpless gave no thought to submarines or aircraft, and I was one of the last to shake off that horrible *mal de mer*. We didn't go through the Bay of Biscay, but described a huge semicircle before approaching West Africa almost head-on.

Now in tropical kit, we heard garbled accounts of trouble ahead. General de Gaulle had asked our Navy to land Free French troops at Vichy-held Dakar, then cancelled the project when shore batteries opened fire – he 'didn't want Frenchmen killing Frenchmen'. We saw nothing more dangerous than porpoises, dolphins, small whales and flying fish, and the *Canton* cut swiftly over the almost motionless, leaden-coloured Atlantic until the coastline of the 'Dark Continent' appeared.

Before entering Freetown the skipper decided to try out his big guns for the first time, and a target was towed along parallel to us. The first salvo not only wrecked some of the ship's crockery but almost ruined our eardrums. Four big splashes appeared, a lot nearer the towing vessel than the target, and immediately a vicious splutter of morse flashed from the threatened craft. We couldn't understand it, but the import was unmistakable – 'You silly bastards what d'you think you're doing?' After an interval, firing recommenced more accurately.

Inside the magnificent harbour we saw a legacy from Dakar in a damaged British warship – the *Barham*, we heard. When our engines stopped and the anchor went down, heat and humidity such as we'd never imagined caught at our throats, and within minutes our drill was saturated with sweat. With two new pals

Sergeants Paddy Magill and Harry Burt, I appraised a scattering
of variegated dwellings against red soil and green vegetation,
with a mountain as background. Sierra Leone, the 'White Man's
Grave'. After being told that the *Barham* was taboo to my
camera, I took shots of natives diving from canoes for coins we
flung to them.

Freetown wasn't our final destination, but we were taken
ashore to be billeted in a girls' school from where the birds had
flown – no doubt hurriedly. Awaiting us were native 'house-
boys' who, although the sky was dazzlingly blue, at once put
everything under cover. We had use of the school facilities, so
needed only our camp beds and huge, bell-shaped
anti-mosquito curtains, which had to be suspended from the
ceiling. Everybody struggled with the things, amid exasperated
oaths in English, Welsh, Scottish, Irish, plus pidgin from the
boys.

Paddy, Harry and I walked into town, and the natives were
proved correct when cool, welcome rain deluged for an hour.
Freetown disappointed Harry and myself, though Paddy had
been abroad before. The town was a mixture of enormous trees,
a few imposing buildings, but also appalling rusty shacks and
shanties. We entered a market, mainly fruit and fish. Flies
swarmed and the noise was deafening. This combined with the
humidity after the rain, made us call it a day, but that day was
not yet over.

Nothing could have been less warlike than that packed
market, yet as we turned to depart a siren wailed. Practice? No,
for gunfire began, and there high overhead was flak bursting
around a plane. 'I can't believe it!' exclaimed Paddy. 'Where the
hell's it come from?' There was now dead silence in the market,
the Africans quite bewildered, and had a bomb been dropped
the carnage would have been indescribable. However, the plane
immediately made off, possibly a spotter from Vichy territory,
and next day's local newspaper bore a huge headline – 'Air Raid
on Freetown'.

*   *   *

A week later we gladly boarded the Elder Dempster liner *Apapa*.
Travelling first class, the cabins and steward service were
greatly appreciated, and that night we slept without the flicker-
ing flames from fireflies crawling on the curtains, and frustrated
whines from mosquitoes. The ship hugged the shore along the

Gold Coast, where at Accra surf boats had the hazardous task of loading and unloading because an incessant heavy swell prevented berthing. The job was done by big, powerful Africans, and while photographing them I was challenged by a Maritime Policeman who'd come aboard. 'I've had permission,' I told him.

Striking a dignified pose, he remarked: 'Then please to take *my* features, sir.'

On the last lap we sergeants were lectured by an officer from the Royal West African Frontier Force, and from what we heard regarding prices, it was obvious why we would be getting extra allowances. He also stressed something of great importance; the way to treat the natives. With new units being formed, recruits would be coming straight from the jungle, probably being forced by their headmen. They'd know no English and would be scared. It would be very trying at times, but we must behave humanely. We were not to cuff our house-boys if they were obtuse, or fine them – they'd get it back with interest when doing our shopping. Above all, we should learn the lingua franca – Hausa – as quickly as possible.

*   *   *

Keep well away from the Bight of Benin,
Few come out, though many go in.

Nigeria, and the Bight of Benin. We entered Lagos Lagoon, and civilians disembarked first. At once we were given a practical demonstration of 'how to treat the native' when a bulky fellow thrust his way to the gangway, obviously out to impress us. Dumping two cases on the deck, he yelled: 'Hey, *you*!' to an African on the quayside.

The man tapped his chest. 'Me, sir?'

'Yes, *you*, yer coffee-coloured crumpet!'

So that, then, was the way to treat them! The officer must have got it all wrong. 'There goes God Almighty!' grunted Paddy, as the fat sod waddled down with everyone hoping he'd fall in the Lagoon. On the station, we heard the *Apapa's* siren heralding her last voyage, for she was bombed and sunk, with the loss of 6 passengers and 18 crew.

We now faced a 600 mile train journey, and at Jebba saw an interesting relic on the platform – the anchor from the first ship taking white men into the interior. After massacring the crew, the locals set up the anchor as a god. Reading the inscription, we hoped for better hospitality!

Nigeria had no railway tunnels, and our engine gave up on one gradient, reversing for another try. Successful, but in their glee the crew missed the next waterpoint and something blew. A lengthy wait for a replacement locomotive was accepted quite philosophically by the civilians . . . nothing very remarkable.

At Kaduna, after two nights on the train, trucks took us to the barracks, half of which were already occupied by the 5th Nigeria Regiment – we were to form the 10th. The few houses were allotted to the officers, and we B.N.C.O.'s (British Non-Commissioned Officers) were accommodated in the evacuated Kaduna College. At first we found the Muslim-type lavatories strange – one squatted with head between knees – but apart from that it was comparative luxury.

There weren't enough boys, so Paddy and I shared a Fulani named Umuru Gombe, who'd worked for a European doctor now on leave. Few of these boys had experience, but Umuru proved excellent, well worth the extra pay we gave him.

Kit was unloaded – beds, nets, chairs, tables, canvas baths and washbowls, buckets, water-filters, and a hundredweight of clothing apiece. Soon we were invaded by Hausa traders, bearded and affable, each with a motley entourage head-loading big panniers of goods, some of which would have made the deprived women at home shriek with delight. I was an early victim, without thinking of the problem of getting the stuff to England.

The traders left at dusk, when a second influx began as thousands of insects converged on our lights and white nets, which should have been dyed green. Though not as bad as Lagos, the air was still much too humid for closed doors and windows, and some of the new intruders were quite ferocious-looking. One big flying beetle was as hard as wood, and if your nut was in his path you knew all about it, but we quickly grew used to these insects, though I was startled by loud thumps when Umuru brought our first early morning tea; he was banging our boots on the floor to shake out any scorpions! Drinking water was on tap, but had to be passed through our filters, the amount of grime removed being astonishing.

*   *   *

We B.N.C.O.'s were welcomed by the C.O., Colonel Evans of the Gloucester Regiment, a quiet man whom most of us liked at once.

A short pep talk, and we were passed on to Captain Forbes who, like most Adjutants, wasted few words. 'As none of you are above the rank of sergeant, there'll be lots of promotion. I'm seeing you individually tomorrow, but don't make out you're this or that because I'll check against your documents. Any appointments will be subject to probation until substantiated. No time now for questions – fall out.'

That evening at dinner, or 'chop' (anything to do with food was chop) it seemed that Harry and I were about the only bods not worthy of Warrant Officer at least; one wondered how their units could have survived after their departure. Paddy was genuine, had been acting C.S.M. and could prove it. He was a career soldier, and admitted it. Harry and I weren't bothered, and it wasn't sour grapes. Both of us considered sergeant to be the best non-commissioned rank, and company quartermaster sergeant the worst. If anything went wrong with food, pay, or stores, the C.Q.M.S. usually took back the can.

Next day I could add nothing to what was on the Adjutant's desk. I'd qualified for Warrant Officer at drill, which wasn't paramount in wartime, although I was itching to find out what I could do with Nigerian recruits on the square – vanity. I could keep Lewis guns in repair, but they were now obsolete, and specialised with the Vickers, which were not to be issued, so I don't suppose Captain Forbes was greatly impressed.

The recruiting officer seemed besieged, and I walked across. Most of the intake had been conscripted by their chiefs, who probably received a backhander. Looking at them, I remembered the Guards Depot, when I was part of the raw material going through the sausage machine. Some of these chaps had only seen a white man when the District Officer visited their remote villages. Most wore shorts, and perhaps a shirt, with a couple in loincloths only. They eyed me uneasily, and I decided to give them all a wide smile. A full set of toothy grins rewarded me, and were so infectious that I laughed aloud. Delighted, they did likewise. Well, that wasn't such a bad start!

Some B.N.C.O.'s were summoned, including Paddy, who arrived late at the college. 'Brigadier?' I grinned, as he took a mug of tea from Umuru.

'C.S.M. of "B",' he answered quietly.

'Congrats. Who got R.S.M., then?'

'Bringing a ready-made from outside, worst luck, but they haven't doled out R.Q. (Regimental Quartermaster Sergeant) yet. I'll be watching.'

'Best o' luck,' remarked Harry. 'Who's your Company Commander?'

'Chap named Carfrae. He's yours too, and Jess's. Wants to see you tomorrow, Jess. You could be his quarterbloke.'

'What? C.Q.M.S.? Worst job in the Army, ain't it, Harry?'

'Wouldn't have it as a gift. Bad enough at home.'

'Better than slogging it on the square, like me,' said Paddy.

'But I *want* the square,' I told him.

'Out here? Your brains need testing,' Paddy replied pityingly.

'Maybe, but no bloody quarterbloke for me – that's flat!'

'Damn' lazyness!' snorted Paddy, departing for a shower and leaving me with a strong suspicion that he'd already 'put my hat on'.

Next day I found that Captain Charles Carfrae, Somerset Light Infantry, had something in addition to a charming smile. 'I think that Magill and yourself will make a good team,' he concluded, and while I was still trying to grope for words the triumphant Magill marched me out. With all vacancies except R.Q.M.S. now filled, in the college that evening there were broad grins from the haves and glowerings from the have nots, and as the sacred cow of seniority had been completely ignored, some new friendships became strained for a time. R.Q.M.S. was eventually given to a junior sergeant, to Paddy's chagrin, but the chap had experience in a Quartermaster Store, which tipped the scale.

* * *

To any quarterbloke, his storeman is vital, and I chose the most massive man in the Company, Abdullai Fort Lamy. Most of the native N.C.O.'s had a smattering of English, and with Nigerian C.S.M. Labo Kontagora interpreting, Abdullai was given to understand that he must guard everything with his life. He did, too, and once I feared for my own when going down unexpectedly after dark. I tapped on the door, and out came my storeman with rifle and fixed bayonet.

Early difficulty. Many men bore the same surname, and for a time paperwork was a nightmare, and I became more familiar with regimental numbers than names. Luckily each Company had a clerk, and ours was an Ibo with the grand handle of Joseph Bramford Annang. He wore civvies and slept in town. Joe, in my office, was quite competent and so invaluable to me. I was able to leave accounts, etc., to him while attending to more pressing matters. He was nearly always broke, but perfectly honest. We were of mutual assistance to each other, and soon I discovered the first of many periodic billets-doux on my desk:

'Dear Colour-Sergeant Shaw, will you be kind and good enough to loan me five shillings until month's end? I am compelled to pay a lady's fare back to Jos and I am pocketless. J.B. Annang'.

'You dirty old devil, Joe!' I told him.

Work now with a vengeance. Two hours of it before breakfast, and ending for the day at 4.30 p.m., or that's what it should have been. The Captain, determined to have the most efficient Company, spared neither himself nor his Europeans. Paddy and I would drag our weary bones up the long pull to the college after others had settled in – it was no joke. 'Wonder if he realises we're missing the lorry?' I grunted.

'New Broom. It'll calm down eventually,' forecast Paddy.

All the conscripted privates and 'carriers' were illiterate, apart from the Head Carrier, Dominic Bachamoku. With the help of him and the vociferous N.C.O.'s I got the whole Company in a queue for clothing issue. None had ever worn boots . . . and what boots! Nearly as broad in the beam as coracles. One enormous pair that might have suited a duck-footed platypus were still in the store when I went on leave two years later. The men hated boots, never wearing them in barracks. During the fitting I found at least a dozen chaps with boots on the wrong feet. They kept referring to shirts as 'shits', and I thought their own Hausa name for them – mai laushi (owner of softness) more attractive.

Well, off they went to their dried-mud huts, headloading gear that included long shorts with slouch hats (for jungle work) and short shorts with Kilmarnock Caps (green fez) for barracks. I also ensured that their old rags went too. Changed, they were at once chased back to the square – Carfrae didn't lose a minute.

Next day they were hard at it when I was grudgingly given six carriers to draw arms and equipment, and scrounged a lorry on being told that the driver understood English. Telling him to take the load to 'B' Company armoury, I went in to sign for the stuff. I emerged to find the lorry was not to be seen, and the carriers began jabbering deafeningly. Nothing was more irritating in the heat, and I yelled two words that had been used scores of times in barracks since we'd arrived: 'Shut up!' One carrier jutted his chin towards the town – bushmen think it rude to point with fingers. Again I yelled: 'Joe!' He emerged to find that 100 rifles, bayonets, machetes, and sets of equipment were on their way to Kaduna Junction . . . and a Lagos train was due that day. 'Joe, I want yer bike.' I slung a leg across. 'Back as soon as I can. Don't let Charley-Boy know.'

'Who's "Charley-Boy", sir?'

'Captain Carfrae, o' course.' As I pedalled off he called out something I didn't catch. No European could ever have biked through Kaduna faster, and with the main street thronged I rang continuously. In those days many natives bowed low when a white man approached, but now their obeisances were wasted – before they were halfway down I was past. Trains, road vehicles, and pedestrians used Kaduna Bridge, controlled by police when a train was due. The only thing happening was a lot of gesticulating going on by the missing lorry, and I now discovered what it was that Joe had shouted after me. After frantically scraping my boots along the ground I hit the truck and fell off. The argument ceased, and chucking the bike into the vehicle I spoke one of the few Hausa words I knew: 'Tafi' (Go). We made fast time, and the square was still echoing to raucous bellows as I tried to galvanise the carriers into action.

Soon the Captain appeared. 'Haven't you got it racked up yet?'

'It'll get better when I master the language, sir,' I said, then sought Joe. 'Your front wheel's buckled, mate. Get it done and I'll pay, and for Pete's sake see about the brakes. Look at my bloody knees!' Most Europeans borrowed Joe's bike. It was the only one around and he should have charged a fee.

Harry and I zeroed the rifles. 'Nice change after the blasted square,' he said. In thin tropical shirts it wasn't easy, and soon our shoulders resembled braising steak. During a break a vulture arrived – uncanny how they scent food. As he regarded us superciliously from a tree I took stealthy aim. That rifle was certainly spot-on, but as the carcass fell I felt like a murderer. The carriers also seemed concerned, talking about 'kudi' (money). 'Is there a reward for every beak?' grinned Harry. It was the reverse, we found – five quid penalty for killing one of these useful scavengers. The men didn't split, luckily for me.

*   *   *

Hausa language books were issued, but I found it better to learn from Umuru. Although the air was much drier than at the coast, the sun was still extremely powerful, yet the country was fascinating. Brightly-coloured lizards ran about on the college walls, and at dusk clouds of bats rose from the ground, settling again after one passed. One B.N.C.O. adopted a monkey, but it had the place in continual uproar and its reign was short. A baby duiker (deer) was brought in from the bush – the parents weren't to be seen. It lived happily with us until it disappeared; we suspected the boys had chopped it. Not to be outdone with gifts, Umuru presented us with a chameleon that grew very friendly.

Another message from Joe, stating that as I was the Adjutant in his office he'd allow only myself to use his bike. Accelerated promotion! And then the Captain himself found a *cri de coeur* in his in-tray:

> Sir, When I and Yanga came here to be soldiers, you put us for carriers, and now these soldiers are laughing at us saying that we Bamenda peoples are foolish peoples. We want you to take us from carriers. If not, send us back to our country. We are, Sir, Private Yanga 38131 and Private Pretru 38140.

So there! And after these lads had been smoothed over, another developed mechanical ambitions:

> Sir, I have the honour to beg most respectfully to write this my humble petition which I hope in this case will be favourably considered. My object of writing is to render me your sincere assistance that I may be admitted as one of the military drivers for 10 Battalion. I hope you will not treat me otherwise. I have the honour to be, Sir, Private Fon Bon 38127.

I began collecting these 'taketas'. Several educated people in town earned cash for writing them, and Fon Bon's application probably cost him half a day's pay – sixpence. I once offered a man help in this respect, and got a polite brush-off.

Unbelievable things occurred among bushmen recruits. One man was circumcised, to the envy of his pal, who by-passed both M.O. and hospital by attacking his offending foreskin with broken glass. It was hospital then, sharpish, for this do-it-yourself merchant. Another bright spark buzzed off to his village and persuaded his neighbour that Army life was Utopia. Cash, food, and clothing, all for nothing, then handed over his identity disc, saying: 'Go there and be me.' The naive one came, was kitted out, and the switch wasn't discovered for a fortnight. The substitute was retained and the absentee caught. Net gain of one.

Despite civilian teachers, the men were finding it extremely hard to learn English, but showed great enthusiasm, drilling themselves by their huts. All drill orders were in English, and a man might march up and down shouting commands at himself, and sometimes it wasn't difficult to recognise which European was being mimicked. The different tribes were fraternising, easing one of our main forebodings. Years before some of them would have been at one another's throats. Of course, there was the occasional scuffle, but discipline was beginning to work, with men getting to parade on time in a country where punctuality seemed a joke. The bushmen were becoming disciplined soldiers, with more money, food, and clothing than ever before. After the war, would they be happy with their former squalor?

*   *   *

'More master coming,' announced Umuru.

'Who told you?' demanded Paddy; movements were secret.

'My ju-ju done tell me, suh,' answered Umuru, stalking away offended when Paddy laughed. A Muslim, our boy should have believed only in Allah, but when I reminded him, said that Allah had told his ju-ju. Many recruits wore ju-ju fetishes, permitted if hidden under uniforms. The bush telegraph was correct, for more Europeans arrived, enabling us now to have a boy apiece, for a dozen new youngsters came. Umuru had to make a decision, and chose myself. At times Paddy could be irascible, for as one responsible for Company discipline he found plenty to irritate him. His new lad, a tenderfoot, made a comical debut. Paddy, squatting like a soapy Buddha in a canvas bath, called for more water, and when it arrived, ordered it to be put on the floor. The boy obeyed literally, starting to wash the floor.

Two of the newcomers were Polish officers, and, at a lecture, one of them told us quite arrogantly that our platoon's firepower was weak. We were too polite to point out that the fire power of the whole Polish Army had lasted about a month after the country was invaded.

A further addition was Sergeant Hughes, whose rich Welsh baritone voice was often exercised, and another colourful chap was Sergeant Panos, a Greek who was instantly nicknamed 'Penis'. As Transport Sergeant he had the job of teaching the men, and us, how to drive, and some of his ways were unorthodox, to say the least. At Kaduna, a burned-out clutch could put a vehicle off the road for weeks. 'Don't ride the clutch,' Panos would order, and if not obeyed would bring his heel down upon one's instep. Whether or not he employed this method on the barefooted Nigerians I didn't know, but can assure any driving school instructor that it brings instant obedience! Most of his learners qualified.

Umuru remained thoroughly reliable – I could leave everything connected with money to him. He obtained dirt cheap souvenirs from the market and gave me surprise items made by himself. One, a pillow, had 'Sweet Love' embroidered on it; despite erotic jokes I used it. His *pièce de résistance* was a big brass bowl, upon which he'd tapped out an intricate pattern with hammer and nail, waiting until several Europeans were present before handing it to me. 'Thank you, Umuru,' I said, 'nice work. Er . . . what's it for?' and should have known better.

'Spittoon,' someone said.

'Pisspot,' suggested another.

Outraged, Umuru gave us the full treatment. 'No for spit, no for piss, no for shit, suh. Master put oranges for 'um.' Well, master still has 'um. 'Um stands on its little brass legs on the sideboard, and . . . no, I don't. I put orange for 'um.

Umuru, entitled to four wives plus any other females he could afford to feed, actually had two spouses. Binta, matronly, was very much the senior wife, but Kandi, very young, used to sit with downcast eyes, never speaking, poor girl.

*   *   *

An unexpected inspection for V.D., with myself ordered to accompany the M.O. and the African orderly. It was outside, and when the Company stepped out of short shorts and raised shirtfronts, a European voice sounded from the open window behind me: 'Oh what a lovely row of coconuts!' The inspection seemed brutal. The orderly, in front, put his hand under the man's crutch and behind the scrotum, then drew his open palm back, pressing firmly. If a speck appeared at the end of the man's penis . . . gonorrhoea.

At times one turned a blind eye. The men's lines were open, and as Duty European I'd seen women leave huts at reveille. Better than chaps finding trouble in town, I suppose.

There were inevitable teething troubles in the first important weeks, and Carfrae, never relaxing, was always the last officer to leave at the day's end, and Paddy and I could hardly go until the Captain did. Dead on 4.30 'Penis' Panos blasted the klaxon, and if no-one appeared within ten seconds the truck roared away to all the pots of char and clean changes. One day, in reply to an order from the O.C., I blurted out that he wanted everything done in an impossibly short time. For once the Captain seemed bereft of speech, then gestured me to leave. Paddy followed me out. 'You silly sod!'

'Just couldn't stop myself.'

Next morning Carfrae said that he'd never before been spoken to in such a manner by a 'regular', stressing the word. I replied that it was also a precedent for myself, but must have looked mutinous, and was put before the C.O. for making an improper remark. Then, as Colonel Evans fixed me with his fatherly eye, the Captain extolled virtues I didn't realise I had, trying to get me off! I escaped with a wigging. No doubt the Captain suffered from frustration during the running-in period, and probably didn't know the college was so distant, but from then on Paddy and I were nearly always on the truck, and Carfrae eventually proved to be one of the finest officers I'd ever known.

Hausas made good drivers, but often changed down needlessly. 'Bloody showoffs!' growled Panos. 'They do it to make the gears scream and scare civilians.' He was unavailable one day and our truck was driven by a learner. It was one occasion when Paddy and I were glad to have missed it, for the passengers were startled by seeing a culvert bridge to the flank and a moment later the vehicle was in the stream.

On another occasion I was being driven through the town when the lorry suddenly swerved violently, stopping on the very edge of a stormwater gully at the side of the street. A shouting crowd gathered, but the driver waited until I'd finished cussing him before explaining that the steering had gone. His quick reaction with the brakes prevented a nasty accident.

Sometimes a balala (whip) was used to punish, but the Captain ordered this very rarely. The 'six-for-arse' was carried out by the African provost sergeant. Some tribes, like Fulanis, would rather die than exhibit cowardice, and didn't even wince, but others, not so stoical, screamed before the balala even fell; it made my flesh creep when I heard it through the window. Actually, some men preferred the whip to other punishments such as physical jerks in full equipment in the heat. They hated working in the sun as much as we did.

The great majority of the bushmen were now clean, smart, and disciplined. Of course there had to be the exception and, just as the Welsh Guards had a Stiffy Shaw, so did the Nigerians have an Abu Makurdi. Life for Europeans out here without patience could be hell, but Abu would have tried the patience of Job himself. Time after time there would be a terrific ruckus outside, then Joe and I would watch half a dozen men hauling Abu to the nick. Frequently N.C.S.M. Labo Kontagora would report: 'Ya tafi daji' (he got to bush) and nobody needed to be told the identity of 'Ya'. Abu always returned, usually when he was skint, but remembering my absenteeism years before I couldn't dislike him!

The monthly pay-day was an event. As a receipt, each man pressed a purple thumbprint against his name, and a large, completed pay-sheet would have made excellent surrealistic wallpaper. The coins would be put into his Kilmarnock Cap, and he'd sit down to count and recount them. If not agreeing the amount he'd return and say: 'Money no reach.' Minor stoppages, such as 'Barrack Damages', might total fourpence a month, but to a man on a bob a day fourpence was a lot. They, not unlike Tommy Atkins, would never believe that these stoppages were essential. It might have been better if they'd received pay weekly, for after a few days most of them were broke.

Some offences were punishable by fines, but Carfrae never did that except when mandatory. Abu Makurdi, with frequent deductions for selling kit and absenteeism, sometimes created uproar, and on one hair-raising occasion up-ended the pay-table; nearly a hundred quid in small-value coin bit the dust. After receiving his small amount one day he yelled at the officer and myself in pidgin, and later I saw the Captain. 'Makurdi believes we're pinching his stoppages?' he asked, astonished.

'The Company think all the deductions go into *your* pocket, sir,' I assured him.

'Oh *do* they?' Summoning all N.N.C.O.'s, he explained where the cash went, but judging from the faces as they exited through my office, not one was convinced.

*   *   *

We sometimes visited the town's open-air cinema, which had extra seats *behind* the linen screen. These were very cheap because the captions appeared backwards! Lizards ran around the picture or stopped on it for a snooze, but films were up-to-date and seldom broke down. One, 'Wizard of Oz', showed witches flying on broomsticks, and Carfrae paid for the whole Company to see it, being assured afterwards that they thought it authentic.

I thought I was making good progress in Hausa, but one morning the Captain took Company Orders without an interpreter, making everyone speak slowly. Green with envy, I heard it going on behind the thin dividing door. He must have done some pretty intensive swotting and was one up on all of us. Soon after that I had a go myself following a complaint about allegedly short rations. I needed a notice – 'Half a Loaf is Better than None' to exhibit by the cookhouse. 'I can't help you, sir,' said Joe promptly, and neither could Umuru, so I enlisted the aid of one of the African teachers who came up with: 'Harbi a wute wutsiya ya fi kuskure'. It looked grand, with words there I'd never heard and, I was quite sure, neither had Captain Carfrae.

While I was nailing up the notice the Second-in-Command of 'B', Captain Pott, came by. He was an ex-District Officer who'd joined for the duration, and stopped. 'What d'you suppose that means, Colour-Sergeant?'

I told him, and he walked away laughing, so I yanked out the nails and sought the teacher. 'Just what is this literally?'

'Shooting in the tail is better than missing.' In other words 'it is better to graze a man with a bullet than miss him altogether.'

'What's that to do with loaves?' I asked blankly.

'There is no Hausa word for "loaf". How about "Better a fool than no fool" which I assure you will be acceptable?'

He went away, and I was about to give up in despair when I spotted Native R.S.M. Ali Bagarami, smartest African in the Battalion. 'Oh . . . Sergeant Major.'

He banged a bare foot. 'Sir?' Although all B.N.C.O.'s were called 'Sir', only officers were saluted . . . disappointing. The R.S.M. listened intently as I explained my need, then suggested that 'Samu kadan-kadan yafi babu' would serve. 'And what's that in English?'

'It is better to eat small-small than not at all.'

'That's *it*! Thank you, Sergeant-Major.' Up it went, but to my chagrin the O.C. made no comment until telling me to remove it. Hausa had a number of amusing idioms. 'Ba ruwanka' (Not your water) meant 'Mind your own business'.

*   *   *

There'd been no chance to explore the college hinterland, but one Saturday afternoon I went out with a Lee-Enfield, and Umuru was unhappy. 'Me come too, suh.'

'In that white cloth? You'll scare everything.'

'Master go lost.'

I ignored the insult, for the nearby jungle was 'orchard bush' – not thick. I set off at the alert, but soon the weapon's weight combined with gumboots and humidity caused me to shoulder it. I saw neither hide nor hair, and later, fed up, fired at some distant feathers – with a 303, mark you. The vulture ducked violently and flapped away, probably annoyed. Returning, I encountered elephant grass taller than myself, then maize 15 feet high. I'd better bring the camera here or those at home would call me a liar. It was cultivated, but by now I'd completely lost my bearings and it was growing dusk. Suddenly Umuru appeared and took the lead – he had been stalking me. 'Master go lost, master go lib for die,' he said reprovingly.

Footsore, sweating, and irritable, I snapped: 'Stop exaggerating!'

'Suh?'

'Sorry, Umuru. I believe you. Take me to a big pot o' char.'

'Me hear gun. No meat?'

'I missed.'

Next weekend the newly-promoted R.Q., still in the doghouse, showed more sense by hiring Ekpo the Hunter, and departed to our ribald cheers. An hour later Ekpo panted in for help. Several boys went, and confounded us by carrying in a magnificent, fully-grown cheetah. Then we mickey-takers were photographed in turn with it, until the impatient Ekpo said that if the skin weren't ripped off pronto, the insects would chop it. Of course, there were people who asserted that Ekpo must have killed the animal with his spear.

*   *   *

I spoke to Captain Pott about certain marks I'd seen on Fulani bodies, and he said they were the result of a rite called the 'Whippings'. Boys were lashed annually so that they could learn to withstand pain. Technically it was illegal, but if every native custom were suppressed it wouldn't help good relations. He suggested that Umuru could take me to Labara, where the custom was about to be held, but Umuru politely declined, saying that his own section of the tribe didn't recognise the rite. However, a boy in the 5th Battalion would take me. Ali turned up on Saturday and as we walked through the bush I asked whether the boys were afraid.

'Dese boys no fear anyt'ing, suh.'

'Have you been whipped, Ali?'

'I got marks, suh.' He added that without them, no boy would find a bride where whippings were carried out. No marks, no missus. The villagers knew of my coming, and two whippers were waiting to look me over. Masked, they wore straw hats, bone charms, and each held a murderous-looking rhinoceros hide whip with a knot at the tip. After giving me the customary: 'Sanu, mai gida,'* (Greetings, white man) they led the way.

The people were in a large circle, and I sat self-consciously upon a large petrol drum placed in front. All except the tiniest naked infants wore gay cloth, and most colourful of all was a group of unmarried girls. It must have taken them hours to titivate; they looked enticing enough to make red-blooded youths agree to torture. A lad entered the ring and sauntered around, studiously ignoring the whippers, who pretended to stalk him warily while he stared fixedly at something in the palm of his hand, and as he passed close to me I saw it was a piece of broken mirror. 'What's the bit of glass for?' I muttered, and Ali said that it was medicine. 'Are you saying it stops him being hurt?' I hissed.

'Him glass plenty good ju-ju. No feel anyt'ing, suh.'

It happened, only six feet from me. A whip descended with a loud whistle and crack, and the boy laughed aloud! A genuine laugh with nothing forced about it. I stared disbelievingly at blood bubbling from the small hole gouged by the fiendish little knot . . . it was absolutely incredible. Crack! went the other whip, with the same result. Not the slightest wince as the blow was treated with disdain.

More savage slashes, then a diversion for a bit of by-play. All the young virgins surged forward, placing themselves between boy and whippers. Ali explaineed that they were begging for mercy, that the boy had proved his bravery. Immediately the lad scowled at the shouting girls, then imperiously beckoned the whippers to carry on. Everybody, including Ali, laughed glee-fully, and I was told that it meant the whip was preferred to marriage. Afterwards I examined the whips – genuine enough.

* 'Mai gida'. Literally, 'Owner of a House'. Used when addressing white men.

Those Fulanis were certainly tough. Ali begged leave to remain, and a small boy led me to the college path. As he turned back in the gathering gloom, he broke into loud singing to ward off evil spirits. An echoing 'tunk-a-tunk' rang out as the leading Labara drum began tuning up for 'play' that would last far into the night. I sometimes lay awake listening to the distant thrumming from some remote village – fascinating and blood-stirring. After dark, the Plough and Pole Star were just discernible, low in the north, and in that direction bombs would be falling on our country. What would those at home give for a few nights of our peace?

*   *   *

The men gave all the Europeans nicknames, and mine was 'Dogo Yaro' (Tall Young Man). Flattering, and my pals scorned the 'Yaro'. Occasionally when wrestling with administration, I'd envy those on the square, until there was a break and they entered my office, sweating and swearing. Delving into odd corners with the storeman, I discovered a crown bird hackle, worn with peacetime uniform; it would certainly decorate my bush hat when I went on leave!

Mail from the U.K. was weeks in transit, and my mother's first letter was so shaky that I could hardly read it. I suspected there was something more than she revealed, and learned years later that people had been killed in the public shelter – luckily my relatives were at the far end. Services were being disrupted nightly, and it was oil lamps for lighting and open fires for all cooking. Bert, in Civil Defence, was in the thick of things. The next letter stated that they'd moved to the Croydon area, near Biggin Hill airfield! The Luftwaffe passed over on their way to town, but there were far fewer incidents.

Just when I was anticipating a break, I contracted malaria on Christmas Eve, with Kaduna's European Hospital all to myself. On Christmas Day, half delirious, I heard someone say there was a B.N.C.O. with a 'temp' of 105. Later I asked her whether 105 not out was a good score. 'Who told you?' she demanded, looking accusingly at the African orderly.

I tried to grin. 'Heard you on the phone, sister.'

'Oh, we get temperatures much higher than that,' she said reassuringly.

My dinner looked fit for the gods, but I couldn't touch it. Umuru arrived with goodies from the Mess, but the sender had forgotten that I was a T.T., and when sister spotted a bottle of booze she went tooth and nail for my innocent boy. To Umuru, and all Hausas, Christmas was merely a time when white men went mad and distributed 'Dashes' (gifts of cash). On Boxing Day, much better, I demanded the spurned dinner, and was told that the cook himself had chopped it; some Christmas! During convalescence at the college I ventured into pastures new and noted how the impeccable daily laundering was done. Boys merely soaked it before walloping it on to a boulder – a wonder it wasn't shredded. Big, hollow flat-irons filled with glowing charcoal could make starched trousers stand up on their own! I discovered my month's supply of sugar lying exposed on paper – ants had invaded it and were being driven out by the sun. I wondered whether Umuru spent all his spare time praying, for whenever I sought him the chances were he'd be on his knees, posterior pointing heavenwards. In town during the sunset glow, the voice of the priest summoning the faithful was romantic – a pity those glorious sunsets were so short.

*   *   *

Came the rains, deluging for half an hour daily just before dusk. A blinding flash of lightning and shrill whistle of approaching wind set all hands slamming doors and shutters before they were battered from their hinges. After the wet season came the scarifying Harmattan Wind, detested by everyone. It cracked skin and rendered dawns freezing; we wore greatcoats before breakfast. Whirlwinds ('Dancing Devils' to the poetical Hausas) filled one's clothing with stinging grit.

Drill now mastered, a route march was held, and I attended voluntarily. Soon all boots were suspended from necks, the Captain allowing it. Nobody fell out. When not chewing kola nut the men sang boisterously, with one leading and the rest roaring responses. The soloist began something concerning the erotic behaviour of a certain dog yaro, and many grins were cast in my direction. Then proudly he launched into English: 'Everybody likes Saturday Night'; second verse: 'The White Men come, the White Men go'; the third must have perished soon after the war ended: 'British Empire it will never Perish'.

Many of the songs were obscene, but so were ours. Worse still, many of our hymn parodies were the reverse of liturgical. The Nigerians loved gambling, swore luridly, appreciated com-

ely females, and were happiest when there was something to
grumble about. In fact, the only difference between us was the
colour of our skins!

After the march, 'B' Company went to bush for a week's
exercises, and I followed with a truck containing the rations and
four cooks. To the rest of the men the cooks were V.I.P.'s, and
Hassan Sokoto, the 'baban cuku' (head cook) was a stickler for
protocol. After the first pay parade he'd informed me, politely
but firmly, that his surname was pronounced 'Sockatoo'. The
cooks brought a scoured, fifty-gallon oil drum, and into it went
meat, fish, vegetables, peppers and palm oil, a glorious soup for
the main evening meal.

Potatoes being unobtainable, the Europeans had acceptable
substitutes in yam and cassava root. I overheard the officers
discussing the various tribal eating habits, and the Captain had
some big hairy caterpillars fried. Several men pounced upon
them and Carfrae won a small wager – possibly Pott put him up
to it!

During training my main task was to ensure that truck and
food were in the right place and on time, and soon learned that
the Nigerians were to be trusted, even in jungle they hadn't
before visited. The men trained enthusiastically, but the Captain
undoubtedly wondered about actual battle. Did he also ponder
on his Europeans? None had experienced enemy action in the
field, except Paddy in Palestine.

Wood and grass 'rumfa' huts were constructed and the
surrounding tinder-dry scrub carefully 'burned back', so it was
puzzling when one rumfa suddenly went up in flames. It
belonged to the arrogant Polish officer who'd criticised our fire
power; he certainly didn't lack any on this occasion!

While the Company were out chasing imaginary foes, I
visited Kajama village for fruit, but it was a tiny place with no
market. Women, naked apart from bunches of grass, kept well
back, and one I beckoned to ran into a hut, from where her
hubby emerged, voluble. 'For Pete's sake, Umuru,' I said
hastily, 'tell him I'm not after his wife. What was that thing at
her neck?'

The man went in, returning with a Napoleon III silver five-
franc piece. 'Four shillings,' I said.

'Suli fudu,' offered Umuru.

'Suli biya,' replied hubby, and I paid out five. Feeling mean, I
added another for the woman. The holed coin was useless to a
collector, but made another unusual souvenir. A fellow passed

with an enormous six-foot bow. 'Tell him five bob,' I exclaimed immediately, and the chap went on his way rejoicing, with more cash than he'd ever before possessed, and Umuru obviously thought I had more money than sense. The arrow-heads were coated with a gluey substance, and he said that a cut from one would bring death 'one-time' (immediately). I doubted that, but handled them carefully! People were now closing in, and I saw something strange hanging from a girl's lower lip that Umuru found was a six-inch nail. 'Bring her,' I ordered.

'No gib fi' shilling for dat nail!' protested the scandalised Umuru.

'No. I want her photo.'

She recoiled from the 'evil eye', then agreed if accompanied by companions. Some glanced away, others placed a fist over their mouth to ward off something. Click. 'O.K.,' I told Umuru, but the girl scowled – I hadn't 'dashed' her. I hurriedly fished out another bob, which she delightedly exhibited to envious pals. The most extraordinary memento I obtained was a pair of ear-rings in Kaduna market. Someone in remote jungle with no use for money had split a shilling into halves and attached wires. Umuru did the haggling, and after he and the Yoruba trader had stopped abusing each other I got the goods for tuppence. 'Me no be here, master pay fi' shilling!' smirked Umuru.

*   *   *

A Battalion exercise was now planned, and there should be no problem about food, for the Royal Army Service Corps were now in the Colony and we wouldn't have to rely so much on 'the land'. Off went the foot-sloggers, with transport following, and soon a peculiar odour filled my cabin. At the first halt the driver went to the bonnet, with myself a close second. Tucked cosily against the manifold was a chunk of meat that the driver grabbed and began to scoff. 'They all do it,' explained Panos. 'Just leave it there while it cooks.' Another dodge was to hang a water-bottle from the outside mirror; the contents stayed quite cool.

On the very first exercise the R.A.S.C. lorry became lost and didn't find us for two days. Bread was dehydrated, and meat more than merely high. Sergeant Maiduguri approached with a grisly, reddish-brown mass and politely requested me to inspect. The inspection was unnecessary – the stink was preced-

ing him. I shied, and dead-heated with other colour-sergeants at
our Quartermaster's truck. Captain Perkins was no novice in the
bush and had lots of that good old standby, bully. The Nigerians
loved the corned beef – 'cawnbiff' they called it. After this the
R.A.S.C. stopped bringing fresh meat on exercises. Meanwhile,
I told the cooks to bury the stuff, which really hummed, but
hardly had their machetes scratched the soil when stark naked
Pagans, both men and women, appeared from the bush and
made urgent signs. They were certainly welcome to it, snatching
the repellent meat and running off pursued by ribald yells. The
women's legs were streaked with red, and they carried bags
containing clay 'make-up' with which they were adorned. Well,
well.

'B' Company's very few Pagans included Sergeant Garuba
Banjira, six feet tall, so no-one took the mickey out of *him*. I once
saw him catch a huge rat that he later ate, and also witnessed a
vicious fight between two Pagans over a similar delicacy. It was
settled when the rat was solemnly cut in half while spectators
rolled around in mirth.

I visited a village called Kachiya. It was large, and Umuru
advised me to contact the 'saraki' (chief) first. The eldest son, a
literate, greeted us at the royal hut. His father was lying on a
dried mud bed, under which was a cavity containing a wood
fire, smoke escaping via the aperture through which I'd almost
had to crawl. The reward from this courtesy call was remarkable, with fruit and eggs ridiculously cheap. Umuru explained
that it was simply supply and demand – everybody grew
nobody bought. Bush people headloaded fruit for miles to sell at
give-away prices. Indeed, on one exercise, 'B' Company Lieutenant Elderton swopped a few cigarettes for a huge stem of
bananas.

Shopping in the bush was wearying – useless to tender
anything above a three-penny piece. Pennies, half-pennies, and
tiny 'aninae' (one-tenth of a penny) had holes bored through
them – you carried hundreds on a length of string. Near the end
of the present transaction I ran out of small change, Umuru
tipping the bag inside out without success. The egg-man
recoiled in horror from the huge one-pound note. 'Won't
anyone change this bloody thing, Umuru?'

'Master see saraki.' Back to the Palace, where the son informed me that in these parts paper money was hated, so would I
agree nineteen shillings? If everybody hadn't been so grave I'd
have laughed, so I accepted. The rate of exchange was doled out

from a biscuit tin in pence, and not, thank goodness, in 2,400 aninae! We left a dash to be given to the chief *after* we had gone – this was strictly *de rigueur*.

I now wanted a picture, but His Majesty demurred, wishing to wear something more Kingly before going outside. An appointment was fixed for next day, and he would arrange 'play' in the evening if I cared to bring along any 'baturi' (white men) friends. Having stayed long enough to satisfy convention, I bowed out backwards through an atmosphere redolent of goodwill and fumes.

In the cash I saw a most interesting penny – Edward VIII, 1936. I was unaware that any coins of his had been minted, so let it be known that I'd give six times their value for any more. First to take advantage of the munificent offer was Abu Makurdi, who went round the Company before presenting three pennies and a puckish grin to the silly white man, and jingled 180 aninae in his palm as he left. For a time I feared a flood, but in four years obtained only fifty. Needless to say, they were in demand when the Duke of Windsor died in 1972.

All the Company's B.N.C.O.'s except Paddy said they would come along to the festivities. 'I'll watch the lines while you gallivant,' said Paddy. 'Lay off the palm wine and women!'

During chop we heard the Kachiya drums tuning up, and everyone was assembled when we arrived. The show was grand, and when girl dancers rolled their bellies I remembered it was one of my own accomplishments. On a crazy impulse I pulled off my shirt and yanked down the top of my trousers. Stunned silence – were they expecting a complete striptease? A yell went up as I rolled energetically, the girls watching wide-eyed. Afterwards I gave them a word of thanks in Hausa, and whether or not they understood it there was clapping. Suddenly the drums started a Charleston beat – Africans have been performing that kind of flat-footed dance for centuries. In a flash the rhythm-loving Kachiyans were up and shuffling around amid a cloud of dust, and we beat a laughing retreat while tossing coins into it.

Umuru had followed us and been busy, obtaining a full-sized tom-tom for . . . fi' shillings. While belabouring it, you produced high or low 'notes' by squeezing strings. Next day I took the photograph and the saraki gave me two gifts – a Prayer Board painted in Arabic, and a Marriage Agreement – he'd been told I was collecting such prizes!

MARRIAGE AGREEMENT

In Rigachikun, Province of Zaria, I, Audu, son of Mallam Musa, desire to marry Ramatu, daughter of Tanku Dillali. 20 shillings were sent as a presentation for the first time. 25 shillings and 3 calabashes of kola nuts for the second time. 150 shillings for the third time. There remains only provision for the Marriage and a day to be fixed for the ceremony.

If, after the Marriage, the girl refuses to render her obligations as a good wife, all those things sent as dowry would be recovered partly or wholly, by mutual agreement or according to Native Law.

Signed: Audu Zaria Son of Mallam Musa

I managed to get a print enlarged in Kaduna and sent it to the saraki. Like the Marriage Agreement, I had to get his letter of thanks translated:

From the Saraki of Kachiya, fine greetings to the Head White Man. My very grateful thanks for the fine photo. At night, in the morning, and all day, Allah will bless you. Goodbye for a long time. Allah guard you until we meet again.

He'd called me 'Baban Baturi' (Head White Man). I'd better not let Charley Boy see this taketa!

*   *   *

More British troops were arriving, and the R.A.S.C. began bulk-buying. Former naive bush dwellers changed overnight into keen businessmen, and the days of cheap food had ended for ever – no more ten a penny oranges, etc. Up went our Mess bills, and there were now two sections of Europeans – one on Colonial rates, with everything to pay for, and newcomers on British Army pay with all food and other extras included.

In Kaduna town there was just one pub – Green's Hotel – and on a Sunday afternoon a thirsty trio entered. I envied my pals their cold beer from the fridge, for my mineral was warm. Esther, the Ibo barmaid, was downcast, stating that someone had broken into her room – she wasn't living in – and stolen her 'rent-house' (monthly rent). Dead silence for five seconds, then: 'How much?' asked Joe Soap.

'Seven shillings, suh.'

Feeling rather than seeing the gargoyle grins of my companions, I forked out, with the girl assuring me that it was merely a loan.

Quoth Paddy: 'Fancy falling for that, Dogo, you silly sod!'

Quoth Harry: 'You can say goodbye to it.'

A month later we again entered Green's, and Esther placed the money on the table. Delighted, I waved it away; worth it to see the other two faces!

The evenings would have been brightened by a piano, but there were none in barracks; I doubt whether there was a tuner for hundreds of miles. We had only the cinema, including Mickey Rooney and Judy Garland singing: 'Don't give up, Tommy Atkins'. As this was in one of the latest films, we hoped it reflected the views of the people in the United States, for it was obvious that without the help of our former great ally there would be a mighty long road to travel, if not an impossible one. Then one day we awoke to the Pearl Harbour sensation, and the news that Japan was now ranged against us seemed small beer indeed compared to the U.S. entering the lists. As to the professed 'unconcern' of the Nazis . . . whom were they trying to kid?

Malaria increased, and suspecting that orders were being ignored, the Colonel decreed that the B.N.C.O.'s intake of quinine would be supervised. There was mutiny in 'B' when the parade was mustered in my office, for when Joe appeared with bottle and glasses he was invited to 'bugger off and drink it himself', Harry adding that if he didn't take the grin off his face he'd get six for arse. In came Carfrae, stating uncompromisingly that anyone refusing would go before the C.O. The door slammed.

'Right,' exclaimed in-charge Paddy. 'Knock it back!' The vile taste lingered for hours, no matter what chaser was used. The only 'B' Europeans to escape malaria were the Captain himself and Paddy, the latter saying that any mosquito biting him would fall off drunk. Actually Paddy never took more than two drinks in an evening.

A great blow to me now was the departure of Umuru, whose former employer returned from the U.K. and at once contacted him. The doctor was at Kano, Umuru's home town. 'I understand, Umuru,' I said sadly.

'Master want I stay end of month?'

'Better not, you might lose the job. Find me another boy first, though.'

'I find master new boy past me myself!' (better than myself).
He brought a replacement named Idi Bida. Although not to be
compared with Umuru, he was still well above average, always
wearing a big grin whatever the circumstances. If you had to
cuss him the grin grew wider. At the change-over Umuru knelt,
thanking Allah for giving him a good master; I responded in
similar vein, without kneeling.

U.K. leave began, but alas, only two officers and two
B.N.C.O.'s could be away at the same time, and in the result-
ing ballot I was unlucky. Four people went, leaving the
remainder fed up and bored. Soccer was tried in the short
evening light, and it astounded us to see those bare toes
larruping the ball.

Abu Makurdi, getting worse, continually caused disruption,
then one day went to bush never to return, rumour having it
that he'd re-enlisted elsewhere. If true, he wasn't the first to do
that fraudulently! Should Abu not reform, how long before the
new unit considered him *de trop*?

An officer from Brigade needed B.N.C.O.'s for Long Range
Desert Patrols. These sounded exciting. Harry and I did well at
our interview until it was revealed that we'd had no leave. 'I
want nobody with leave on his mind,' said the officer, and was
adamant. The first quartette returned, with one sergeant
bemoaning the loss of his fiancée to a Pole. I think a number of
our original volunteers for West Africa had personal problems.
When I asked one chap why he'd left a cushy U.K. post he
answered tersely: '*Cherchez la femme.*'

The next leave departures included the C.O., and a locum
arrived who inspected each company in turn. After looking 'B'
over, the acting boss ordered that they be congratulated. Carfrae, instead of utilising Captain Pott, shouted it in fluent
Hausa, to the Africans' delight. Eventually Colonel Evans and
co. returned, and I was to be next from 'B'. Any day now!

I'd sometimes wondered whether Carfrae really waded
through all the B.N.C.O.'s missives home; hardly a morning
without several in his 'in tray' for attention – censoring was one
of his duties. One 'mail day' I'd just finished an urgent letter
and found that the orderly was already on his way to the
Adjutant, so chased after him, having hurriedly scribbled the
Captain's initials on the envelope – a daft thing to do. Soon
afterwards Carfrae was summoned, and when he came back
and shut the door something made me gesture to Joe for silence,
but what went on was not distinguishable. Soon the door

opened and Paddy appeared. 'Dogo, you're under arrest!' and I broke into a cold sweat.

Later, the C.O.'s expression was grave, and so was mine as I looked at his desk – my hasty scrawl hadn't deceived Captain Forbes. Our kindly Colonel, I'm sure, considered himself in *loco parentis* to us B.N.C.O.'s, and now found it difficult to speak. Finally he tapped the envelope. 'You know why you're here?'

'Yessir.'

'Why on earth did you do it?'

'An urgent domestic matter, sir. I didn't want to miss the mail.'

'You've missed it now. You realise how serious this is?'

'Yessir.' (I realised it, all right!)

'Well, I don't know, Shaw,' the C.O. murmured in perplexity. Then: 'How is this B.N.C.O. doing, Captain Carfrae?'

'Very well indeed, sir,' was the prompt response from Carfrae, bless his little cotton socks!

'Only one thing saves you, Shaw,' observed Colonel Evans. 'There was nothing that needed censoring. Had there been, it would have meant courtmartial. Never do it again.'

'Thank you, sir,' I muttered, the luckiest individual in Nigeria.

*   *   *

Leave at last. My souvenirs, apart from the six-foot bow, were in a huge box. Harry was taking over, and then, while checking ledgers, I felt an unmistakable grip, and groaned in dismay. 'What's up?' asked Harry.

'Malaria, blast it!' In hospital, I heard that Paddy had taken my place on the boat, and could have wept. Time crawled, and on our second Christmas Day we went to the Officers Mess for drinks, a chance of which the boozers took full advantage. Some had to be lifted into the lorry on the return trip; luckily redcaps were unknown in Kaduna.

Captain Carfrae, Harry, and I were the only three from 'B' without leave, and suddenly we were off, with Joe begging another favour at the last moment. 'Please post this in England, sir.'

'Why England?'

'It's to the King.'

'What? I know you wear civvies, Joe, but you're still in the Army. It should go officially.'

'But would the King get it?'
'Depends what you've put in it. Let's have a dekko.'

To His Majesty King George VI,
King of England and Emperor of India.

This my humble petition is forwarded for your favourable consideration.
1.   I am a British Subject under the flag of Great Britain.
2.   I have greatly determined to be faithful and loyal to the throne of England, having enlisted as a Soldier Clerk with a view to moving with my Company to anywhere I may be called upon to serve.
3.   My family, my wife and two children, are in a state of melancholy, and I have to support them by allotting a certain sum monthly. The pay for an Enlisted Clerk is not up to £3 monthly, and I earnestly ask Your Majesty to considering giving me a proper wage that will enable me to support my family. I do not ask for myself alone, but for all Enlisted Clerks in West Africa.

        I am,
            Your Majesty's very humble and devoted servant,
                Joseph B. Annang.
                10th Nigeria Regiment,
                Kaduna, Nigeria.
                7th March, 1941.

'Here, this is dated over a year ago.'
'I've been waiting for somebody I could trust.'
'Waiting for someone daft enough, you mean! Well, listen, Joseph B. Annang – I'll do it with one condition – don't mention my name if there are repercussions. You know I had a narrow squeak myself. Goodness knows how many regulations we're breaking here.'
'I promise, sir.'
'It's grubby. Type it, sign it, and I'll keep this one.'
'How shall I address it?'
'Buckingham Palace, of course, and don't be surprised if you're put in the nick!'
'I wouldn't mind, if we got a rise.'
'You'll be lucky, mate!'
At Lagos transit Camp Harry and I waited miserable weeks, meeting the Captain in town one day. Frustrated by the possibility of his efficient Company going to seed during the delay,

he said that he'd paid for an air passage. And, naturally, the day after he took off, the *S.S. Cuba* sailed majestically into the Lagoon; joyfully we boarded her. All this time I'd jealously guarded my six-foot bow, despite flippant remarks. Into the messdeck it went.

CHAPTER EIGHT

2nd (West African) Primary Training Centre

Captain Carfrae laughed last; we had a sweltering fortnight at Freetown while a convoy assembled – nobody allowed ashore. One optimist, knowing that onions were scarce at home, bought a netful from a canoe, hanging it in the messdeck. Soon they had to be jettisoned through the porthole – what a stink. Suspecting a plot to send my bow after the vegetables, I tied it to my hammock hooks; Brian knew it was coming. The convoy moved slowly, without incident, and at Bonnie Scotland I posted Joe's 'hot' letter, then sent a wire – the leave would be spent at my mother's new home. On the train, impervious to Harry's grin and sour-grapes jibes from others, I affixed the crownbird hackle to my bush hat.

London's grisly approaches looked even worse with bomb scars, and at Euston there was a queue for taxis, but the lovely green feather was magical – people just beckoned me to the front. At Croydon another taxi, for although the big box was to follow, I still had lots to hump. At the house my four-year-old dashed out . . . oh hell! I'd left it at the station. 'Never mind,' I told howling Brian, 'some poisoned arrows coming.'

'What's that?' demanded wife, mother, and sister in unison.

'It's all right,' I whispered, 'they're scraped!' A week later the box came, more than compensating Brian. I was also happy, for Customs hadn't opened it!

*   *   *

During the leave I had a nasty malarial relapse, badly scaring my relatives. Worse, a horrible abscess formed, and instead of reporting for Nigeria it was Woolwich military hospital. Arriving during visiting hours, people treated me like a wounded Anzac hero before learning that I was a miserable Cockney with a boil in a very vulnerable spot. After red-hot kaolin poultices had worked I was in charge of the ward for disciplinary purposes, and was asked to give talks about Nigeria to staff and up-patients. Three whole months elapsed before I got away, and found to my chagrin that I was medically downgraded. Back to blasted odd jobs now, of course. At a Royal Sussex unit in Colchester I at once applied for a regrading and was told to wait. I was still waiting weeks later when attached to Royal Engineers at Preston, and at Fulwood Barracks was put in charge of an office. The O.C., Captain Walker, introduced me to my staff, and what a staff . . . four A.T.S. girls! As the Captain left, there was a quiet female gravitation towards my hackle, which was obviously in danger, so I locked up the bush hat and drew a cap.

What a set-up! I drew my pay under false pretences, for the girls made it clear that neither tuition nor supervision was necessary. Occasionally, when someone who mattered entered the office, I'd stick my nose over a girl's shoulder, but the work was always faultless.

*   *   *

He that drinketh the water of Africa,
Must needs return after many days
To quench his thirst thereat
(Old Arab saying)

Christmas again, with no lack of Lancashire hospitality, especially when I attacked the piano at the Withy Tree pub. This super-cushy job could have lasted for the duration, but I was determined to get back to Nigeria. My new friends thought me scatty when I successfully applied for regrading. Again A.1, so goodbye to those luscious girls. Back at Colchester, I was promptly returned to Lancashire to claw back an absentee. After repeated visits to the Orderly Room, where there was no Fuzz Marshall to help, the posting at last came through.

Embarkation leave, during which Brian demonstrated the sending of messages via tom-tom – what did the neighbours think of it? Soon I was off, and had never imagined that a ship could hold so many humans until I boarded the *S.S. Stratheden*.

Already in her bowels was a unit of Indian Infantry, doubtless enjoying the heat. With everyone on deck as we sailed, it was like being in a football crowd, and one half-drunken fellow burst into song:

> Homeland, Homeland, when shall I see you again?
> Land of my birth, the sweetest place on Earth;
> I'll dream of you, breathing your name with a sigh,
> It may be for years, and it may be for ever,
> Dear Homeland – goodbye.

An encore began, which was more than flesh and blood could stand. Something weighty hit the back of his neck, and he spent several hours trying to discover the thrower. We were again in convoy, and on the first evening a match was struck on deck, with the effect of a searchlight in the blackout. Of all people, the culprit was a Warrant Officer, who was immediately broken down to private; the C.O. of a wartime trooper had plenary power.

At Lagos nothing was known of me, for my C.Q.S.M. post with the 10th had long before been filled. After saying that I was ready to revert to sergeant in order to join them, I searched the transit camp. I knew only one man, from the 5th Nigerians who'd shared Kaduna Barracks with us. The 10th had moved to Sokoto, he said, and the next few minutes were extremely depressing. 'Did Captain Carfrae return?' I asked.

'Promoted Major. 7th Battalion.'

'Paddy Magill?'

'Gone. I don't know where.' He also knew nothing of Harry. Dismayed, I began to realise why letters hadn't been answered, and grew more gloomy as he went on. Poor old Joe Annang had died – malaria, and Taffy Hughes' rich baritone had been silenced for ever by blackwater fever. The final item was startling: 'Your old C.O. is in the officers' quarters. He's off to Blighty, and so am I. Good luck, Dogo.'

I found Colonel Evans, and suspected that the smile he gave me was his first for some time. He confirmed what I'd been told, and so ended a most dispiriting day. A miserable fortnight followed. I didn't know a soul, but one evening spoke with a sergeant of the Gordon Highlanders and we were soon pally. Attraction of opposites, perhaps, for he was short and stocky. I've heard remarks about the Welsh and Scottish being mean, but most of those I've met have been the reverse, and this particular 'Jock' Mitchell would have shared his last bob. 'First time here,' he said. 'How about ye?'

'Second tour.'

Although Colonel Evans added his weight to my request for the 10th, I was of course sent nowhere near Sokoto. Jock and I were posted to a training centre near Enugu, and after another circuitous rail journey I made a beeline from my new Orderly Room to the sergeants mess. There, in solitary state at a belated lunch, sat Regimental Sergeant Major Magill, a monarch of all he surveyed. 'If I'd known you were coming I'd have baked a cake,' he greeted me.

Luxury here, for B.N.C.O.'s had their own houses. I at once wrote to Umuru, just in case he were free, and he duly replied, regretting being unable to join me. He'd heard that all boys refusing to enlist had been sacked (true). He didn't believe in war and would never be happy in Ibo country. Well, good luck to him. Meanwhile I'd been given an Ibo boy named Sylvester, who proudly wore a crucifix and proved first class. I'd been very fortunate in my boys.

*   *   *

Another office, where the amount of paper work was so colossal that sometimes all Europeans helped with the bumf. Most of the African intake were literate, and not much Hausa was heard, the great majority being Southerners. My new O.C. had the same surname as myself, and many recruits thought he was my father! His stiffly starched bush hat caused Europeans to refer to him as 'Wild Bill Hickock', but anyone less wild than Captain Shaw would have been hard to find.

The C.O. was a Colonel Taylor – 'Snip', of course, and, I was assured, a 'proper bastard'. I found him scrupulously fair, but a fanatic as far as cleanliness was concerned. Everyone was on tenterhooks while one of his periodic raids was in progress. After each explosion the standard shot up to a height impossible to maintain, gradually slipping until the next balloon went up. Apart from these unheralded blitzes, life was uneventful until I acquired an unexpected interest. Cigarettes arrived from U.K. schools, and although a non-smoker, I was asked to thank the donors and incautiously invited replies. Two months later a deluge of letters came; I was swamped. Learning what was afoot, Captain Shaw loaned me the office typewriter after hours. Postage was free, and I stuck at it night after night. Jock sometimes dragged me away to play Scots songs in the Mess, saying I'd go crazy.

The house light being poor, I bought a spirit lamp that gave extra glow but also attracted more insects. Absorbed in tapping, I leaped up in alarm at movement by my foot. An enormous toad was advancing leisurely, but there was nothing slow in the way his flicking tongue was snapping at incinerated remains as they descended from the murmuring lamp. I picked him up, his legs waving feebly, but when replaced he merely went on feeding – baked flying-ant seemed to be favourite. Occasionally he emitted a sibilant 'Crick' that sounded comradely in the quiet night.

Sylvester arrived – did I need anything before he retired? 'Come and salute Ted,' I invited.

'Which place dis "Ted", suh?'

'Look um.'

Sylvester looked, hissed, and swooped. 'Whoa!' I shouted. 'Put him down. He's my friend.'

Sylvester looked incredulous, then wooden. The amphibian was replaced none too gently, making for the ever-open door. 'Master want anyt'ing?'

'Bottle of ginger ale and some ice.'

'I do go-come, suh.' (Go, to return quickly.) He left, and I could hear him complaining to Jock's boy: 'My master done shout me.'

'What t'ing you do him?'

'I no do him not'ing. Himsay put down his toad. Himsay lef' um.'

'Toad? Whyfor himsay lef' um?'

'Himsay dis toad be friend for him. My master no get sense for head any more. I t'ink he be cress (crazy).'

After that, Ted the Toad arrived whenever the lamp glowed, and a rapport was established, but I was never able to find his daytime habitat.

*   *   *

A nearby village, Abakpa, was a thorn in our side. With Enugu township out of bounds and patrolled, it was thought that absentees were shacking down in Abakpa, so Snip decided to raid it. At dawn we stealthily surrounded the place, and a number of chaps were caught with their trousers (literally) down. A large amount of Army property was recovered, and a frightful hullabaloo arose from one house, an outraged woman protesting that a pile of drill was legitimate laundry, and indeed she had a contract. An interesting find was several wooden idols – a native sergeant had supplemented his pay with spellbinding and blackmailing. We were ordered to burn them, but I snaffled two towards my second store of mementos.

War seemed far away, but Enugu wasn't distant enough to prevent rumours. I paid little heed until I heard the 7th Nigerians mentioned, then sought Paddy. 'Heard any of this Burma palaver?'

'Only vague talk.'

'Well, I just heard the 7th are there. If so, I'd like to join Charley-Boy.'

'So would I.' Paddy seemed uncommunicative, and probably knew more than he'd admit. Soon afterwards, to my regret, he was posted to another unit, and I became the senior C.Q.M.S., but when relieving a Warrant Oficer who went on local leave I found his paperwork almost equalled my own. It was just administration *ad nauseum*.

Jock was also restless. 'Heard the latest, Dogo? Some of our lot are wi' Wingate.'

'What? *Chindits*? No Nigerians with last year's Expedition.'

'Well, there should ha' been. I bet they'd be tougher than the Japs in jungle.'

'Agreed. Look, I'm going into the Orderly Room for a month. I'll find out what I can.' And I found out nothing.

Hardly had I rejoined Captain Shaw when Snip struck again, after an unusually lengthy interval. There was almost complete silence as we trooped after him, until he spoke. 'Europeans to the Welfare Hut.' The officers went in first, and emerged looking grim. Now our turn. Deadly quiet, but at his most scathing, Snip said that if things again sank to the level he'd just seen, the Night of the Long Knives would be a Sunday School tea-party by comparison. Then, for good measure, Second-in-Command Major 'Jerusalem' Holyland lashed into us concerning administrative discrepancies.

'I'm fed up!' exploded Jock later, as our boys brought pots of char.

'You can't blame Snip,' I replied. 'The place was bloody awful.'

'Admitted, but nothing happens here except spit and polish. It isna my idea o' soldiering.' Jock had seen service in the Middle East. 'I was a bluidy sight happier i' the desert.'

'Jock, old Snip would've made a damn good Guards officer.'

'He should've joined 'em – ye too, ye long drink!'

I burst out laughing. 'You don't know what you're saying!'

'Well, it wasn't meant to be funny,' was the angry response. 'Listen. If the Burma tale is true, they're sure to want reinforcements. Be honest. Wouldn't *ye* like to go?'

'You bet. I've done office work for years.'

He shook his head commiseratingly. 'An' ye'll do it for duration while the crown's on ye arm. Get it off, Dogo, or ye're doomed.'

That evening I stopped typing, chewing over Jock's words and remembering the classic 1914 recruiting poster – 'What did You do in the Great War, daddy'? One day my own kid might ask, to be told that my backside had been firmly glued to a chair. Removing the school's letter, I inserted a new sheet of quarto.

'What's this for?' asked Captain Shaw next morning.

'I'd like the square, sir. I've done nothing but administration since 1940.'

'I'll tell you something in confidence. Two Warrant Officers are being recommended for Commissions. Aren't you next for C.S.M.?'

'Yessir, but that's nearly all paperwork too.'

'I understand. It's a pity, but I'll put you in front of the C.O.'

Soon I was feeling piqued, having fully expected Snip to try and dissuade me. All he said was: 'You wish to revert to sergeant? Granted.' Then I was marched out to remove the crown.

'Jock,' I remarked later, 'old Snip wasn't a bit upset.'

'Good fra you, Dogo,' laughed Jock. 'If I'd known ye were going to do that I wouldn' ha' said anything. All that extra pay ye've lost, too!'

I got my squad at last, but Colonel Taylor was never in any great hurry over promotions, and for some time I was forced to divide my time between office and square. One morning I was taking particulars from a batch of new entrants when Jock pushed through and nearly upset the ink. 'Hey! Heard about the wire?'

'Barbed wire?' I asked blankly.

'He leaned over, whispering: 'Telegram. Top priority. Sergeant volunteers.'

'What's the job?'

'Doesn't say, but it could be Wingate's lot.'

I was certainly interested now. 'What makes you think so?'

'Got to be able to carry 65 lbs long distances.'

'What?'

Jock looked exasperated. 'Ye wanted a change, didn't ye? Come on, let's get in first.'

After an African clerk had taken over, Jock and I met Sergeant 'Taffy' Hitchens leaving the Orderly Room. He stuck down his thumb. 'Snip' thinks it might be for the Pioneers.'

'Blimey, Jock,' I said. 'The old Labour Corps. That's not for us.'

'Rubbish! Would "top priority" be Pioneers? He doesn't want to lose any Europeans,' and a minute later, in Snip's sacred sanctum, we tossed up sizzling salutes.

'Well-well-*well*,' smiled the Colonel, who sometimes leg-pulled when not in a predatory mood. 'Imagine *you* carrying 65 pounds, Shaw – you've a foot in the grave already!'

'Four years' office work, sir,' I replied, very firmly.

'I see. And you, Mitchell?'

'I'd like a change too, sir,' piped Jock blandly.

'So . . . you both want a change, eh?' grinned Snip sardonically. 'If you land this, you'll certainly get one. Off to the M.O., both of you, and Shaw . . .'

'Yessir?'

'No hanky-panky with your age.'

'The blighter knows what the job is,' I muttered outside.

'So do I. Chindits for sure.'

After an extended examination the M.O. handed us written guarantees. '"Fit for severe and prolonged exertion in any part of the world." How about that, Dogo?' grinned Jock.

'How about it? Chindits, Commandos, *or* the Pioneers!'

'Shurrup!' chirruped Jock. 'Watch old Snip's face when he reads these!'

But the C.O. had gone. Captain and Adjutant Hardy took the slips, and gravely dismissed us with no hint of any kind. 'An' that,' forecast Jock gloomily, 'is the last we'll hear of it.'

* * *

With my C.Q.M.S. vacancy at last filled, my first job after leaving the office was in charge of a bearer party – a recruit had died. Clean, spruce, and starched, we were handed picks and shovels at the mortuary. 'You're diggers as well as bearers,' announced the wardmaster. We went by truck to the cemetery, and as the men dug, the sun mounted and the starch dismounted, until they resembled wet scarecrows. Back to the mortuary, where a coffin lay outside, unattended. As the recruits placed it into the truck there was a loud burst of Yoruba, which I sternly suppressed. 'That's enough. Treat this coffin with reverence, *and* that Union Jack!'

At the cemetery the padre, stained with sweat, awaited us, and halfway through the ceremony an ambulance approached at speed, with the wardmaster leaping out when it stopped. He beckoned furiously. 'Help,' I thought, 'we've brought the wrong body!' and tiptoed across. 'What's up?'

'Nothing in that bloody coffin – that's what's up!'

I looked at the padre, still droning away in the heat, and went over to interupt. And all he said was: (I'll always remember him with admiration) 'Good gracious!'

Exasperated, for these bearers were literates, I hurried them into the truck. 'Why the hell didn't you fatheads tell me?' One replied that although they realised that there was nothing in the coffin, if white men wished to bury an empty box it was nothing to do with Yoruba people.

'They probably thought it was an old English custom!' laughed Captain Shaw, then gave me surprising news. 'You leave here at six tomorrow morning, with kit limited to 70 lbs, so you're off somewhere by air. Find Mitchell. The C.O. wants both of you.'

I raked out Jock, whose accusation that I was a 'bluidy liar' changed to a whoop of triumph. Snip told us that we had to be at Lagos by Thursday, thanked us for our work, hoped we'd win lots of medals, wished us luck, shook hands . . . and buzzed off. Infuriating. 'Sir,' I said to the Adjutant, 'we heard this could be for the Pioneers. Surely not?'

He looked amazed, then laughed. 'Pioneers my foot! You're for the 3rd West African Brigade. They're in India, part of Special Force.'

'Special Force of what, sir?' asked irrepressible Jock.

'Chindits,' was the laconic answer. 'Best keep that under your hats.'

We left in a daze, with Captain Hardy smiling after us. 'Whoopee!' said Jock. 'Told ye so.'

'Wingate?' I muttered. 'I can't believe it.'

'Dogo, as a regular ye know ye shouldna volunteer for *anything!*'

'Why, you cheeky sod, it was you who started it all!'

*   *   *

My squad's good wishes touched me, but Sylvester wouldn't believe that we were parting. An immediate urgent problem was whittling kit down to 70 lbs. A large packing-case was already stuffed with souvenirs, and the new C.Q.M.S. said he'd send it to England. Knee-deep in jumble, I looked out at the sunset glow on green and red landscape, at a prostrate follower of the Prophet, at a line of coal-black, bare-breasted Pagan women headloading jars of palm wine. This country had fascinated me, and I was probably leaving it for ever. Chindits? The very idea seemed incredible.

I began typing at breakneck speed, but Jock had no such last-minute task. He'd written only two letters since landing – one to his mother, the other to some mysterious lassie whom, he said, was 'supposed' to be marrying him.

The mess had got wind of our destination, and we agreed enthusiastically with those who said we were mad, and kept things going until well after pumpkin time. Finally, after accompanying Jock in a last 'Scosh' song, we broke up for what was left of the night.

The first available train would not reach the capital in time, and Snip commandeered a lorry from a passing convoy. It contained six men from a Gold Coast unit, bound for Lagos but nothing to do with our project. To these were added our boys and camp equipment, to which we'd cling as long as we could. There was room for Jock and me beside the driver and, being Sunday, the only witnesses to our departure were two sleepy vultures and Private Okon Akpan of my late squad, proudly guarding the Orderly Room verandah with its bright paint and tropical blooms. Okun grinned, giving us an unsentry-like wave as Jock cocked a snook at all the splendour. 'Goo'bye Enugu an' all ye bullshit,' he exclaimed, then added, 'I bet we'll soon be wishin' ourselves back!'

That 'bluidy' Scot could never have spoken truer words. Dear Reader, what is it that prompts men, presumably sane, to abandon safety and luxury for something that promises only danger and discomfort. I honestly don't know . . . you tell me!

*   *   *

Onitsha's streets were filled with gaily-clothed Ibos, and we crossed the Niger on a small ferry that could hold only one vehicle, then continued along a good road through the Southern jungle country, sleeping overnight in a small hamlet that, rather surprisingly, proved to be a Hausa community. During my courtesy call on the Saraki, his henchmen brought a gift of fruit to our encampment, and Jock, not knowing the language and thinking that the man was trying to sell it, finally told him to bugger off, so we had to go along together and soothe the insulted Chief.

Next day a frightful racket arose from inside the truck. Stopping to investigate, we found group all-in wrestling going on, with our boys at the bottom of the heap. Apparently, after the time-honoured start of calling one another bastards, they'd gone on to decry regiments; nothing makes blood flow faster among troops of any nationality.

Two days later we reached the dazzling white mosques of Ibadan, and after chop took the whole party to a cinema in Abeokuta, where Jock and I resembled bushwackers amid the spick-and-span Europeans.

Lagos at last, where eight other sergeants had already arrived. Notable among them were a huge fellow named Keevil, looking capable of handling a dozen average-sized men, and a young chap named Mew, who possessed unquenchable curiosity. Studying these new comrades-in-arms, I thought a more devil-may-care bunch would be hard to find. Jock would be in his element among them.

We were to travel first-class, by B.O.A.C., and next day a few officers joined us. We sergeants possessed quite a hefty sum between us in West African currency, so Jock and I obtained a camp truck and went to town to change it. Our boys begged a lift, saying they had 'sisters' in Lagos, but Africans refer to anyone of their own particular tribe as 'brother' or 'sister'. If a real blood relation they add: 'Same mother, same father'.

It was Saturday, with the Paymaster sailing on the Lagoon – we must wait. Hearing a loud market-like noise, we discovered a native-filled soccer ground, and, to our amazement, *women* players! Of the Calabar tribe, they had long hair that waved wildly, and we appreciated the attempts to head the ball. One goal was scored, past a keeper wearing high-heeled shoes, who kept up a wordy warfare with spectators massed by her goal because they'd impeded her attempt to save. Weak with laughing, we obtained our British quids and overtook the boys trudging back to camp. To Jock's 'innocent' inquiry as to their sisters' health they answered gravely: 'Dey t'ank God' (for being well). It was now dark, and at the canteen a furious avalanche descended upon us. The others thought we'd been at the fleshpots with their cash.

Reveille was at four a.m. next day, and somebody made a good haul from abandoned camp kit. The boys wept, and managed to get into both truck and airport, and a whip-round among us produced a good amount in left-over coins. It was cold, but our blood ran warmer at sight of a floodlit Sunderland flying-boat. We boarded with some civilians, and Sid Mew, exhibiting more insatiable curiosity than Kipling's 'Elephant Child', was promptly ordered away from the pilot's vicinity.

None of us had flown before, and as we soared into a blazing sunrise, Jock and I looked back to where the pathetic figures of our boys were rapidly dwindling. Through the thin mist there was the faint gleam of white goalposts; had that fantastic game taken place only a few hours before? Goodbye, Nigeria.

CHAPTER NINE

3rd West African (Chindit) Brigade

At Leopoldville, I doubt whether the hotel residents appreciated our noisy session around the piano, though next morning several wished us 'good luck in Burma'. Top secret indeed! There had been some imbibing overnight, and 'when the wine's in the wit's out'. More luxurious accommodation at Stanleyville, where at dusk we strolled down to the Congo river. As in Nigeria, drums throbbed in the bush, and it was my last glimpse of Darkest Africa.

Next day the jungle gave way to monotonous desert, and at Khartoum the officers went to an hotel, and we sergeants to a transit camp. Looking round our hut, lit by one low-powered lamp, the grisly contrast was comic. Keevil, sitting down upon his 'charpoy' (wooden bedframe) found it collapsed under him. Naturally the chaps wanted the town and any fun that was offered, and we all piled into, or nearly into, a taxi. On all sides was sand, but at last the driver found a pavement. Keevil again, the only one with piastres, paid the fare, spending the next hour working out how much each of us owed him.

We'd actually been deposited outside the officers' hotel, and a resident standing there stated that our tickets entitled us to the same accommodation, arguing with the management until he got his way. Jock and I weren't anxious to go night-spotting, so obtained a truck for the kit. An hour later the hotel vestibule was unrecognisable – bags, bundles, boxes, boots, sweaty drill, undies definitely not whiter-than-white – and they brought outraged protests from the staff. 'Well, what the bluidy hell d'ye expect *us* to do wi' it?' demanded the hot and exasperated Jock.

'You can take it up to the rooms.'

'*Ye* tak' it up,' flared Jock. 'That's what ye're paid to do.'

'We don't know their rooms,' I pointed out. 'Let 'em grab it as they come in.' So the huge pile stayed, with some residents laughing, and others very disgusted. As well, perhaps, that we had an early breakfast.

I'd never expected to see the Pyramids and the Sphinx from above, but now here they were, and soon Cairo's white and yellow buildings looked magnificent in the sunset. The officers went to Shepheards Hotel, which in 1952 was destroyed, with the B.O.A.C. building, by rioters. The sergeants went to a hostel, and were invaded by guides, offering delectable entertainment. Some accepted, to return after midnight cursing at being conned. 'Serve ye right, ye stupid bastards!' snorted Jock, awakened by the uproar. Next day we were booted out and into a transit building, sleeping on a stone floor with blankets only. A solitary bed was occupied by a Commando, and Jock innocently inquired whether he'd fought everyone else for it. 'I'll fight *you* for it if you like, Scottie,' was the grinning rejoinder.

Leaving Cairo in an Ensign monoplane, we had a glimpse of the Suez Canal, and at Basra Jock and I shared an air-conditioned room in another sumptuous hotel, our last taste of luxury for a long time. Off again at four a.m., to breakfast at Bahrein in the Persian Gulf before ending the flight in Karachi.

*   *   *

After living the life of Riley, it was back to hard fact with a train journey through the Thar Desert region, then a lorry ride to Rear Brigade at Talbahat. To our chagrin we found that the Nigerian columns had departed for Assam – we were replacements if needed. Left behind at this camp were sick and non-combatants, plus a handful of Europeans who were unashamed malingerers. There were thinly-veiled sneers about our sanity, which ended abruptly when Keevil showed that he wasn't amused. These fellows asserted that when news of casualties was received, no Africans would go with us as reinforcements. Well, time would tell.

I ascertained that Major Carfrae was indeed leading a 7th Battalion Column, and stressed my keen desire to join him. In vain. Jock and Keevil were allocated to the 7th, Sid Mew and I to the 12th – sheer, deliberate, bloody-mindedness in the Orderly Room! 'Stop moanin', Dogo,' grinned Jock. 'I'll keep an eye on the Major fra ye!'

Weapon training now. First a flamethrower, then an American invention called a Bazooka and equally lethal. Engineers were geligniting the rock-hard ground, and when their bugle sounded you had seconds to dive for cover and avoid showers of flinty shrapnel. Actually, by arriving late, we'd missed quite a lot of backbreaking jungle work, with Wingate determined that all personnel would be fighting fit.

Evenings were deadly. We fished a lake with improvised tackle. When I sent an airgraph to England for proper hooks and gut Jock roared. 'Ye must be saft!'

'Not so soft. Looks as though we're stuck in this dump for good.'

'Oh no. When chaps start gettin' bumped off we'll go in fast enough. But anyway, why are *ye* bletherin'? No-one over thirty-six can go in.'

'What? Where's that come from? Nothing said about it in Enugu.'

'I've got contacts,' was the airy answer.

'Then shut up, or they'll hear you. It's all right for you and Sid.'

Our draft was summoned – was this it? No, just the final medical I was fearing. A.1 wasn't enough – one must pass A.1 'Plus'. Lieutenants Galbraith and Campbell, bosom pals, entered first. Galbraith wore spectacles, so if *he* made it, why shouldn't I? Both emerged grinning. Jock and I were first of the sergeants; there were two M.O.s. The tests were the stiffest I'd ever known, with Jock also going through the mill. Finally, when asked my age, I groaned inwardly. No use lying, for my Army Book 64 was in his hand. 'Forty-one, sir,' I muttered.

He scribbled. 'That's all.' I went out without tying my bootlaces, quizzing the book as the others gathered round – A.1 Plus! I subsequently learned that in the first expedition all over forty, except Wingate himself, had died, and much later also heard that I was probably the oldest 'other rank' on the second campaign. Oh well, when ignorance is bliss . . .

Then came the eagerly awaited information. The curtain had gone up, and the Columns had been put down 200 miles behind the Japanese front lines, some by American-piloted gliders – what a job in the dark! The Chindits were now severing vital enemy communications and aiming to hold on. Then suddenly – disaster. Barely had we in the rear absorbed the first reports when stunning news came through that our Leader had been killed in an air crash. Wingate dead! The whole project seemed doomed, but it was now too late to pull back; a General Lentaigne took over. Meanwhile, at prearranged times the Columns called Rear Brigade with powerful radios. Plenty of desperate fighting was taking place.

For us, Vickers tuition now, and during the first lesson Lieutenant Brown of the 12th arrived and pow-wowed quietly with the instructor before beckoning to me. I followed him with my heart bumping and Sid looking after us; Jock was slinging grenades around somewhere. Said Browny: 'Our Vickers sergeant, Freebody, is a casualty. You're recommended.'

Since I'd ten years' experience of the weapon and Sid about half an hour, this wasn't surprising. Browny went on: 'Here's a list of things you'll need. Go and draw them. You won't be able to write from where you're going, but we'll arrange to send a monthly airgraph to your next-of kin, unless you get yourself killed.' He smiled, ever so nicely.

'Thank you, sir!'

Keevil and a 'Taffy' Hawkins joined me, having been chosen for the 7th and 6th respectively. We drew extra gear – two big containers to sew on the pack, and a canvas water-bag (chagul) to augment the bottle. We were told that watches, compasses, and torches had run out, but as an ex-quarterbloke I was sceptical. We couldn't even get important 'panic maps', so-called because anyone lost could make his way in the general direction of safety. 'General direction' was correct, for the scale was one in two million! These maps were silk, of handkerchief size. We were given Sten guns, unpopular because an accidental knock could cause them to fire. Finally, we collected morphia needles . . .

My pals were waiting. 'What's cooking?' demanded Jock, glaring at the heap on my charpoy.

'Beaten you to it, mate,' I said, not without a touch of malice.

'Me wi' campaign experience, an' ye a forty-year-old greenhorn!'

'D'you know anything about a Vickers?'

'Well, no,' admitted Jock.

'Stop chuntering then, or I'll stick one o' these needles into yer!'

Despite all the banter, I was feeling quite a pang – when would we three meet again?

Next day Keevil, Taffy and I were jolted over an appalling road to Special Force H.Q., where, infuriatingly, we weren't expected. Officers for British units yes, sergeants for West

Africans no; in vain we protested. Was I going back over that bone-shaking road to hear Jock roar? Finally we were told to turn up at dawn, and slept on stretchers. At daylight no-one protested when we boarded a lorry with the officers, and on alighting, walked with them towards a waiting Dakota. An airman standing by it had no passenger list, but was probably counting bodies, and we brought up the rear closely. 'It's a Yank, look you,' murmured Taffy. 'Good!'

'Three sergeants,' smiled Keevil politely.

'O.K. buddies.' We were into the plane before this worthy nephew of Uncle Sam could change his mind, and soon landed in Assam, right on Burma's doorstep, having merely hopped from Rear to Forward Brigade. As we dumped our kit in a bamboo and grass hut (a 'basha') an air alert sounded that everybody ignored.

Although not expected, we weren't sent back, and joined a most peculiar queue by a bamboo cookhouse. Carrying messtins were British, Africans, Burmese, Chinese, Ghurkas, and Indians, a Tower of Babel yacketing in chorus. To our astonishment some officers joined us – apparently no-one below Major could feed at their mess. Another strange sight arrived – an armed padre, and when Keevil ventured to ask why he wore a pistol he said it was to protect sick and wounded in his care. Adding to this bizarre scene were a dozen circling vultures, and yarns I'd disbelieved concerning these Eastern 'shitehawks' were proved true when one swooped and snatched bread from my tin. I felt only the wind of its passing, then emulated Oliver Twist by going back to beg for more.

Partly flooded rice-fields surrounded the camp, with jungle beyond. We weren't far from the Khasia Hills, with their record annual rainfall. Each evening it deluged until dark, when jackals came out and howled around the paddy. Promiscuous shooting was taking place, so we went and tried our Stens in the direction of the bloodcurdling row. A business-like Asian civilian fried eggs and chips on a tiny oasis – to reach him you wore rubber boots. We were now using rupees (chips) for currency.

Reports from the Columns continued to enthrall us. They'd cut road and rail, constructed air strips, and were repelling furious attacks. The blocks had been given names – Piccadilly, Broadway, Aberdeen, etc., and with great excitement I learned that the 12th were in the biggest stronghold of all – White City. The 6th were at Aberdeen, and the 7th were rovers, their *forte* being to stalk enemy parties, kick their backsides, and scarper.

Soon we were startled by hearing that Carfrae's Nigerians had ambushed and destroyed a whole convoy. 'Missed it,' groaned Keevil. 'Just my luck!' The details were fascinating. After the short, sharp action, the Major ordered the trucks and enemy bodies to be burned. With no time for interring, he wouldn't leave them lying around. He also left a note for the enemy Area Commander, assuring him that the men had been cremated *after* death – some of his own Column might one day be captured. 'What about that?' marvelled Keevil. 'Japs could've turned up at any moment. He must be a cool customer!'

'He is,' I replied, 'as you'll find out!'

'When the hell are *we* going in? There *must* be casualties.'

My name was called. At last – this was it. Five minutes later I was back. 'I'm off, and not to see the Wizard!'

'Lucky sod.'

'Think so? I'm off all right, to build a shithouse!'

'Eh?'

I exploded. 'I'm to find six Africans and construct an extra latrine. I've come ten thousand miles, first-class, to build a shithouse!'

Soon some grumbling 'volunteers' were hacking the ground, while I mooched around with feelings unutterable. A strange officer arrived, and spoke to the men before calling me over to interpret. 'I'm Ricketts – Deputy Brigadier,' he announced. 'Who are you?' After asking further questions, he said that I appeared to have been 'enterprising'. Involuntarily I replied: 'It hasn't got me very far, sir. I didn't forfeit promotion in order to dig a latrine.'

He might have stuck me in the bamboo nick for that remark, but merely smiled. 'I'm as anxious as you to go in, and can promise that it will be soon.'

'That's something like it!' commented the others at my report, then we threw ourselves flat as an adjacent ammunition basha unaccountably went up in flames, blowing itself to bits. An hour later Keevil dashed in. 'C'mon, you two. Off tomorrow. Lots to do.' First, everything white had to be dyed with a horrible woadlike muck – towels, undies, even handkerchiefs. Keevil accidentally plastered his face, and for several days resembled one of Queen Boadicea's heavy mob, enough to scare the pants off a whole enemy platoon. Extra bombs, bullets, plus five days' hard rations were rammed into the equipment, total weight 65 pounds without the water-filled chaguls which went another five. We should have broken down the various containers, for more room and less weight. We were tenderfeet, but by hookey we learned fast. My pack was too bulky for the truck cabin when we left for the airfield next day. With each of us were eight Africans.

Three planes would leave at hourly intervals. At dusk a shadowy figure approached – Brigadier Ricketts had come to wish us good luck. 'Aren't you coming, sir?' I inquired.

'Not this time,' he answered regretfully, 'and I may not join you at all, for you'll probably be flown out before the monsoon breaks. Here's a telegram for you, Shaw.' Birthday greetings from my mother, re-routed several times from Nigeria. With difficulty I made it out – 'Many Happy Returns'!

*   *   *

It grew dark. Keevil's Dakota roared off, then Taffy's. Soon my own friendly American crew arrived, and one super-optimist gave me his name and address, saying he would like to acquire a Japanese flag or sword! Inside, we sat on benches, the interior lit dimly and windows blacked out except for a tiny peephole in each. I listened to my eight men conversing quietly in Hausa, and wished that those miserable know-alls in the rear could see and hear them. But what were their private thoughts at being dumped behind enemy lines? My own were a mixture of excitement and trepidation. Jock, with his happy knack of easing tension with flippancy, would have been welcome just then.

We took off, and for some time there continued the muffled roaring, until the souvenir-hunting airman came back to me. 'We're over the front line, buddy. Look out – you may see something.' I stared down through a peephole, and suddenly from the black depths brilliant red splashes belched – one, two, three, four. 'Mortars or artillery,' yelled the airman from the next hole.

I couldn't reply; this was my first glimpse of fighting in the field. Those missiles below were meant to scatter death among men who were probably desperately in need of sleep, and soon I'd be down there too. I sat down rather shakily, with a nasty sensation in the pit of my stomach.

Later I began to feel ear pressure – we were descending. The Dakota touched, slowed, and stopped with a jerk as we groped for equipment. When I left the aircraft in front of the others I became conscious of an automatic weapon pointing at my guts and glaring eyeballs behind it. A huge beard opened in the middle and a voice demanded: 'British?'

'Yes,' I answered hastily.

'Any mail?'

'The crew have it . . . I say . . . where am I?'

'Aberdeen to you!' he threw back over his shoulder.

'So I'm a Chindit at last,' I thought, but not very exultantly.

CHAPTER TEN

Chindit

Boots, boots, boots, boots,
Moving up and down again . . .
Oh my God keep me from going lunatic . . .

(Kipling)

THE CHINTHÉ

*According to ancient Burmese legend, a Princess was kidnapped by a
'Nat' (evil spirit) and taken into the mountains. All rescue attempts
were unsuccessful, so the despairing King summoned the Chinthé – half
lion, half dragon – that lived in the jungle in those times. The Chinthé
succeeded where all the King's horses and men had failed, and as a
reward was appointed Custodian of Burma Pagodas for all time. Its
effigy can be seen at the door of all Temples today.*

*Since the Chindits were fighting to release Burma from the Japanese,
General Wingate's adoption of the Emblem seemed appropriate. In fact,
Wingate was referred to by the Burmese as 'Lord Protector of Pagodas'.*

*I could not attempt a comprehensive account of the Second Expedi-
tion, for I joined them when it was already under way. But maybe the
General himself, had he been spared, could not have written a full
description. Parties were ambushed, dispersed, and unable to reform.
Individuals became lost, and were never again seen – the jungle
engulfed them.*

*Special Force, 1944, expected to be flown out of Burma before the
onset of the monsoon. Because of the death of General Wingate, they
eventually had to make their way on foot from 200 miles behind the
Japanese front lines. The next few chapters describe the struggles of a*

Column from the 12th Battalion of the Nigeria Regiment, with which I had the honour to serve.

Taffy's voice sounded, and we followed him into an unlit basha. I groped my way to where I could hear Keevil. 'Park yourself on this stretcher, Dogo. Not allowed lights. What a stink in here.' At this point someone else spoke, with cultured irritation – did we know there would be a stand-to at four-thirty? This consisted of taking up defensive position around the basha, shivering in intense cold for half an hour, until an M.O. arrived who turfed us all out. It was his Casualty Clearing Station – hence the smell.

So this was 'Aberdeen'. Several wrecked aircraft lay around, and we learned that an arranged light plane flip to White City was off – we'd have to walk the 17 miles, which included a mountain. With us were two lost chaps who'd constructed the word 'LAND' with bamboo. An intrepid Yank, chancing the surface and possible enemy tricks, brought down his light plane successfully.

We said goodbye to Taffy, already in charge of a 6th Column Bren, and set off, the jungle permitting of nothing more than single file. Gurkhas led, and every time they negotiated an awkward patch just belted off again, so that those behind had to accelerate or lose touch. The pace was taxing the powers of even marching-fit men, and I was in early difficulty. My shoulders were becoming numbed and, leaning ever further forward trying to ease the crushing weight, I could see only the boots of the African in front of me. At the mountain the pace hardly lessened, and during a heaven-sent ten minutes' halt the British officer commanding the Gurkhas came along. 'How's it going, sergeant?'

'Pretty warm, sir.'

He grinned. 'The rear's always nasty. Keep count of the men who fall out!'

Off again, and soon the track became steep. I wasn't the only one in trouble, for within the next few minutes we passed a fallen, ashen-faced Tommy, and then an African. During the Campaign the enemy took full toll of such unfortunates, and coming upon yet another I felt naked fear. I *must* stay on my feet, but it certainly wasn't Kipling's 'heart and nerve sinew' that kept me going, but the sheer dread of being captured. I was now paying dearly for all that office-lazing.

Keevil was in front of me, and I occasionally glimpsed him on the twisting track. He appeared unaffected, to my unjustified irritation. 'Blast this murderous pace!' I muttered savagely, having lost the initial taut feeling that every bush concealed a Japanese. At the summit we again halted, and I lay like a log, watching an enormous spider hanging near my face. Tarantula? I couldn't have cared less. The officer again. 'How many?'

'Eight Africans, five Europeans.'

'We'll stay half an hour, and if they aren't in by then, they've had it. I relaxed, head against the pack I'd been cursing, and gave my own group a word of praise for being intact. Suddenly the sky darkened and an out-of-season storm burst with great violence. We made no effort to extract ground-sheets, letting that glorious downpoor crash upon us as aches and pains eased magically. No move was made until the rain ceased, by which time all the revitalised fall-outs had rejoined.

The sun returned, glinting on huge drops plopping upon vegetation, and going downhill the packs were even heavier from the soaking. All except those indefatigable Gurkhas were exhausted when we stopped near a village, where inhabitants came out and shyly offered cooked rice in big leaves. 'How d'you feel?' I asked Keevil.

'Bloody! How the hell did you manage it, Dogo?'

His reply gave me momentary satisfaction, but I was very relieved when it was decided to resume the trek next day. Sleeping by the hamlet could be hazardous, so we left the track and formed a square in bush with H.Q. and non-combatants in the centre. After scratching slit trenches, it was dark when I posted my first sentry. Soon I wondered how long one could go without proper sleep, for despite warnings the look-outs chatted, and every hour made more noise awakening reliefs. At dawn stand-to I found that because of an unfavourable slope, some men had slept with their heads facing inwards. Had there been an alarm, H.Q. might have been shot up by our own side!

Off went the Gurkhas next morning. We'd collected a mule from somewhere, so as 'Tail End Charlie' I was no longer looking at boots but a donkey's backside – permanent. There wasn't the slightest breeze, and when the mists dispersed the sun beat down with terrific power. The leaders missed a junction, and we had the pleasure of seeing the Gurkhas come back and push past us, grinning like gargoyles at the joke. The officer said, *en passant*, that the enemy must have camouflaged the junction and that we would have met an ambush. To save retracing the whole distance he decided to cut through the bush by compass until hitting the right track. It was hellishly tough, especially for the poor old mule. Suddenly he wrenched free from his minder, and was gone.

*   *   *

> I will lift up mine eyes unto the hills,
> From whence commeth my help.
>   (Psalm 121)

A loud explosion ahead, and Keevil glanced back at me; the White City wasn't far away. I was nearly bent double under the pack, while my belt, weighty with explosives, was beginning to paralyse my hips. All feeling was leaving my legs. If I could only throw myself down – anything to ease this torment. Then the ghastly face of a fallen man, plus more bangs, forcibly reminded me that the surroundings held those who would show scant mercy. At some huts we halted and were told to lie flat. I didn't feel the earth when I flopped; I could have lain there for eternity. Stragglers rejoined, fell, gulped water . . . whoever invented the chagul saved the sanity of many.

I rose and staggered forward at a shout for group commanders, to hear that we were about to enter open paddy. We would see White City directly we left these huts, and could be sniped at from Mawlu village to the right, and should keep a good interval between groups.

The Gurkhas advanced, and there was no firing. When my chaps emerged last, they extended into line with myself in the centre. Ahead lay the block, a cluster of hills with tiny figures watching our approach, and to the flank was Mawlu, dominated by a large golden-coloured pagoda. The paddy was full of giant cracks, and the jolting made the pain at my hips excruciating. A yell, and everybody dropped as three planes raced low over the hills. The ground shook as a single bomb burst, while we lay expecting a shower of cannon shells that didn't arrive. The engines faded. Oddly enough, I wasn't scared – like everyone else I was seizing the chance to drink. Keevil, fifty yards ahead, looked back and waved his chagul. 'First pint under fire!' he yelled, and, so help me, he was grinning!

We moved, though I'd barely the strength to stride over the cracks. A stumble, and I'd never get up again. Either the Japanese would loot and leave the body, or our side would bury me on the spot, and old Browny would notify the next-of-kin. 'Shall we *never* get there?' I kept muttering, and have only dim memories of the last hundred yards. Through smarting eyes I could just make out the defenders looking down at us, and to me, the White City was no beleaguered fortress, but Mecca. My very life depended upon becoming besieged. Crazy! Somehow my feet carried me over a road and a shattered railway track. Then I stumbled through some wire, and that was the lot for the moment.

                              *   *   *

I was sitting on my pack, watching a line of men and mules going to and from a stream. British, African, Asian, with every white man bearded. Upon the bank there was a succinct notice – DEAD JAPS IN THIS RIVER. ALL WATER MUST BE CHLORINATED.

A European asked my name, and wearily I told him. 'Stand up when you speak to an officer,' he said sharply. I nearly asked how I was supposed to know his rank when, like all other humans in sight, he was bare from the waist up. Just then a second white man arrived, much more of a gentlemn than the first. After shaking hands, I learned that he was my new C.O., Colonel Hughes. What could I do as regards weapons? I said that I hoped to be useful with a machine-gun, and was told that I certainly could, for the Vickers sergeant, Freebody, had been flown out sick.

Twelve Battalion consisted of two Columns – 12 and 43. I was in 12, and its Commander was a Major Taylor of the Royal Sussex! I heartily agreed when he said that the South Downs were to be preferred to the White City hills! He introduced me to my officer, Lieutenant Hugh Gordon, who in turn passed me on to Captain Bence, commanding the Brigade's machine-guns. He'd show me my gun site tomorrow, and indicated a hole that would be my home until then. He said that my team were on fatigue some-where, and recommended a man named Anton Antonadi as an orderly.

Still more dead than alive, I bathed at the waterpoint, then returned to find that the team were back. Beyond a curious glance they ignored me, so I called a sergeant and asked his name. 'Haruna Numan, suh.'

'Were you told to report to me, sergie?'

'Yes, suh.'

'Why didn't you?'

Silence. So to indicate that I was no rookie, I inquired in Hausa for Anton Antonadi, and was told that the man had stated that he didn't fancy the job. At the moment the last thing I wanted was an unwilling orderly and, still feeling very ill, told the sergeant to leave me. Soon I heard argument, then another presence loomed up. 'Dis orderly work, suh. I fit do um.'

I was surprised at the English, for the speaker was a Munchi, a backward tribe with a dialect few Europeans mastered. Training them wasn't easy, but they made good soldiers who believed that death met bravely ensured afterlife. Their women were equally courageous, prepared to be buried alive with deceased hubby! I smiled at the man, who returned an enormous grin. Like most of his tribe, the skin on his face had cicatrized over cuts inflicted when he was an infant – a playful Munchi idea of decoration. 'Hallo,' I said, 'what's your name, Munchi?'

'Zaki Yabo, suh. I hear Hausa too.'

'Good. Zaki, all I want now is some tea and sleep!'

While he brewed, I gazed around. A rough cross marked an African's grave, and large mounds of earth covered mules, scores having been killed. There were many mortar bomb craters and bigger ones from aircraft.

I drank the smoky, milkless liquid thankfully, then found that my hole was silk-lined! Hundreds of parachutes, some silken, had been dropped, and naturally the lads had seized anything offering a modicum of comfort. White City's title had been derived not from the London dog-track, but because of all the parachutes caught in the trees during the initial fighting.

I'd been fortunate indeed to last out this day, and it was some time before I fully recovered. That night, despite roaring, supply-dropping Dakotas, I fell asleep at once, easy meat if the Japanese had attacked.

* * *

Next day I spoke with some of the defenders who, we'd heard in Assam, had been fighting mad when repelling the enemy. They said nothing about their own individual feats, but were enthusiastic about others. All agreed that the Japanese were brave to the point of fanaticism, but had contributed to their own failures. All attacks came over the same routes, which had of course been ranged to a yard. Whoever chose the White City site was a genius. It cut both road and rail supplying enemy troops confronting 'Vinegar Joe' Stilwell, the U.S. General commanding Chinese in the rear.

Zaki's account of the last assault was hair-raising in more ways than one: 'De Japans run. We run, catch dem. Chop off heads wid machete!' He grinned ferociously. Later I learned that though Africans did indeed carry back severed heads, Zaki's team had not yet been in action. I made no comment, for my orderly's yarns provided welcome entertainment.

The hills bore unmistakable signs of sustained battling, crater-pitted and with flattened shrubbery. A very few trees remained upright, but with subnude branches. Everywhere was the filth and litter of war – empty tins, and cartridge cases by the thousand. Large canvas containers held water against further attack, and latrines were hastily dug. You'd find several different nationalities squatting over holes and trying to converse, in which case you awaited a vacancy . . . all very different from Birdcage Walk!

Although literally surrounded by the enemy, there was no 'Mafeking' atmosphere. Supplies, including a Battery of Artillery, Bofors A.A. guns, jeeps, had been brought in by Dakotas – even mules arrived by glider. Sick and wounded went out in light planes. Far from besieging, the frustrated Japanese were in frequent uproar when perambulating Chindits pounced from nowhere, took a deadly toll, then withdrew at speed. Mysterious bangs rang out from the jungle, and defenders would crack off a few rounds for no apparent reason, but what I found really amazing was that people wandered about in full view of the enemy.

A corporal of the Leicestershires came up to me, carrying the tail fins of an enormous mortar bomb. 'Just in?' he asked.

'Yes. Nearly feet first!'

'Take a dekko at this cowson. We call it a "coalscuttle" and it's all hell where it bursts.'

None of these fighters were specially selected troops, but ordinary Infantrymen like myself. Looking at the haggard faces, I felt that joining them was a privilege.

Captain Bence arrived, and after pointing out Lieutenant Gordon's position on a rise called Pagoda Hill, took me up another at the eastern side of the block. 'Here you are —' he began, then paused, for I was standing open-mouthed. Enmeshed in Dannert wire were bodies, distorted and grotesque. Within touching distance were naked Japanese – suicides who had crawled up to sever the wire. Behind them were others fully accoutred, their skulls grinning inside steel helmets. With a sudden chill at my spine I remained staring, for there was something puzzling about these remains, and Bence explained: 'Hellish stink. We had to use flamethrowers. Couldn't recover them – the wire's full of boobies.' Dangerous work for the flamethrowing men, I thought, for the wire held a miscellaneous assortment of explosives. Among the ghastly skeletons a small brown bird was hopping, giving sparrow-like cheeps. Bence continued: 'This is O.P. Hill, your position. The Observation Post was here until things grew too warm. It's where the Japs finally broke through. They invariably come this way.'

'Thanks, mate,' I thought, and inquired about a nearby Vickers position.

'They're Gurkhas, but they don't cover Mawlu. As soon as you're in, they're pulling out. Well, sergeant, it's your palaver now, so get cracking.'

The team watched my contortions on the crest – the field of fire must include both Mawlu and the eastern jungle, and between that same jungle and myself dead ground dipped out of sight – not at all nice. I called Sergeant Haruna, who listened without comment before haranguing the men, and to the accompaniment of the usual rhythmic grunts and bawdy songs they attacked the baked crust.

During stand-to next morning Zeros swept in at 2,000 feet and the team dived for cover. Curiosity stayed me, until Zaki bellowed from his hole and I shot into mine, belatedly remembering that a bullet travels 2,000 feet in less than a second – a quick sergeant was better than a dead hero!

Up again to the dig. 'Which place your hole, suh?' asked Zaki.

'I'll see the Gurkhas first.' They invited me to inspect their site – a pity I couldn't use it. Those little fellows took incredible pains when digging (so, unfortunately, did the Japanese). A small cave was liberally lined with parachuting. 'This is our bedroom,' I told Zaki, who went off for our packs while I cast around for an O.P. 'Here you are, Sergie Haruna.' He demurred, saying that the escape hole from the trench would serve, but I'd already rejected it. 'No good, Haruna. I can't see Mawlu.'

'Japans no come from Mawlu. Japans come from bush.' He indicated the dip.

I dug in my heel. 'I'll have it *here*.'

'Master sit for dere, master soon go lib for die.'

'That's my palaver, Haruna.'

He persisted doggedly. 'Dey bury plenty Japans for dis place.'
But the O.P. was completed without disinterring anything

grisly. Despite his obstinacy, I didn't dislike old Haruna, for if anyone else tried to emulate him by being awkward the sergeant gave him short shrift. I could understand his resentment of my arrival, for with Sergeant Freebody evacuated, Haruna had expected to lead the team for the rest of the Campaign.

Lieutenant Cameron, whose rifle platoon adjoined my site, agreed with me that the dip was a menace, and pointed to a distant tall tree that he thought might hold an enemy O.P. Needing railway sleepers and steel, I was told to see Lieutenant Rowbottom of the Royal Engineers, but he was out trying to plot hastily-laid boobies. During the morning an explosion rocked the block, and Rowbottom's leg had to be amputated. On hearing that I took the team to the railway, where the usual sentry was now missing. All's fair in war, and three times the Gunner headloaded the coveted wood and metal to O.P. Hill. The site was completed and the roof camouflaged. What we needed now was a gun!

Luxuries were being taken into the newly-covered position – groundsheets, parachutes, and a large tarpaulin were dragged into the bowels of the earth, but how about the exposed front of the site? The Gurkhas had a large piece of netting, wonderfully garnished with imitation shrubbery – ideal. Things my chaps were sticking in the ground would be flattened by our own muzzle blast; we'd be sitting ducks. The Vickers arrived, and I checked it. Now, how about the team's expertise? 'Who's Number One?' I asked.

'Me be, suh,' answered Private Ali Banana. 'Me be for dis "mai ruwa"* seven years.'

'Glad to hear that, Ali,' I said, and meant it. He and his number two stripped and cleaned the weapon, and soon I saw them in difficulty while reassembling. Quietly I put them right, to receive covert smiles of thanks. The pride of the Banana tribe was saved, and at least two friends gained.

The air siren blew, and I jumped into action. If simple adjustments were made to the tripod, the Vickers was quickly converted into a handy weapon against low-flying aircraft. Fixing it within seconds, I yelled for a number two, who was essential when firing the gun in that way. Nobody appeared at my bawling, and meanwhile planes were wheeling overhead and Bofors banging like mad. Loud crashes and the slap of blast against my face made me join the others in the trench. We

* 'Mai ruwa'. Literally 'Owner of water'. The gun held water as a coolant.

emerged to see smoking craters, and among the casualties was Corporal Matheson, again from the unfortunate Sappers.

*   *   *

Before joining Carfrae outside, Keevil climbed up to say good-bye. Noting the fireswept bodies, he hoped to see plenty more. Many people, including the Press, came to view the spectacle, and once we had a V.I.P. in Jackie Coogan. 'The Kid' had piloted one of the first gliders behind the lines. But for myself, those mute, roasted skeletons dominated the hilltop. Always conscious of their presence, I ate and slept within feet of them. At times the cheep of the little brown bird rang through my head like an anvil and, flamethrowers notwithstanding, there was sometimes a nauseating stench.

The Gurkhas left, amid a deafening hullabaloo between the two teams. My lot yelled in Hausa and the other in Gurkhali, so no-one knew what insults were being flung. Once it threatened to be machetes versus kukris and I gathered that the synthetic vegetation had disappeared overnight. After the uproar I annexed the cave, but Zaki, electing to sleep in the trench, made off. I unearthed 14,000 rounds of ammunition, boxes of gre-nades, and some frightful glass prussic acid bombs. The cave held masses of silk – I felt as though I were at the Ritz. Loud laughter outside, and I emerged to see Zaki dragging an extremely well-made camouflage net, quite the equal of the Gurkhas'!

A night patrol of Cameron's hadn't returned. 'Lying doggo or captured,' he surmised. 'I'm relieving a listening-post. Care to come?' I followed him through a gap in the wire and at once saw the reason for the stench, for in the dip lay dozens of enemy bodies that hadn't been 'treated'. Looking around, I felt sick-ened by the horror in that bright sunlight. Some were shattered by grenades hurled into the dip, and included an armless private, a sergeant with both feet severed, and a Lieutenan-Colonel who had certainly not been bringing up the rear. Further down, mortar bombs had left more broken remains, with one legless man a nightmarish sight, his empty waterbottle flung from him in a last agony of thirst. Cameron posted his men in this huge charnel-house, leaving them to an unenviable task. Returning, we had to lie among the dead as another air attack took place. The water-point was crammed with troops and mules, but only one African was wounded. That evening a

water-buffalo came out of the jungle to drink, and to prevent
him touching off a whole series of mines the poor beast was
shot. Two days afterwards, swelling to twice his enormous size,
he burst, fortunately downstream.

The missing patrol returned, having heard metal being struck,
and it was thought that transport was being repaired, so our
Battery of 25-pounders went into action, the shells whistling
over our heads. The enemy must have hated this Battery, for
their positions were wirelessed to it by the rovers. A Black
Watch Column encountered a strong dug-in force and radioed
for air support. From O.P. Hill I had a grandstand view as
Mustangs and Mitchells strafed in a low-level raid before the
Scots went in with bayonets.

After several requests I was given leave to try the gun. All the
team fired, and I told Haruna to go first. He happily got rid of a
whole belt of 250, and after that we were friends! Cameron's
platoon afterwards stated that something fell out of the tall tree.
I missed that, for the noise inside the turret was earsplitting,
and when the water-condenser was accidentally up-ended we
were smothered with steam. Entering into the spirit of things,
one of Cameron's chaps slung a four-second grenade into the
dip, and the listening-post became violently abusive on the field
telephone.

How about the approaching monsoon? Everybody was convinced that it would render the block untenable, yet there were
rumours that we would stay. 'We'd be flooded,' said one
Tommy to me, 'except you on the hill with your bleedin' gun!'
Then an even stronger rumour was scoffed at – we were to trek
north to help the Chinese, who were being held up. All agreed
that no such operation could be feasible in the rains, and that
airdrops could not be used. They were wrong, for confirmation
followed – Mahomet must go to the Mountain. 'They're daft!'
asserted my informant. 'Wingate wouldn't have put up with
this. What the hell d'they think we are, bloody ducks?' It was
now that I first heard the phrase 'Forgotten Army'. These men
had done an incredible job, and the cutting of the railway was
the primary cause of the enemy's ultimate rout. The chaps felt
cheated, sure that Wingate would have had them evacuated.

It grew even hotter, and the stench stronger. I never got used
to the idea of men lying unburied, whatever the nationality.
Similar feelings animated somebody outside the block, for one
day Cameron took me through the wire and pointed . . . the
sergeant had gone. There lay his boots, with feet still in them.

Whoever dragged away the body – maybe a relative – had first dodged the listening-post before crawling to within yards of us. The next day a young wounded Japanese was brought in, and a bad job was made of searching him. While being tended by our M.O., Captain Tait, he suddenly produced a bomb, which luckily was dud. Leaflets had been dropped to the enemy, inviting them to surrender. What a hope!

All our men feared being taken prisoner, but a captured document proved surprising:

> British. Stands on formality and gives careful consideration to everything. Has a strong sense of patriotism and nationalism. Must be treated as if he were a gentleman.
> American. Offhand and hail-fellow-well-met in manner. Acts on impulse without deep consideration. Is without reserve and takes everyone as friendly on sight. Must be dealt with in the same fashion.

This, of course, related to interrogation in the field. P.O.W. camps were quite another matter! An officer's diary wasn't quite so flattering:

> British prisoners say they must win with their big material resources. They are bastards, but to some extent I admire them.

Zaki got busy with blue silk, saying that before the block was abandoned there would be tribal 'play'. After making me a pair of shorts, he produced a wonderful hat for himself. At sunset a party of Munchis sang and danced, while the Hausas banged anything that would make a din. All hell was let loose, and O.P. Hill became crowded with appreciative Tommies. I looked across at Mawlu's glittering pagoda, carefully left undamaged by Allied airmen, and asked myself if we were indeed in the heart of enemy-held territory? The Japanese in Mawlu must have thought us stark mad!

All Europeans except myself were armed with U.S. Underwood carbines, superb automatic weaons. I persevered until I got one, but was still without compass, watch, and panic map. I was given a compass that proved erratic, so left it, hoping that some Japanese would get lost, then slung my Sten over the wire and tried out my carbine – the Sten bounced about satisfactorily. We were all given 50 silver rupees, for buying food or information if needed.

News of the trek had been received by the Africans with philosophical grunts, until we heard that No. 12 Column would hold the block for a day after everyone else had left. Even happy-go-lucky Zaki pricked up his ears at that! Just in time, Jock flew in, but left at once to join Carfrae and we didn't meet. Freebody also arrived, but Major Taylor decided that he would go to Lieutenant Macauley's rifle platoon while I stayed with the Gunners. Freebody, surprisingly, seemed unconcerned.

Dakotas were now landing, and it was possible to send airgraphs. Seeing me busy, Zaki approached, with all the team hovering within earshot. 'Master send word for his people for England? Master please salute dem from me.'

'Thanks, Zaki. I will.'

'Me want send word for my wife for Makurdi.'

'All right. I'll do it for you two-time.' (shortly)

'I send t'hree pound for her.'

'What d'you think White City is – a post office?'

'If I go lib for die, de paymaster keep my money for his hand.'

The others edged forward, fully in agreement, having had no pay for weeks. Their accounts were heavily in the black, and all were convinced that in the event of their demise the Paymaster would grab the lot. 'You're not going to die, Zaki,' I said, 'and even if you did, your wife would get all the kudi. Hear that, you lot over there?'

Yes, they heard, but I could have spouted until the Day of Judgement!

CHAPTER ELEVEN

White City Abandoned

On 10th May every spare man toiled all day, dismantling the Battery and preparing heavy stuff for Dakotas. Everything not being taken was destroyed or boobied, and at sunset No. 12 took over all the defences built for three times our number. I was told to concentrate upon Mawlu – the dip would be looked after by riflemen. Terrific noise went on for hours after the Daks arrived, with Africans yelling at one another. During this distraction, at dusk the rest of the Garrison sneaked over the paddy and into the jungle. With them went 43, our sister Column, commanded by the C.O., Colonel Hughes. We were now alone.

The last Dakota roared away about midnight, and an uncomfortable night was spent. Apprehension at dawn, but no enemy appeared – they must have thought we'd been reinforced for the monsoon. Actually, at that moment, a brand new Japanese division was in Mawlu, preparing to assault the block. Our top brass must have known, but very little vital information trickled down to us small fry. Understandable, for if prisoners were taken, the less they knew the better, but there is no doubt that if the enemy commander had had the faintest notion that our Blue Peter was hoisted, our present skeleton defence would have been overrun.

Making as much display as possible, we lit fires, but the usual moves to and from the waterpoint were much less, so men were sent down regularly as a blind. It became difficult to enforce, for many Africans had worked hard overnight, and knew another sleepless one lay ahead. They began to hide in holes. I spent the day in the turret, wearing only the silk drawers and observing the Japanese with binoculars. Equipment lay ready. Having been wearing canvas shoes and taking little exercise, most people viewed the coming march with misgiving.

The sun beat down mercilessly and the hot air seeped into the turret, and around noon loud explosions broke the torpor. Boobying piles of stores and ammunition, the unlucky Sappers had accidentally started a fire. A huge black cloud of smoke rose, and all afternoon the White City re-echoed to bursting shells and grenades. Surely the watching Japanese must think we were destoying equipment prior to withdrawing? I went outside, where Ali Banana was lying on the roof, quizzing the village through the range-finder. 'See anything, Ali?'

'No suh. Dese Japans foolish mans.'

'Good job too!' I went back, and soon received a galvanic shock as a section of steel-helmeted Japanese walked from the jungle by Mawlu and stood upright, looking toward us. I instantly tapped the sights on to them, for one good burst, with its cone of fire, would hit the lot. But . . . orders were that we mustn't shoot without permission. As I watched, there was a hasty scrambling, and Ali Banana was in, gibbering excitedly and bursting to get behind his gun. 'I know,' I said quickly. 'Ask Captain Bence if we can fire.'

Ali misunderstood, and went out yelling: 'Abokin gaba sun zo!' (Enemy they come!) Everybody dashed up to the parapet and the Japanese, satisfied that the block was indeed occupied, strolled back into the bush. Haruna and the team were furious, saying they'd been told in Nigeria to kill as many 'Japans' as they could, and now they'd been allowed to walk away. 'Me wait seben years for dis!' yelled frustrated Ali.

'I've waited twenty,' I replied. 'No good cussing *me*. I can't understand it either.'

Final preparations. We smashed surplus stores, and when destroying the valuable range-finder I felt quite a pang. 'Me leab dash for Japans,' grinned Zaki, pulling the pin from a grenade before wrapping it tightly in a blanket and putting it in the cave. Anyone incautiously investigating would end up as dead as any comrade in the wire.

The sun sank, and on Pagoda Hill I saw Gordon's pre-arranged signal – we were off. As the team dismounted the gun I went to read a note pinned to a sandbag by some humorist. It was an advertisement from an old newspaper:

WHITE CITY STADIUM
GREYHOUND RACING TONIGHT

*   *   *

Speed was paramount, for the enemy would soon note the absence of stand-to Very Lights. We formed up in a valley, with several mules fractious for a few seconds. People spoke in whispers and everything seemed ghostly in the half-light, reminding me of a silent film. Some Europeans had blackened their faces, but I hadn't. Hallo, these youthful features were familiar, and Sid's hand gripped mine. There was little time for talk. He'd flown in with Jock and was now with Cameron.

Well-timed movements. Within minutes we were complete and making for the exit, keeping strictly to the centre of the path. Here a jeep, there some boxes, all primed for death at a touch. Suddenly we tensed as a vehicle approached the bridge over the stream, but it stopped just short of it. Lucky occupants! Then we were through the wire, over the road and wrecked railway, and no greyhound at the real White City could have shot faster out of its trap!

A smashed glider, stinking animal carcasses, then bamboo jungle and real trouble. The Reconnaissance Platoon, leading, mistakenly thought that the mules were using a different route. Moving by compass, they went lickety-split through the bush, and we in the rear were soon in great difficulty. Mules distend themselves when first loaded, and usually a routine halt was made after half an hour to tauten straps. We didn't stop for over two hours, during which mules slipped, loads swayed, and we cursed treacherous tendrils tearing at our boots. Surcingles loosened, requiring frantic readjustment to avoid losing contact with those ahead. Meanwhile, our dumb friends were suffering far more than we realised, but at long last we halted at a stream, the animals drinking as though they'd never cease. The moon having risen, we were a splendid target with everyone standing in the water cooling their feet.

The re-start wasn't so precipitate. Delayed action explosions had been sounding from the block, and around midnight the bridge went up with a tremendous roar. Later we formed a square, and I hadn't realised how tired I was until lookouts were posted and I flopped to earth in the cold. At daylight we learned that during the breakneck scramble, Major Taylor himself, with his complete H.Q., had become detached. If they didn't rejoin soon, we'd have to push on to a 'five-days rendezvous', pre-arranged for just such an emergency.

The stream, or 'chaung', we expected to find was dry, but when we dug, water seeped through. Chaungs abound in

Burma, a few holding water all the year round. In the dry season one of the Column Commander's important jobs was to reach water at dusk, the ideal time. It was often a problem, but in the monsoon his headache was trying to get away from the stuff! Another name for chaung was 'hka', but as that's pronounced like a hiccup we'll stick to chaung (chong).

Captain Dickson and Sergeant Pomeroy, in charge of 'dokis' (mules), were furious, for many had been badly galled during that forced march, and mules were our sole transport for heavy stores. Other Chindits ahead were in action, for we heard the unmistakable Japanese machine-gun nicknamed the 'wood-pecker'. Bangs still sounded from the White City, where the Sappers had done such deadly work that when the Japanese 'attacked' the empty block the day after we left it, they gave up trying to enter. Actually, months later, when the enemy division itself withdrew before our advancing 14th Army, a Chindit officer familiar with the layout had to be sent before the Mawlu area could be occupied.

Headquarters failed to rejoin, with our situation growing dangerous. Mules brayed, and another hazard was the engine recharging wireless batteries. Inquisitive natives peered from the bush and ran when beckoned; sentries were doubled. Desultory shooting sounded in the night, but our own positions were undisturbed apart from brays and snores. Once the square was formed, no-one left it. In the first expedition a Column was given away by a man who went outside the perimeter to defecate.

Next day the Second-in-Command, Major Miles, took over, and a guide led us through a hamlet called Haungton. Arrival at the next place, Samaw, was delayed; a Reconnaissance warning of movements ahead. They proved to be the Black Watch, disporting themselves in a pool! We pressed on, the heat terrific and nobody marching fit, and the 'Reccy' found water just before dark. In charge of this vital body of 'Burrifs' (Burma Riflemen) were Lieutenant Harrison and Sergeant Roberts, both Rhodesians, with Oscar Minas, an Armenian civilian from Burmese Intelligence, who spoke the language fluently. The Column consisted of Headquarters Group, Reconnaissance, Signals, Engineers, Medical, Mortars, Vickers, with 4 rifle platoons. Last, but certainly not least, were a few R.A.F. personnel who kept contact by radio with Air Base. I greatly admired them for volunteering for a job so very foreign to them.

Leading or bringing up the rear being equally hazardous, the order-of-march was changed frequently. Communication within the Column was by walkie-talkie radio. The Gunners' was carried in turn by Zaki and Abu Bamenda, Gordon's orderly. It weighed 5 pounds and they had no love for it.

Everyone, including the Column Commander, humped a 65 pound pack, for the mules had more than enough to do. The Vickers' dokis had by far the heaviest loads, an ammunition mule carrying 200 pounds. After the Dakota, the poor old mule was the Chindits' best friend.

After the Campaign, a book by a Brigadier – *not* Ricketts – stated: 'The only Nigerians I had seen who were not cheerful were those carrying the British N.C.O.'s packs as well as their own' – unquote. I strongly resented the slur, implying that all B.N.C.O.'s were alike. It certainly didn't take place in No. 12 Column. Indeed several of our chaps, including Sid Mew, humped the pack of an ailing African on more than one occasion. It would have been much fairer had the author named the actual unit concerned. Why didn't he? Could it be because the identities of the officer permitting such conduct would have been revealed?

*   *   *

Off at dawn, and soon it was hotter than hell. My aches returned, but this time everyone suffered. My stomach was troubling me, and while Gordon worked like a beaver all day I was of little use to him. I'd quickly found that this dour Scot had the heart of a lion. Handicapped by knowing no Hausa, he knew that nobody was more obtuse than an African pretending not to understand English, yet he managed to enforce instant unloading at routine halts – the Gunners were irritated when riflemen flung themselves down with no animals to bother them.

Leaving the bush, we entered a long, furnace-like valley, and the crocodile of men and mules crawled at funeral pace, but just when it seemed that I could bear the crushing weight no longer there was another halt. Noon. Not a vestige of protection from that brassy, cirrus-streaked sky, and my ears rang with heat and the organ-like hum of insects. Again I felt the horrid fear of falling out – unforgivable in a regular soldier. To Gordon I must seem a confounded nuisance. We were losing so much sweat that Doc Tait told us to eat salt, and also put it in drinking water. Horrible at first, but we grew used to it. Warnings against unauthorised drinking were well founded – it brought intolerable craving for more. The worst torture was waiting twenty minutes for sterilising tablets to exterminate the bugs – by then the water was nearly hot.

Approaching the end of the valley we stopped, for this was the five-days rendezvous. If H.Q. didn't turn up within forty-eight hours they'd have to be written off, a deadly blow. The bush at the side of the valley was so thick that the Nigerians had to come into their own with machetes and the square was laid by compass. Gordon smiled away my apology, saying that many people suffered similarly during training.

Another unit who had bivouacked here had been betrayed by a mule's bray, the enemy firing upon them promiscuously. Consequently there were wounded awaiting evacuation from a light plane strip on the valley. I lay in a cool chaung, surrounded by jungle-covered mountains that for sheer grandeur surpassed anything I'd ever seen – why couldn't I stay here for ever? But my stomach malady worsened, and I repeatedly clambered in and out of a crevice, cursing Burma and the Japanese while Gordon's satirical smile said plainly: 'Well, you damn' fool, didn't you ask for it?' An enforced wait proved a godsend. After Tait had given me tablets he bluntly said that if I hadn't improved when the planes arrived he'd send me out. What? Turn up at Enugu with a lame story about diarrhoea? Tait's warning did more than anything to straighten me out.

A huge pyramid of stores left by preceding Columns that had lost mules had to be buried – Vickers, mortars, radios and medical chests. The mortar officer, Lieutenant Barker, and his henchman Sergeant 'Hoppy' Hopgood, took a powerful wireless set to the square but obtained only squeaks. A bagful of airgraphs from White City awaited the planes, but none that I wrote were ever delivered.

It was anxiety time, for the Burrifs forecast that the monsoon would begin on 16th May. However, light planes buzzed down, removing every afflicted man, and it was good to see them go. Still we couldn't leave, for an air drop was expected, and the Column was getting hungry. Having eaten practically nothing since leaving the block, I had spare tins. Zaki loved 'cawnbiff'.

But for this delay, less than a dozen dokis could have tackled the Chin Hills, immediately ahead. Some mules aggravated galls by rubbing them on bamboo, and Sid and I were amazed to see dozens of maggots on the wounds. We were smartly slapped down by the harassed Dickson and Pomeroy for suggesting that they be removed; actually they materially assisted a cure by consuming gangrenous flesh!

The Burrifs were right, for on the 16th a shower fell with a force that warned us of what to expect, but then there was a great boost to morale when our H.Q. walked in, with Major Taylor unperturbed . . . hadn't this been pre-arranged? Yet there were certainly enemy about, for a Burmese officer who tried to contact a village for food didn't return. The Column grew more famished, for the air drop hadn't yet arrived, so Burrifs made another attempt to forage. Suddenly there was a loud bang – an incurable mule had been shot. Doc Tait pronounced it edible, so I sent Zaki along. He came back with a big doki steak. 'Master he no chop dis?' he asked, shocked.

'Master he will, but I'll have it cooked.'

Loud jabbering started when the Gunners were told to draw their meat, and the indignant Haruna arrived. Apparently it wasn't kosher. 'Suh! Duka mutamen sun che babu,' he exclaimed vehemently.

'What's all that?' asked Gordon.

'All men they say no.'

'Why, Haruna?'

'No man fit chop horse. Very bad t'ing.'

'All right, sergie, they don't have to. Why is it a bad thing?'

'Nigeria mans no chop deir horse, suh.'

Remembering that no-one objected to pork loaf in the rations, I seized a chance to riposte. 'How about the tinned pig, Haruna? The men are Mohammedans.'

Unabashed, Haruna stated that the Nigerian Emirs had granted a dispensation for the duration of war. 'Touché!' I muttered to Gordon, as the sergeant stalked away triumphantly, eyeing my mess-tin with disgust as Zaki passed him, averting his nose from the smell. I just couldn't get my teeth into something as tough as an old boot; Zaki had merely warmed it. Finally I slung the steak into the bush after offering it to a doki who was no cannibal. Gurkhas were also affected by food problems – tinned mutton was dropped for them.

The Burrifs returned with rice. It wasn't cheap, but Wingate's rule of paying well brought better results than the enemy's commandeering. However, the bullion mule's 'treasury' had been depleted, and H.Q. demanded the return of our issued silver rupees. Good. They weighed 1¼ lbs!

At length came the welcome roar of a Dakota, and to the normal dry ration were added bread and jam. I licked my lips, having developed a craving for sweet food. Things went wrong when the Gunners got Gordon's and mine as well as their own. Returning from the dropping site too late to salvage any, I saw them scoffing wedges of bread and cawnbiff, spread thickly with plum and apple. Worse, there was mail for all Europeans except Sid and myself. Some rations were missing at the check, but there was no time to look for pilferers – the Japanese invariably saw air drops and would turn up sooner or later.

*   *   *

A quick meal and we left, soon entering jungle and tall teak trees. When mounting the first hill it was like climbing into a great, murmuring cathedral, but despite the shade we were soon sweat-soaked. Next morning the hill resounded with barking deer, disturbed by our movements. Occasionally there was a whirring overhead and we glimpsed a big eagle. Animals and snakes kept clear of so large a party, but at dusk millions of insects combined to make an incredible racket until dark. We could have passed unheard within yards of the enemy. And after nightfall, of course, came the inevitable mosquito.

Next day I was startled by seeing a group of armed natives, but they were friendly Kachins, the rifles having been given them by Wingate. Besides defending their villages they attacked small parties of Japanese.

It wasn't just one hill, but a long succession of razor-backs, with dry chaungs between, but I was much fitter, and we bivvied by a village called Hkaungtonsi. Animosity had arisen between the two orderlies. Abu, an Ibo, held Munchis in contempt, and Zaki hated Ibos. Of the 20 Gunners, all but Anton Antonadi, from the Cameroons, were Hausas, like the six muleteers and their sergeant, Kamanda Garuwa. Abu, the only southerner among that lot, was much on the defensive.

During the long mid-day halt it rained heavily, and Tait at once ordered that groundsheets would not be worn while we were marching – heat exhaustion was deadly. In any case, every Infantryman knew that capes were worse than useless in rain, but we made use of them as shelters during the night, and soon everyone had thrown away his sodden blanket.

Slopes became slippery, with intervals between groups lessening as conditions underfoot worsened. Several people, African and European, were in difficulty, but I was now able to give Gordon the assistance he needed.

The Column avoided paths when possible, but were forced to use a track with a steep drop to the left. In front of us a Signals mule fell, a single bamboo saving it from the chasm. Just then the Column halted, and Gordon and I tried to help Corporal Barlow and his men, handicapped by the spasmodic struggling of the animal. The harness was released and the mule rose, but its load went into the depths. 'That's the engine,' groaned Barlow in despair. 'Most important load in the bloody Column.'

Yes. The charging engine was a vital accessory. Without speaking, a Signaller lowered himself from the edge and began descending through the thick bamboo. 'He'll be lucky not to break his neck,' said Gordon, as the Column moved and we had to leave Barlow to it. The gradients were now so greasy that many of the usually sure-footed dokis capsized. We would pass one lying on its side, eyes blinking pathetically through plastered mud while people fought to free and then replace the filthy harness and loads. The muleteers had a frightful job, leading their charges while gripping a rifle with the other hand, taking inevitable face-down plunges. But one big grey of ours carried his 200 pounds like a feather and took everything in his stride, including us if we weren't wary.

A long, exhausting day – we covered only five miles before reaching Puaji. Mugs should have been inside equipment, yet at a chaung every African held one full of untreated water. Doc Tait, justifiably incensed, whacked down mugs with a stick. 'Isn't there enough trouble without typhoid?' he shouted. After that no mugs appeared, although it made no difference whenever we passed over a stream – bush hats held a lot!

By the time we'd watered our mules and reached the square it was pitch dark under the teaks, and Gordon beetled around for a parking plot with men and mules following closely. As we trod on every group in turn, I'd not heard such picturesque language since leaving the Guards. It was utter confusion, during which a hoof, or a boot, came down hard on my heel – the pain was intense. Out came machetes, the noise bringing down more curses on our heads. However, the Column Commander, with information that no enemy were very near, allowed us fires for thirty minutes and told us to limit their number. The other group, having fed, knew nothing of the concession, and directly the first flame shot skywards there was a concerted bellow from Europeans and Africans alike. Gordon ordered Zaki to use Abu's fire, and Abu reacted predictably. Hardly had their bit of all-in wrestling been sorted out when

Barlow and Co. arrived, and again the welkin rang. 'How did you find us?' I asked Barlow as he sipped from my tin.

'Didn't have to. Like Piccadilly Circus on Saturday night!' His man had actually headloaded the engine up to the track, a wonderful feat, but it was broken, and an S.O.S. winged away for another. The night was dry but not very comfortable, with one European sounding delirious, and at daylight we found that several groups had jammed into a small space with plenty of room elsewhere. Fortunately we didn't often bivvy in the dark.

                              *   *   *

Before resuming, many people lightened packs, and some 'indispensable' items that 'went to bush' were astonishing. Gordon suspected that some ammo and grenades were being cast, but had no time to check. Today's target was Tangba, at the summit of the hills, where we expected another air drop. The Gunners certainly worked this day, with every doki except the grey falling several times. How on earth were the R.A.F. chaps managing with their big, unwieldy panniers?

As usual, rumours buzzed during the mid-day break. B.N.C.O.'s were debating their individual plans should the Column be attacked and dispersed. Hoppy's was the most original. He'd collar the Bullion mule and gallop to where there were no jungle or Japanese before starting a harem. 'How about Sid and me as eunuchs?' I suggested.

'Count me out,' laughed Sid.

We were seated on a log, repeatedly brushing away red butterflies that persisted in settling on our arms. 'Why the heck d'they want to drink sweat, Sid?'

'Heat exhaustion, o' course!'

Along came Major Taylor, and the never-reticent Sid tackled him about the rumours. 'Ignore everything not given out officially,' he was told. 'I know nothing except that we're to make for Indawgyi Lake.' Away he plodded.

Out came a map. The lake was prominent, some miles north. 'I'd say the Jap navy was there,' said Hoppy, 'but it'd only start another rumour!'

A news sheet was sent round, taken from the BBC short wave. It was mostly about the anticipated second front in Europe; our antics weren't mentioned. Nearing the summit, hefty Ali Banana collapsed, to be put on one of Tait's spare mules. At Tangba, cool, clear water trickled enticingly from a bamboo pipe constructed by villagers. Of all people, Sergeant Kamanda Garuwa dashed to it, followed by half the Gunners. The sergeant obeyed my order to return, but it took cussing and barging to dislodge the others, during which exhibition the next group passed us. At the bivvy site an exasperated Gordon was rounding up stragglers, and after I'd explained, said that reorganisation was needed; certain personnel were unsatisfactory.

Bad weather at Air Base; the drop was again late. Flying operations were mainly by the 10th U.S. Air Force, but neither they nor the occasional R.A.F. plane had failed to arrive at all. They were our sole lifeline.

Meanwhile the friendly Tangba headman, assuring us that no Japanese were near, sold us rice. The Dakota came after dark, in blinding rain when our ground signals must have been difficult to see. The crew, taking appalling risks, were faced with an equally hazardous return to Base; I prayed for them.

Rum was dropped, and thereafter came with every supply. I filled my waterbottle, using only the chagul for water itself. Rum might come in handy sometime. Not everything could be collected, and at daylight evidence of pilfering was clear. Besides food, 5,000 silver rupees were missing, together with their chute. Those carrying cash, mail, or documents had coloured ribbons attached. But, bullion or not, we had to get mobile before Japanese turned up.

CHAPTER TWELVE

Monsoon

Mud, mud, glorious mud,
Nothing quite like it
For cooling the blood;
Follow me, follow,
Down to the hollow,
And there let us wallow
In glorious mud.

We started downhill in heavy rain, having had no respite from it for two days. Although there was only a small abrasion on my banged heel, it had become quite painful. Others were also handicapped. An R.A.F. man was riding, while Ali Banana looked as though he'd topple from his mount – he now had double pneumonia. Two Gunners had to watch him, so we were shorthanded at halts. Although, during the ensuing filthy night, no ingenuity with covers prevented us being soaked, the way the Africans got fires going at dawn was amazing. Fortunately the dry season cold snaps had gone, or few of us would have got much further. Both rain and mud were warm.

Kaungra should have been the next overnight stop, but we didn't reach it. Surprisingly, going down was far more difficult than ascending, especially for the rear groups – the ground was a cocoa-like mess when we tackled it. On those gradients you first teetered, then your feet shot away and you sat down with a splash and slid, probably whipping away the legs of the chap in front. The bamboo resounded with curses, yet it was still possible to raise a laugh when someone went down with a particularly loud smack. Luckily the mules found it easier and there weren't so many spilled loads, but we soon lost all resemblance to human beings, and later became known in the

14th Army as the 'Shitty Chindits' because we were always caked with the stuff.

Rifles and carbines, choked, had to be attended to at every halt, and then we heard of a wide chaung ahead – those with heavy loads would undress and manhandle them. After lengthy stops our group reached the bank, finding the water some four feet deep. The naked Gunners first took over their clothing and equipment, then returned for the stores, headloading without trouble. Gordon and I carried the rangefinder and spare parts, but not on our heads – nor were we nude! The mules, once in, were no trouble.

Gordon left a message, asking those following to postpone crossing until we'd cleared the far bank, which was steep. It would surely be ignored, for the 'Tail' also had dokis and loads, with the chaung steadily rising. As well as the slope, the far side was thickly overgrown, yet somehow the muleteers found spots to stand their charges. In almost indescribable conditions the Gunners had to dress, then load up, slipping, sliding, and cursing in Hausa and pidgin as rain sheeted down inexorably. Fortunately the mules usually stood dejectedly still during such downpours.

Behind, I heard Major Miles sounding off about the congestion; as Second-in-Command he'd be last to cross. Gordon went off ahead to maintain contact, and over came the Tail to filter through us, swearing at us for blocking the the track and being sworn at for barging past. Fists were swung. At that moment the Japanese were not only secondary, but pretty bad seconds at that!

Each step upwards now spewed back a grout-like cascade of slush over the next man's boots, and as I reached the halted Column I slid into a gully and stuck knee-deep. The united strength of Zaki and Abu yanked me out, with the grinning Gordon wishing he had a camera. Down came a taketa: 'Brew up, then make Kaungra before dusk'. Wondering about Miles's reaction, we intercepted the runner on his way back. Miles had scrawled: 'The Tail isn't half over'. Groups therefore just bivvied where they were, for no square could be formed on such a gradient. And, due to the atrocious conditions, the Column Commander was now forced to waive cast-iron Chindit rules. Unavoidable.

The Vickers, our first consideration, were in a frightful mess, and we now met a new and vicious foe in the leech, which was able to crawl undetected upon one's skin and gorge blood until it burst. One of the worst hit was Pomeroy, his denims saturated. Before dark, Major Taylor clambered around praising and encouraging. One important thing that must have pleased him, and all the Europeans, was that tribal prejudices had gone. Hausa, Ibo, Yoruba, Munchi and other races now pulled for the common cause.

Intelligence reports were favourable, and the Column Commander ordered that no-one need sleep in contact with the ground. At once the hill re-echoed as bamboo charpoys were constructed. The rain ceased, and mules began scoffing the tender bamboo shoots as fast as they could tear them off. Zaki and Abu, now chatting amicably, built a big fire inside a hollow tree.

To my dismay the heel had turned septic, and Tait said it would remain troublesome until we could lay up for a day or two. I limped back to my position, thoroughly fed up with this bad luck when I was otherwise fit. Glancing at several leeches being forced away by the heat, I thought of my house at Enugu, of the cool bedsheets, of Sylvester bringing iced water . . . and of Snip's sardonic words: 'So you'd like a change, eh?'

I didn't wallow for long in self-pity, for the two orderlies managed to set the tree on fire while Gordon and I were wearing only boots while drying clothes; luckily the flames kept mozzies at bay. Chindit rules were again bent next day when prickly bamboo, the most impenetrable jungle there is, forced us to use a path. The enemy were known to be track-minded, and I didn't envy the Reccy, nor the leading platoon's scouts. It quickly became too churned for us in the rear, so out came machetes, the worst spots being packed with branches. At the long halt a check revealed that some ammunition had been thrown away, with the Gunners equally guilty. An exception was Corporal Dan-Boy Fort Lamy who, stout fellow, was carrying two extra bombs, and hoping to use them. We radioed for more ammo, and severe punishment was threatened for future offenders, but the men understood far better that the more metal the planes brought, the less food.

Two miles only that day, for all the track to Kaungra had to be bolstered. All these hamlets were probed first by Burrifs, to buy food or information, and engage a guide for the next stretch. Wingate's doctrine paid rich dividends; he even refrained from punishing natives who helped the Japanese, unless it were done gratuitously.

No chaung, and the well-water looked so dubious that we

used twice the normal amount of evil-tasting powder – tablets were unobtainable just now. Doc Tait opened his surgery, and I was again in the queue, noting that a new malady was attacking some Europeans – 'naga rot' (jungle sores).

* * *

We heard that Brigadier Calvert, who'd left White City some time before the Garrison, was attacking Mogaung, and we were to assist him. Even if we got there, what kind of fighting shape would we be in? However, Mogaung was rail-linked with Myitkyina (Mitchinar) where there was an airfield. With those two places taken, nothing could stop us being flown out . . . except orders to the contrary!

The next day was rainless, and I found the increased pace difficult. A cheering thought – we'd reached the last hill of the range, and bivvied at the foot. On the far side lay the deep Namsang Chaung, but we'd heard there was a ford. Burrifs, going over to view it, reported it fast-flowing. We couldn't begin climbing next morning because of heavy rain overnight, and while the track was being bolstered all groups were searched for the missing rupees. Gordon and I were astounded by some of the stuff the Gunners were humping; things like Japanese steel helmets and binoculars – no wonder other items had been thrown away, and Gordon insisted upon all 'heavies' being jettisoned.

Most men had a few coins, but none of the missing bullion. Abu, not expecting to be searched, stood grinning at the angry Gunners, but received an unexpected jolt when Gordon when through his kit and found 14 rupees. It was too much for the proud Ibo, who stalked into the bush unseen by his boss. I intercepted him. 'Where are you going, Abu?'

'Me go Major Taylor. I no be t'iefman.'

'Nobody called you a thiefman.'

'Whyfor Mr Gordon put my name for paper?'

'He put all names with money – sergeants too.'

Not mollified, Abu made for Column H.Q., to return looking chastened, studiously ignoring Hausa ribaldry over his loss of face. Later there was uproar when he found that his belongings had been raided and the 14 chips pinched. Furious, he vainly demanded that another search be made for his missing cash.

An unexpected order – mules would be taken to the hilltop, ready for an early start next day, and I set off with our six and their muleteers. The gradient was the steepest yet. Near the summit there was a sudden yell and the grey knocked me into the bamboo, where I received an excruciating blow on the heel. As I rose painfully, Major Miles appeared. 'Get your chaps back at once for their kit. We're crossing the chaung tonight in case of more rain.'

Sound sense, yet my heart sank at his words. By the time I'd reached the Gunners the Column was ready to move. 'How's the foot?' asked Gordon, as Zaki helped me into my gear.

'Rotten. Just had a nasty knock. That damn' grey. I doubt whether I can make this hill again tonight.'

'Get to the river somehow. For God's sake don't get left on this side.'

I took position, but lost ground at once, keeping to the edge as others overtook, but Zaki refused to be waved on. Soon further climbing became impossible, and I crept into the bamboo and sat. Zaki followed. 'Go back,' I ordered.

'You stay, me stay. Sleep for here. Ribber no trouble tomorrow.'

I stopped protesting, in the depths of misery at falling out. The Tail – Cameron's platoon, crept slowly upwards, with Sid the very last man. None of them noticed us. Then Sid, too, was gone, and the muffled sounds died to a jungle silence that seemed to crash against my eardrums.

*   *   *

We had to move in case the enemy were trailing, so went some way to the flank. Zaki quickly made a big charpoy on a comparatively level clearing. It was now fine, the sinking sun casting mottled shadows. With luck, we should get over tomorrow. We had little food, but Zaki brewed tea in thick bush. Later he slept at once, but before I dozed there was a faraway rumble. We were awakened by a heavy shower that ceased after an hour, but again I was startled by a second monsoon that arrived with a deafening swish, bursting with even greater force than the first. Water from the sheets was blown on to us before the wind tore the coverings away, and we just sat there enduring it – no alternative. Lightning stabbed the surroundings into green brilliance amid stunning thunder. When it finally stopped I lay listening uneasily to a faint, distant roaring that emphasised the nearby silence.

At dawn we left without attempting to brew and something seemed different; no barking deer. A monkey, with others behind it, made me jump, but they were merely inquisitive. After that, not a tree or shrub stirred – the jungle could have been wax . . . there was only that sinister roaring.

My heel was sore, but began to ease after we crossed the summit. The roaring grew louder, and as we reached the bottom the Namsang Chaung burst into view, a filthy brown flood whirling along all kinds of rubbish. Any tracks had been washed away and I could see no ford. Zaki jabbered, but I was beyond words as we picked our way past boulders. Zaki's torrent of Munchi turned to Hausa – he'd understood there were boats! His harangue became so unbearable that I slapped his face, instantly regretting it. He probably felt like returning the wallop, but merely sat down on a boulder, without speaking.

We had no map or compass, and one day's rations. I felt panic, for if the Japanese caught us they would certainly try to obtain information. But there was nothing we could do at the moment. Oh well, when in doubt, brew up, I'd heard. 'Let's have some tea, Zaki.'

Silence . . . 'Brew up, Zaki.'

'Match catch water,' he growled.

'I saw you smoking this morning.' I then tried a new tack. 'Zaki, I'm very sorry I slapped you. Would you like tea, or rum?'

'Hur?' He looked more animated. 'I t'ink dis lum. My chiki (belly) done trouble me. Lum good for chiki.' Soon water bubbled in my tin, but we left our food untouched. In kids' books I'd read, the hero kept himself alive with wild fruit, but I'd seen none since entering Burma, proving I suppose that I was no hero!

The rum made Zaki talkative. 'Me no fear die, but we no fit cross dis ribber. Not till monsoon he finish.' He advised returning to Tangba, where the headman would hide us if we paid well.

'How much kudi have you got, Zaki?'

'Master know I no catch kudi.'

'I catch seven rupees.'

That shook him. Many Africans think white men are all millionaires, living in places like Buckingham Palace and only drawing pay as a formality. I also reminded him that between us and Tangba lay the first wide chaung, now probably in spate. He grinned when I said he could tell his admiring home village that he'd been the last Chindit coming out of Burma, then stated that he could hear a cock crowing to the right. I told him to investigate and be careful while I explored the left. All I found was more horrible prickly bamboo, so returned. Suddenly smoke rose from the bush opposite and I banged two shots into the air. The startled face of an African appeared, and I kept yelling: 'Ina hanya?' (Where's road?) against the roar, until he waved and went back. Nothing happened, and the smoke ceased. 'Selfish bastards!' I thought – I badly needed to know the position of any ford. In fact the man belonged to a section detailed to watch the river for a time, and they made no report about me! Zaki returned hurriedly, inquiring about the shots; he'd found no village. The water was gradually receding and we argued about the ford. It was settled when a small tree swirled along, checking momentarily before going on – Zaki was right.

The river sank a foot an hour – would rain hold off? At length Zaki tried, though I favoured waiting. Repeating that he didn't fear death, he entered water that reached his armpits, headloading his pack. He was forced to return, still balancing his burden. Later we made an attempt together, wearing full equipment. We'd cut a long bamboo and Zaki led, holding the thin end while I gripped the base. All was going well until the bamboo snapped and Zaki went under. No swimmer, he'd have been gone if a few strands hadn't held. He reappeared, still hanging on to the pole and fighting the current while being half-strangled by his rifle sling. Despite my heel I managed to keep my footing and Zaki was swept to the bank. We clambered out and he sat scowling.

The sky began to cloud, and with my companion uncommunicative, I had a go, but halfway across the current tugged so alarmingly that I gave it best. Zaki said something in Munchi that sounded uncomplimentary, then brewed tea. He had a water-proof tin for matches. We opened our last tins of rations, and the unhappy orderly was also out of cigarettes.

Gloom lay over the river during our next attempt – successful, but at a price. On the far side we were swept off our feet, and although we managed to scramble out, my carbine and Zaki's rifle now lay on the murky bed of the Namsang Chaung, so we skipped into the bush, sharpish.

During the night I awoke from an uneasy doze, to the sound of heavy footsteps. It was pitch dark, and as I sat up with a jerk Zaki chose to snore. As I jabbed him, a loud snort sounded. I felt Zaki tense. 'Master, master —'

'Yi shuru!' (make silence) I hissed, and we remained still as the thing plodded down towards the river. 'What was it?' I muttered.

'I t'ink maybe bush cow, maybe tiger.'

I laughed, the first for days. With no tigers in Africa I doubt whether Zaki had seen one. When the animal returned I ensured that Zaki wouldn't snore, and then a familiar spatter of rain made me feel safe.

* * *

Zaki followed the Column's tracks with little difficulty. I intended to treat my foot as gently as possible, but he stopped me from removing boot and sock at a shallow chaung, then ferried me on his back. How much did I owe my grinning orderly? But although the heel was improving, I felt extremely vulnerable without my carbine; we must catch the Column.

Cautiously peering across a large clearing, we saw huts and movements ahead. 'Africans,' asserted Zaki. This hamlet was Maungtheingwy, where Lieutenant Dunkelly's platoon had been left to guard the wounded and sick awaiting planes – a strip had been constructed. At the moment it was fine. 'Hallo!' Dunkelly greeted me. 'You got over then? Can you do something for the sick while I fix up smoke?'

'Sure, but how about the Column?'

'Three miles away, expecting a drop. Just round up my chaps.'

The wooden houses were on stilts, and native faces looked down at me. Lying beneath the largest building were the afflicted men, multi-racial and a pitiful sight. The ground was dry, but surrounded by black, stinking mud upon which dogs, pigs, and chickens were encroaching to snatch at half-eaten food. New ration packets lay around, for these poor chaps were far too ill to eat. A large can of tea simmered over a fire, tended by a medical orderly who was himself awaiting evacuation. Flies swarmed about the whole appalling place, and within a few feet was a small cross over a rough grave.

While we cleared unspeakable litter, the sick watched us dully, their expressions hopeless. Several seemed mere skeletons, and Ali Banana, eyes closed, resembled death itself. A corporal of the South Staffordshires rose painfully, then stood for minutes staring into the distant jungle. What could he see – a vision of his home in the Midlands? It was Whit Sunday, and I also felt nostalgia . . . England, on the verge of June.

I was startled as three figures emerged from the bush, one being aided by the others. They were Tommies, and the sick man had dysentery. He wore only a shirt and wrap-around blanket, his clothing having become too foul. His pals left immediately to rejoin their unit, if they could find it.

Dunkelly was experimenting with a new type of smoke bomb. 'They've taken away the detonators, blast it!' Ramming in explosive from a Mills grenade, he was rewarded with a faint plop. 'Haven't seen one of these function yet, but I will.' He tossed it on to an adjacent fire! It 'functioned' all right when a streamer of phosphorous missed us by inches as we leaped aside. Dunkelly being more dangerous than the Japanese, I scarpered. Our Signals officer Lieutenant Johnstone, awaiting evacuation with more jungle boils on his skin than a Dalmation has spots, had a companion in a Major from a British unit. Johnstone, struggling with an abandoned radio, was trying to raise Air Base. 'How about the enemy listening in?' I asked in my innocence.

'Don't be naive,' he answered pityingly. 'D'you really think I'm sending it in clear?' A few minutes later he anounced, as casually as though he'd asked someone to lunch: 'They'll be here at noon.' Far more excited than Johnstone, I hastened to the sick with the news.

Dunkelly handed me a Very pistol, and it was full marks to Johnstone when two planes arrived punctually. When I fired, a dud cartridge fizzed, but down they came. Ominous ruts appeared on the strip as the aircraft taxied to the far end, where they stuck fast. I went out with the platoon, and we pulled, pushed, and cursed, as the engines deafened us and slipstreams tried to tear away my beard. The jungle re-echoed, but we were too busy for apprehension, and finally got them into a position from which to take off. Both pilots were U.S. sergeants, and I fully expected to be blistered for bringing them down on to the gluey surface. Instead, I received a friendly: 'Howdy:' and they even kept straight faces when Zaki brought them some of that awful tea that had been stewing for days. 'I doubt whether we'll get off with three apiece,' observed one, 'but we'll try.'

A loud outcry, and an African approached, fell to the ground, and with rolling eyeballs and heartrending groans, gave us to understand that he had great pain in his chiki through swallowing some poisonous root. 'Worst man in my outit,' muttered Dunkelly. 'Trying to get evacuated. Take no notice.' He knew his man, for after more heartrending noises plus covert glances towards his unimpressed platoon commander, the fellow got up and walked away, to the hilarity of the pilots.

The Major couldn't walk, and was lifted into a plane. 'Good luck, sir,' I said. 'You won't be needing this now,' and cheerfully annexed his carbine. He replied with a wry smile that I'd probably need plenty of luck myself. The first plane taxied slowly past us, with Johnstone one of the three passengers. His wave to us was premature, for there wasn't a chance. It teetered to a stop at the end of the strip, to be joined by the second. Out we went again. Those pilots were game, trying with two and then one patient before deciding to wait a little, undoubtedly most unhappy at the distinct possibility of joining our march – if you could call it a march. Their fears were increased when Dunkelly's Burrif spoke to natives who'd crossed the Namsang. Japanese had entered Tangba after we'd left, and executed the headman for helping us, so they couldn't be far away.

The sky darkened, with rain threatening, and with one passenger each the airmen tried again. One plane gathered speed of a sort, rose, and just cleared the trees. The other did a repeat performance with his buddy hovering; a waggle of wings, and they were gone, to the clapping of the platoon. Rain fell, and Johnstone did not speak as we left the strip.

One of the sick burst into wild lamentations, as Africans do on the rare occasion when they weep, and I looked helplessly at that scene of utter misery. Compared to theirs, my recent troubles had been negligible.

'Rejoin and report,' ordered Dunkelly. 'We'll make stretchers and carry them, but without a miracle some of them won't last much longer.' Zaki and I swiftly collected surplus rations, and when he asserted that the family above had the rifle of the evacuated man I went up the wooden steps to collar one of two Lee-Enfields I found. Coming down, I saw Corporal Dan-Boy approaching, carrying a note telling Dunkelly to send men back over the river to look for me. I still have that taketa, proving that No. 12 weren't selfish bastards after all!

Dan-Boy took us to the column, where Major Taylor, after welcoming me, expressed astonishment. 'Only *two* got away? I've heard engines all afternoon.'

'Manoeuvring on a bog, sir. Mr Dunkelly is making stretchers.'

'They may not be necessary. I'm expecting some elephants.'

What? The miracle was about to happen, and the day ended on a happier note when a cave opened in the middle of Gordon's beard as he and Sid greeted me; I helped them with ration packets. In the dusk I could just see Zaki regaling the

Gunners with the events of the past 48 hours and obviously adopting the star role. Haruna came over, saying how pleased he was that Zaki had saved my life.

*   *   *

Flying had become so dangerous that no more drops would be made at night. Next morning the sick came through, en route for goodness knows where. Four men on each elephant were on a kind of scaffolding – it was grand to see those great beasts pick their way to avoid hurting their charges. Johnstone decided to remain, but for the last time I saw Ali Banana. To my surprise he waved feebly, and when I hoped that he would soon be well he replied: 'Allah Ya che.' (God He say). Ali himself must have had the constitution of an elephant, for he eventually reached India and recovered.

Another day lost, and next morning we were aroused long before the usual hour, for an unexpected move. For the Column to leave in the dark, and with no breakfast, was unprecedented. Haruna appeared from the gloom, planted himself in front of Gordon, and rattled off. 'Speak English,' he was told.

'If we no drink tea now, which time we drink tea?'

'I don't know, sergie. Go and watch the loading.'

Haruna instantly went berserk, an astonishing performance. He wrung his hands, wept loudly, uttered hysterical cries. I spoke in Hausa but he turned away, while Europeans who'd known him for years were equally unsuccessful. 'Leave him,' said Gordon tersely. 'Load up, you men,' and as they started, Harruna gave a wild yell and went to bush; we tied his equipment to a doki.

It was a forced march, and with firmer ground my heel became sore, so I removed boot and sock at a chaung, resisting Zaki's offer of a pickaback. A rumour had developed – the Force would be evacuated by flying-boat from the lake and it would be devil take the hindmost. 'How about this latest yarn, Dogo?' called Sid, splashing across.

'Like the others – bullshit!' I replied irritably, yanking on a sock.

Over came the Tail, sweating and swearing. 'I'm having jungle boots sent for you,' said Doc Tait as he passed. After three hours' hard slog we learned the truth. Hazelwood, the R.A.F. oficer, had radioed a new site for the delayed drop and we were hurrying to prepare it. Again it wasn't our day. Those with food left ate it. I had sugar and bully beef, bartering the latter with Captain Bence for his biscuits to make 'porridge'. The Column had now been going 21 days on 13 days' food.

Haruna quietly rejoined, but was inevitably broken down to private by the Column Commander. On hearing the sentence he grabbed someone's rifle and again went to bush, but was cornered. After he'd quietened down, he was sent to the Reccy, where his subsequent work was so good that he eventually regained his stripes, to the joy of Gordon and myself.

Meanwhile, three well-laden Dakotas arrived, with the U.S. crews in jocular mood on the radio. One chap, announcing a 'free drop' (without chute), headed straight over us – it must have looked funny when we dived for cover. Away they roared, and an African, caught in flagrante delicto while creeping away with a box, was whipped. Harsh, yes, but these were harsh conditions; pilfering wasn't unknown in British Columns. One idea of Wingate's was to remove part of an offender's rations, and then, when his comrades helped him, conscience was an added punishment.

As well as lots of grub, clothing had been sent, and I was given a badly-needed shirt. The jungle boots also came, and my discarded clodhoppers were pounced upon by several men asserting that their own leaked; I had to separate the contestants. Some Chindit Commanders radioed Biblical quotes to one another; Wingate started it in the first expedition. On this occasion I could have broadcast one of my own choice – 'Having food and raiment let us be therewith content' – (1 Timothy, 6–8) – until I discovered that during the boots fracas, some passer-by had swiped my lovely new shirt. Zaki, who should have been guarding it, was too deeply concerned with cawnbiff.

The rations were U.S. 'K', in strong packets withstanding weather and hard knocks. I gave my cigarettes to Gordon and Zaki and exchanged tins for sugar and biscuits. Many and various were the 'dishes' invented, with Sid a cordon bleu. He'd happily shove all kinds of stuff under my nose for a verdict.

We cooked and ate, with the Nigerians, living for the day as always, stewing themselves huge meals, and Zaki managed to baffle his prodigious appetite. When I remonstrated, he said it would be less in the pack!

Information was really good, for a surprise message stated that there was no veto on noise. Instantly the men gathered in laughing, talking groups, assuring one another that no more Japanese would be encountered. Anyway, for the Europeans it was a welcome change from 'Yi shuru' (make silence), 'Beri magana' (stop talking) and the exasperated 'Shut up'!

Suddenly my lost shirt was forgotten when Hoppy, with a facetious remark, thrust a bundle of 80 letters at me. Dozens from pupils, and several from teachers. Those from the kids had one thing in common – affection, and great concern for a soldier whom they'd never seen. How I blessed the impulse that had started this avalanche. 'Wait 'till they learn how their letters came down by parachute!' smiled Gordon. Yes. If only I could reply. And I managed to get all the schools' letters out of the jungle, protecting nearly 400 with waterproof anti-gas wallets.

Next morning the yacketing drowned our new charging-engine, and when we set off the jungle boots were soft and comfortable. However, after splashing gaily through the first chaung the novelty began to wear off as water seeped through – they'd been made for patrol work in the dry season. We were now nearing the lake, passing through acres of tall weed that gave off a horrid stench when touched. In one stinking patch our group was attacked by wasps, hundreds of them; not a man escaped as we slapped our way through. Corporal Cody of the Sappers, wearing shorts with denims in pack, had an agonising time. Struggling through another patch, we dived into the weed as an aero-engine roared. A low-flying Dak appeared, and someone at the entrance waved. How we all envied him, without a thought for the risks *he* was running. What did he think of our crawling crocodile of scarecrows?

As we made bivvy an hour-long monsoon crashed, but this time I wasn't in the medical queue. Tait and his sergeant, Harwood, worked in the rain until well after dark. Captain Bence was groaning all night with stomach disorder – my bartered bully beef? Few slept through a second cloudburst, and when that ceased the mozzies swooped to take blood transfusions. I lay on my hard charpoy, thinking of home:

> And it's O! for a glimpse of England
> The grace of her dewdrenched lawns;
> The calm of her shores where the waters wash,
> Rose-tinged by a thousand dawns.
> And O! for a glimpse of London Town,
> Though it be through the fog and the rain,
> The well-thronged streets and glittering shops,
> That pageant of pomp and pain . . .

And O! O! O! for some fish and chips!

Dawn, and not rose-tinged. Everybody tired, soaked, irritable, fed up, and if the spirit of Wingate were watching us, it must have groaned in despair at the charpoys and other rubbish left behind. Skidding down and crawling up chaung banks, we cursed Burma, the war, and Japanese in that order. Conditions underfoot reduced our 'speed' to a mile an hour, and that was when machetes weren't being used. The next drop was on time, and jungle hammocks for officers fell, with more promised. Many ingenious Africans had already constructed hammocks from parachute cord. I watched Gordon suspending his between two trees. Top and bottom were rubberised cloth, separated all round by a yard of fine mesh netting. Closing it with a lengthy zip, you had complete protection against weather and mozzies. Gordon, trying it, said there were two snags – he couldn't get out very quickly and it weighed 5 lbs. My one snag, I told him, was that I had no hammock. Again we were indebted to our American Allies for this priceless item of jungle equipment.

The night alternated between rain and mosquitoes while I listened in envy to Gordon's snores. He emerged dry for stand-to, while I rose stiffly from my frame, and for some reason took a one and only swig at my bottle, filled with neat rum, to be nearly choked. Noticing Gordon's quizzical grin, I had to say that it made me feel a little more lively.

CHAPTER THIRTEEN

Indawgyi Lake

A new block had been formed at Hopin, some miles north, and the grimly defending Garrison included our 6th Battalion, with casualties sent to Mamon Kaing for possible evacuation by flying-boat. Enemy were reported in other lakeside villages, but we entered Mamon Kaing without opposition. Once again we were to hold the fort while others forged ahead. There was a superb view of the huge lake, with mountains beyond. Gordon was to put one gun by the village and the other on an uninviting spit of land jutting into the lake and almost bare. 'Sorry, Dogo,' he said. 'I'll come with you and pinpoint your site or you might get strafed after dark.' We reconnoitred with Dan-Boy, to find the spit impossible, so made for a small islet with bushes. The water reached to Gordon's shoulders, but as he was about five feet six I was better off. Dan-boy, in the rear, was headloading rifle and shovel. When carrying things as awkward as these, the Africans made themselves headpans of grass. Dan-boy was also gripping a bomb with one great fist, though what he proposed to do with it while neck-deep in a lake I couldn't imagine. On the islet we found a site after by-passing some rotting cattle, and I indicated the place by yelling to the team, watching us from the bank.

After making the damp detour in reverse, we reached the spot to find they'd gone, together with my pack. One man, Tu Tingu, came paddling up in a dugout that Gordon had already vetoed. With him were two chaps returning for the gun and tripod, but Tingu's wide grin vanished when Gordon intervened; 'No gun in *that!*'

'Me big waterman for my country,' protested Tu Tingu vehemently.

'Never mind what you are. Out, you others.' Moman Jaruwa and Gamadadi Ambusa disembarked, crestfallen, but to me the possibility of my gun resting on the lake bed was more than enough. 'Bon voyage!' grinned Gordon as I got in and the canoe rocked. 'I'll send a runner with any messages and he'll yell for the ferry.' Tingu took me, and Zaki insisted that he dry my clothes – we must not disrobe tonight because 'big-big moskeeta he lib here'. I peeled to the blue silk drawers, now attractively mottled, and having grown quite respectable whiskers must have looked enticing.

The gun arrived too quickly – no need to ask how. We dug positions, knocked up beds, and hoped for the best. The novelty of this independence appealed to me, though a fish's skeleton indicated that my kingdom would eventually be inundated. Tu Tingu whittled a hook and began casting unsuccessfully. 'The fish see you,' I suggested. 'Sit down.'

'Master let me take boat,' he pleaded. 'Me catch plenty-plenty.'

'Wait 'til tonight. I'll come with you.'

We went out to examine a larger craft, containing a Burman, his wife, and two children. The man spoke fractured English, gave us some carp, and refused my few rupees. When I smiled at the kids they looked scared to death!

After stand-to we went out again, and one carp was Tingu's solitary catch but the interlude was its own reward. From a cloudless sky stars were reflected in placid water, and tree silhouettes seemed to emphasise the silence as a single light twinkled on the far bank. It was Sunday, 4th June, maybe around noon at home. The speck of a lark in a blue vault, a muted cowbell – I could hear them. And as I sat there, miles behind the enemy lines but at perfect peace, thousands of Allied troops were poised for the invasion of Europe.

As we landed, my idyll was shattered by conscientious sentry Abdullai: "alt! Oo going?'

'Why you ask we?' yelled Tu Tingu. 'You *know* we. You blood' fool!'

'You blood' *big* fool!' was the belligerent retort. Later a screech sounded from the shadows, and Tingu went for the message. A drop was expected next day. We must beware of all boats.

It was again fine in the morning when a flying-boat came, shivering the mountain reflections. Sick and wounded, including Ali Banana, were packed into it; any discomfort must have been worthwhile. Slowly it rose on its hazardous flight to the Brahmaputra, and got there. Our drop came, and I was told to collect the team's share, but felt amazed when Tingu asserted

that the canoe would hold eight as well as the stuff to be
brought. Taking only weapons, seven of us made for it, with
Zaki left in charge. 'If Japans come and you can't hold them,' I
said, 'take out the lock and gudu (run).' (The lock was a small
but vital bit of mechanism. Without it the gun was useless.)
When loaded, the canoe had about three inches of freeboard
left, and too late I saw the unholy glint in Zaki's eyes. 'Hankali!'
I yelled, but he pushed us off anything but 'gently' and amid
terrific cursing, we turned turtle in five feet of water.

'You blood' Munchi shagi!' (bastard) bawled Tu Tingu, shaking a wet fist as Zaki shouted insults about watermanship. I slid
on to the bank like a zoo sea-lion and grabbed Zaki's rifle. 'Clean
my carbine or you'll get no grub.' It took some minutes to fish
up several weapons before Robinson Crusoe and four Fridays
paddled to the village.

Hopin, nicknamed 'Blackpool', was perforce abandoned after
the enemy surrounded and bombarded point-blank with artillery. We heard ghastly accounts of mortally wounded men
being shot by comrades before the remaining garrison fought
their way out, with 6th Battalion Africans headloading
wounded on improvised stretchers. The only route to the lake
was via the Kyusanlai Pass, and a race for that was won by the
Leicestershires, who ambushed the hurrying Japanese.

A batch of letters, plus hooks and gut I'd written for – they'd
arrived at just the right moment. Tu Tingu gave one look and
snorted in disgust: 'No be strong!'

Another shirt for me, and one for Zaki, which he merely
pulled over the shirt he was wearing! We paddled to the
Burman's hut to buy eggs with rupees, but he kept tapping his
chest and one of Zaki's shirts paid for the goods. After I'd failed
to get the kids to approach, we left the little family to their lonely
life.

That afternoon I dropped my tackle into the lake with some
confidence, catching one fish after another; Tingu had not a bite.
Suddenly he ejaculated: 'Big-big rain he come,' and, hissing its
way, it nearly beat us to the islet. Later, Zaki toasted my soaked
denims for the second time that day, afterwards giving a
horrible groan before clutching his stomach. 'Blimey! What's up,
Zaki?'

'Dis chiki done trouble me much, master.' His voice was *very*
faint.

'Take the canoe then, and see Doctor Tait.'

'Me no want doctor. Me t'ink dis lum be good for chiki.'

I remembered that after issuing the team's rum, a half bottle remained. 'Here you are, you scoundrel.' And for one suffering acute internal disorder he made a remarkably agile beeline for the main fire. A yell at midnight – the runner. We were off again. Reville at 4 a.m. The message ended: 'Don't trust that blasted cockleshell', but a better route to the mainland had already been found. Ashore, as Captain, I was last to leave the ship, and was about to knock holes in it when the Burman unexpectedly appeared, gesturing urgently; probably it was his canoe, anyway. Soon the guns and tripods arrived, headloaded by the rest of the team.

We were leaving because the return of the flying-boat was uncertain, and a skeleton defence remained with the sick. Tait, with two other medical officers, had worked for hours, sometimes operating in revolting conditions. Nevertheless seven men died during our short stay here, unavoidable in this hellish warfare with no rear line of communication.

As we left for Nammun more wounded were arriving, all having to pass a steadily growing cemetery. But I had now completely shed my former malaise and was feeling fit.

During the day the Gunners' walkie-talkie was unaccountably damaged, and Abu, who'd been humping it, vigorously denied responsibility; neither he nor Zaki wept when it was flung to bush.

By Nammun stood an enemy basha-barracks that they'd obviously expected to re-occupy, or they would have destroyed it. Most bashas leaked, but Gordon and Cameron invited Sid and me to share a smaller one, well made and easily the best. Why hadn't some bigger bugs annexed it? 'Because,' grinned Gordon, 'it's right against the village – first to be attacked from there!'

That was no deterrent, and later we found that it had been the officers' mess. The kitchen was comandeered by the four orderlies, who handed our mess tins through the serving hatch with exaggerated aplomb. Preceding troops had left stores in a pile, including hammocks. Luxury indeed. 'Far too good to last,' forecast Sid, 'but "sufficient unto the day" . . .'

Villagers approached, and women offered rice, eggs, and tiny chickens, but refused money. 'Well, what *do* they want?' asked Sid in perplexity, then obtained a chicken for some thread, understandable with all the parachuting around. A young girl came to me as I forced bachelor buttons to my denims, and beyond blushing these days. 'She wants your pants, Dogo,' laughed Sid. I tried to tuck my shirt further beneath me, then found that safety pins were her need. Cheerfully she parted with a chicken, which Zaki grabbed. Meanwhile, the two orderlies had unpicked a filthy old jersey and carefully disguised a lot of short lengths as one long unbroken one round a stick. After haggling, they scrounged about two pounds of rice. A huge joke – they giggled for an hour. Then Tu Tingu unearthed an abandoned rifle and quickly struck a bargain with a villager. I'd never expected to see a perfectly serviceable Lee-Enfield exchanged for two bantam-sized eggs, one rotten.

The Pass was being manned by the Black Watch, and we were to relieve them. The place affording no suitable positions for Vickers or mortars, Hoppy and I would stay in Nammun, taking up supplies on alternate days. 'Some news for you,' said Major Taylor as the daily conference ended. 'The Second Front's opened.'

Dead silence, until we were outside. 'What's the hell's the good of the Second Front to *us*?' demanded Barker pithily of the jungle. Far more important would be the capitulation of Mogaung.

Anticipating restful sleep, I insinuated my lengthy self into the hammock, then groped for the zip. Leaning out too far, I was slung to the floor with a thwack that shook the basha, also my companions. Anyway, I learned, and it was grand to be free of those blasted malaria-carriers and to listen to their frustrated whines.

*   *   *

The Column left, and a British one occupied the bashas for two days. Zaki fraternised, unaware that these Tommies were among those who repelled the first fanatical White City attacks. 'De Japans run,' he told a smiling audience. 'We catch, cut off heads wid machete.' Then he glanced back, and saw me eavesdropping! These men confirmed a rumour that we'd heard and ridiculed. Some of their wounded had been captured, and the Japanese let them go after treating their injuries. They'd been lucky indeed in encountering an enemy officer who, unwilling to be burdened by sick prisoners, was also humane. Actually, the brutal truth, in these conditions, was that ailing men, even your own, were a far bigger handicap than the dead.

Shots sounded from the Pass – how were the lads faring? Gordon badly needed to know whether our guns were undamaged by the march, but wasn't allowed to test them, so we cleaned and overhauled. Rain having penetrated the ammunition boxes, Gordon had 8,000 rounds removed and the belts dried. At White City he'd jettisoned loaded stripless belts in sealed containers, saying they were unreliable. Having fired thousands of stripless, it was the one decision of his with which I didn't agree. Some of the gunners and African N.C.O.'s were angered by Gordon's zealousness, convinced that when Mogaung fell we'd meet no more enemy, but Gordon remained adamant.

Next day three Dakotas came, with villagers helping us, and there was no theft. One large tin of biscuits became detached on the way down and disappeared with a plop into flooded paddy, but was dug out. With this drop came some delicious toffee which many Africans disliked, so I did well.

I set out with the Column's grub, and the importance of the Pass was soon apparent – cliff to the right, and abyss to the left. Nearing the Column we began to get wet from a drizzle which, they said, was incessant. Worse, water wouldn't boil properly at that height, but on the credit side the air was cool. I crept forward with a letter for Sid, in charge of a listening-post. He was looking harassed – one man had made the other men jittery by firing without reason. Later an enemy patrol did emerge from the bush, and each side was so surprised that they stared at one another until the Japanese turned and fled. Nerves must have been taut in the Kyusanlai Pass!

British composite rations had been dropped, and the Africans marvelled at tinned goods and other delicacies. The way they'd adapted to unaccustomed foods was remarkable.

Somebody at Base had had the cheek to send leaflets – 'How to make Tea'. To us, who'd brewed up water ranging from boiling, hot, tepid, greasy, soapy, chlorinated, to animal-manured, it was as big an insult as telling Americans how to 'make' coffee!

Tommies, perusing a notice pinned to a basha, were doubting its authenticity. It was signed 'Army Council' and heavily marked 'Secret', so of course I took a copy:

> You have killed more Japanese than you have suffered total casualties and sick. By destroying the enemy lines of communication and harassing his rear you materially assisted in capturing Myitkyina. But the victory is not yet complete and much hard work lies before you. In spite of hardship caused by present

conditions the task must be pushed forward with rigour and bold endeavour to a successful conclusion. You are Chindits. You can take it and make it.

'And you've bloody-well had it!' somebody had inevitably scrawled, and if the message had indeed come from Whitehall they were counting chickens, for Myitkyina was still in enemy hands, nor did they relinquish it until a month after Mogaung fell.

A new order, disobeyed by many, including myself, decreed that all mail from home must be destroyed immediately after being read. What a hope. The idea was that captured letters might contain moans about air raids, etc., to be twisted into propaganda. I didn't throw away a single schools' letter, and was also bending rules by keeping a rough diary. The enemy wouldn't have found anything useful in it, and I also took jolly good care not to write anything derogatory about them . . . just in case!

Another British Column passed through. Bent shoulders, sunken eyes, beards, exactly like emaciated old men. Not a dozen lifted their heads as they plodded past. Gordon spoke quietly: 'My God, do *we* look like that?' He himself was tireless, rigidly enforcing stand-to, keeping sentries alert, never sparing himself. I felt great admiration, especially on learning that he was unwell. Grumbling Gunners and N.C.O.'s had to toe the line, and at length Gordon took pencil and paper, poring over names. Sergeant Musa Damboa arrived with a taketa – apparently two men were hankering for fresh woods:

> Report by the Sergeant Musa Damboa. 16.6.1944.
> Please sergeant I want you to take me to Mr Gordon and see him. Since I was come to this Machine Gun I never get any better place. I want to go back to Rifle Company. I do not live in this Machine Gun because you too much trouble me. Tu Tingu.
> Private Abdullai Fort Lamy he say want see you too. Please Sir, you see, these two men report to me they want see you. O.K.
> Sergeant M.U. Damboa.

Neither could have known what had been written – they were illiterate and had been misled by someone. Gordon had no intention of losing two of his best men, and his suggestions were agreed by the Column Commander. Exchanges took place. The muleteer sergeant was replaced, and Corporal Dan-Boy was given another stripe; from then on the atmosphere improved.

With Blackpool abandoned, nothing could be gained by holding the Pass; if properly blown it would be unusable for weeks. The track to it was frightful by now, and Africans were shovelling slurry into the depths. The Column was relieved by the Black Watch, and on coming down appeared to be all in. Cameron, a husky Scot who 'celebrated' his 21st during the march, had lost a stone since leaving White City. He and Sid went off to a chaung to bathe, and Cameron's shirt, containing a compass and 200 rupees, vanished. It was found next day, complete with compass, but not cash. He laughed. What was money here compared to that little instrument? As Bill Shakespeare put it: 'Who steals my purse steals trash'.

Sickness was hitting Europeans, and Lieutenants Heap and Briggs were made Captains in consequence. A new cemetery was greviously increasing in size, and even the Nigerians, born and bred in the jungle, had had more than enough.

New maps and more rupees were issued, but with no pockets left in my denims I changed coins for notes. Lying among new rations was a paper heavily marked 'Top Secret'. Unbelievably, it gave details and timings of the Black Watch takeover. 'Burn the damn' thing!' growled Gordon. As we left, I gave the kids some more 'toffees from heaven' as their parents scrambled for salvage. Major Miles and Captain Heap, too ill to march, remained in Nammun with the Sappers. The hammock's extra weight was noticeable, but I was feeling fit, and received a shock on finding Gordon stretched on the ground and almost weeping with vexation. 'Go up front, Dogo, my guts are giving me hell.' Abu stayed with him, leaving Zaki to hump the new walkie-talkie without relief, and at the very first halt he sorrowfully showed me a ruined instrument. Accidental? But of course. Butter wouldn't have melted in that Munchi's mouth!

Gordon struggled late into bivvy, looking ghastly. I knew what stomach trouble could do. Next morning he wriggled into his harness, and despite my protests was about to add his pack when Tait uncompromisingly ordered that it be placed on a mule. Gordon gave way with reluctance; his Gunners were there.

Owing to trouble with the new maps, the Column deviated, spending the long halt in a village called Moman Ywakyet. Gordon made it, and on resuming placed himself with the leaders. Falling back at once, he waved me on without a word. The bush gave way, first to the former stinking weed, then loathsome black water two feet deep. Slowly we splashed along, halts being taken standing and without unloading – the dokis must have suffered. How about Gordon, and the frightful possibility of not reaching terra firma before dark? However, we squelched out of that liquid filth at dusk. Gordon went straight to his hammock, and Doc Tait's 'surgery' closed down later than ever. God, how welcome was sleep that night!

*   *   *

Next day Gordon felt better and kept position. Dakotas were circling at Nammun, dropping explosives to the Sappers, and violent crashes sounded as the Pass was blown. The day's march was shortened by news that the Japanese were coming towards us with elephants, and we prepared an ambush as heavy rain started. Gordon put both guns where they commanded the track, and I didn't envy Sid, out ahead with orders to let them through before opening up. We waited tensely, then less tensely, and finally not at all tensely – in fact we waited all night and were soaked. No hammocks, fires, or tea. Cold grub. After arranging to take alternate watches, Gordon and I finished huddled against each other. At daylight a semi-nude figure came round – imperturbable Major Taylor. From one bare shoulder a carbine hung, upside down, and a pipe between his teeth was also inverted. His other adornments were boots, shorts, bush hat, and prickly heat, an extremely irritating rash for which rainwater provides relief. Well, it was literally bouncing off him. 'O.K., you two?' he inquired, as usual, and went on. Absolutely unflappable!

The ambush was taken off, and it was found that one of Cameron's men had disappeared . . . he was never seen or heard of again. Before we moved, Miles and Heap turned up, preferring to rejoin rather than await a doubtful take-off from the lake. They'd skirted the hills and so missed the marsh.

Soon we came upon elephant spoor that had turned towards the hills. The enemy were probably alarmed by all the explosions ahead. The going became more than ever hazardous with water-filled holes from elephants' feet, with mules again the chief sufferers. At midday, most of us spent a glorious half-hour lying in a chaung, and later I read an article that stated it was useless to bathe and put on the same dirty clothes. What rubbish. Lying in those soft, swiftly flowing streams promoted wellbeing that lasted for hours. The same author wrote that to grow beards brought sores. Well, every European in No. 12 had a beard, but none had trouble beneath it. Wingate's view, that to go unshaven meant extra sleep, was sound, and in our case a beardless white man among Africans presented a prominent target.

Surprisingly, despite all the exposure and mosquitoes, there was very little fever. A notable absentee was the louse, possibly because we were nearly always wet through. I was told of a European in another Column who became lousy, asserting that there were valuable chemicals on the skin that should not be washed off in the bush. True or not, No. 12 preferred to be without chemicals *and* crabs!

We reached a derelict bivvy site where there had obviously been trouble, for arms, ammunition and even unopened mail lay around. A 6th Battalion man staggered from the jungle with a garbled account of being attacked while awaiting a drop. We took him along, and later those following from Nammun saw African and Japanese bodies. When we neared our own bivvy the Vickers stayed behind to guard a fork – no chances were being taken. As the Tail crawled by I was struck by the absence of noise. Mules seldom brayed on the move, and men and animals resembled phantoms in the half-light. Sid was again 'Tail-end-Charlie', and his grin vanished when I said there was still half a mile to go. A minute as the crow flies, but an hour for a Chindit 'marching' on superglue!

A phenomenon here was phosphorescent bark, that we wrenched off to place by the guns so that posts could be taken quickly in the dark. The hammocks were slung on a precarious slope, the zips almost level with our heads. When Gordon and I did hourly stints, each time I vaulted and swung I expected to roll into water yards below.

Breakfast was taken standing – the ground swarmed with red ants. The march was again short, in anticipation of a drop that was delayed 72 hours; any tapeworms must be getting impatient. But a strong conviction was growing that we'd leave Burma as quickly as possible, for Mogaung had fallen and Calvert's gallant Brigade were mopping it up. The noise going on when we rejoined the square was terrific, and even cautious Gordon was sure that there were no enemy for many miles. But the one person unaffected by the wave of euphoria was the calm Column Commander, who at all conferences stressed his conviction that there would be confrontation.

A village was contacted, and Lieutenant Macauley, Gordon, Freebody and I found ourselves in possession of a small chicken, and solemnly debated whether to draw lots or divide. Sharing won, and Freebody volunteered to fry it. As we watched hungrily, a blinding shower broke, and all dived for cover except the valiant cook, protecting his fire with a cape. As the rain ceased, he triumphantly emerged with a blackened mess that we tore apart with gusto.

In this area, stand-to was the signal for thousands of minute flies to become airborne and attack our faces – the irritation was intense. Occasionally they'd explore during the night, passing through the net mesh with ease, and the air would curdle!

*   *   *

The drop came, and we stayed overnight. After an hour's spell as Duty European I was awakened by C.S.M. Potter, who'd relieved me. 'Sorry, Dogo. Message. Japs coming this way, still a long way off. Be prepared.' Dozing again, I had another shock when a loud twang sounded by my ear, followed by two more – ill-used hammock strings were going. I lay expecting to land head-first, and next day replaced them with parachute cord.

Again no enemy came. Our next destination was Lakhren, which we approached gingerly after hearing shots. Gurkhas were responsible; they like to bang off at every opportunity – probably the reason why they're such good marksmen. The residue of 6th Battalion were here, and said that our sister Column 43 were on their way. After they'd rolled in, noisily, I found the mud around my hammock commandeered by strange Munchis. 'Dis mans my brudders,' announced Zaki. 'Dey all salute for you.'

'How do you do?' I asked politely, and rows of pointed teeth appeared.

'I tell dem,' went on Zaki impressively, 'dat you be good master for me. Master gib small-small lum please?' Removing what should have been a brimful bottle from my harness, I looked ostentatiously at him. 'Yes, suh,' he said sadly. 'Plenty t'iefmen be for inside dis Column.'

Monsoon conditions demanded special attention to weapons – a jam could be fatal. The platoons' small mortars had been jettisoned – weather had ruined them. We were given canvas covers for the Vickers. Sid still had a Sten, and as I hadn't tried out my second carbine, we potted at various objects and must have resembled brigands. I had full and flourishing whiskers and Sid an inch or so of scrub he called a beard. Here in Lakhren it was loud talk and laughter as Dakotas dropped tons of stuff to a central dump. One Gurkha amused himself for hours by sounding fractured calls on a bugle, but who cared? This track led to Kamaing and Mogaung. No more Japanese! But one worry was the news of flying bombs being launched against Britain – what would be the next horror for those at home?

Suddenly, in the midst of all the *joie de vivre*, came a crunch – Major Taylor was correct. We were to negotiate a second range of hills and attack the enemy, known to be in strength on the Mogaung Plain. Stunned, we listened in silence as the objectives were named, but on emerging everyone spoke at once: 'They're mad!'

'We'll never even get over, let alone attack!'

'How about the dokis?' groaned Hoppy, for the mortars also had animals. Gordon and I pored over the map until the closely-knit contours sickened us, and the only happy soul around seemed to be Sergeant Dan-Boy.

Rumours. Lentaigne and Stilwell were at loggerheads, with Vinegar Joe also being handicapped by Chaing Kai Shek. Were politics gumming up the works too? A subdued group of Europeans gathered for the final evening conference, to get a further shock when Major Taylor, trying to keep the regret from his voice, said goodbye. His rash was now so bad that he couldn't wear a shirt. Again, Doc Tait's order had to be clinched by Colonel Hughes, still leading 43. With Taylor went Captain Doyle, Intelligence Officer, and Johnstone, with a number of Nigerians, all aiming to reach an American field hospital near Kamaing. Major Miles, far from fit, again took command, and Tait, looking quite as ill as any of those he was sending away, insisted upon carrying on.

CHAPTER FOURTEEN

Catastrophe

How oft, when men are at the point of death,
Have they been merry.

(Shakespeare)

After the first expletives, most people viewed the latest plan
with the average soldier's wry fatalism – if a bullet had your
name on it, you'd be hit. So instead of the anticipated route, we
headed for the mountains. The villagers maintained we'd not
get over, but hadn't Wingate formed his Force to tackle the
insurmountable?

The night before we left was dry, and there was a European
bottle party. Officers and B.N.C.O.'s had been on first-name
terms for weeks – it was that kind of Campaign. A big fire,
lots of rum, and entertainment. I won a tongue-twister contest with 'I rattled my bottles round Rollocks's Yard', and
Potter gave a spine-chilling account of looting Japanese bodies
after they'd been in the White City stream for days. I glanced
around at the ring of bearded faces. What a spectacle with
flames glinting on gigantic red anthills against the black background. Things degenerated when someone wondered how
many of us would get out. 'The War Office won't care if we're
all dead,' was one remark. 'All they care about is their Second
Front.'

'Wrong. It's just as important to keep the Japs out of India.
That's why the Government's paying to keep us in *here*.'

'Government? It's British and Yanks taxpayers who fork out.
The trouble is, Wingate's dead. That's why we're being shoved
around like bloody pawns!'

A vote was taken, the result being met with cheers and boos.

Then an acid note came from Miles – if we needed no sleep, others did, and the party broke up with laughter and higher spirits.

* * *

Next day No. 12 led, with 43 next, followed by Brigade Headquarters and 6th Battalion; intervals between Columns would be two hours. The going was so bad that by bivvy time we'd merely reached the first hill, and next morning had to haul ourselves up by gripping bamboo. Conditions were similar to those on the first range, but resistance had greatly weakened. Men and animals skidded yards before falling like skittles. Fearing surprise, Gordon had the canvas gun-covers removed, and soon the weapons were muck-covered. Once I rendered hurried first aid by sloshing them in a chaung, enough to give any Vickers man a fit, and Sergeant Freebody, seeing me at it, nearly had one!

Inevitably 43's leaders, belting away from their heavily-laden groups, caught up with us, but their cussing availed them nothing. Then a prolonged stoppage made me go forward to investigate. A wide chaung. Though slow-moving, the far bank rose steeply for 20 feet. Mortar mules were in the water, with Hoppy and Co. trying to drive them out and up. On our bank were two elephants, fortunately with no stick, their mahout having been stuck there for two days. The huge beasts ignored the turmoil, placidly accepting some of my toffees.

Clapping as Hoppy got a mule out – but our turn was some way off. 'Get the stores across,' ordered Gordon, and I went back to bring our group along. Riflemen protested at the queue-jumping, not realising how fortunate they were. Gordon was in the chaung, waist-deep with the mortarmen. The other bank looked so hazardous that I suggested to the Gunners that the loads be split. Abdullai Fort Lamy looked insulted, placed 85 pounds on his nut, and safely made the climb; the rest followed. Headloading was invaluable, enabling African Columns to take heavy equipment over obstacles where other units were forced to jettison.

Soon every remaining Column mule was in the chaung, with their masters washing them, having developed a real affection for their patient charges. The ubiquitous Gordon, to his annoyance, had to go forward to Column H.Q. at a shout for Group Commanders.

Another hour, and it was our turn. Suddenly I thought of the grey, in fine fettle after his bath. Holding the halter, I told his muleteer to go up and wait. Bang at that mini-cliff went the grey, evaded groping hands, and went off up the track, followed by a grinning master and two grumblers headloading ammunition. After that, four more dokis were yelled up successfully. I couldn't find the last, and hoped I'd miscounted.

We climbed steeply, on a track so narrow that every time a mule fell nothing could pass. After one spell, when a muleteer, Sergeant Sokoto, Zaki and I struggled while naughty language floated up from behind, I came upon four Gunners taking advantage by having a private brew-up. After promising them six-for-arse from Miles later, I was able to see the funny side of it.

Far more serious, an ammunition mule slipped over the edge of a chasm, but landed in a clump of bamboo a few feet below. One carrier remained on the track, but the second toppled down – we could hear it crashing. The muleteer was game, rescuing the doki and harness. We had a problem, for no mule could carry such an uneven load. Just when Miles appeared, taking in the situation at a glance. 'Dispose of it.' With chagrin I heard the second carrier go down to join its fellow – 2,000 rounds chucked away after dragging them from White City. I reached Gordon, who took it philosophically – we still had 6,000.

The missing mule was there, its master engaged in acrimonious argument. Apparently he'd gone along the chaung edge and found an easier crossing, and when I asked why the hell he hadn't come back to tell us he looked blank. The Sappers' hoodoo was persisting, for Lieutenant Thompson, their one remaining officer, fell and broke a shoulder. With only enemy ahead, he was patched up and, with two Africans, retraced the tortuous route to Lakhren. He must have endured hell.

The distance covered on that horrible day was 1½ miles, and I asked Gordon: 'How d'you rate our chances?'

'No more than fifty-fifty, but I'm determined about one thing.'

'What is it?'

'Doesn't matter about that ammo, but if we do get out, we'll have the guns with us – tripods too!'

After we'd slept in sodden clothes, the monsoon still raged next morning, but at long last the rain ceased, and we rose stiffly after the midday halt. The afternoon marches were detested by all, and Sid and I were both depressed by news that the two close pals, Lieutenants Campbell and Galbraith of our Lagos draft, were now equally inseparable in death, both killed on the same day.

We bivvied in an old enemy camp, where the mud was repulsive reddish super-gluey slush. Bathing in a shallow chaung, we exhibited jungle sores to one another. Sid had two colourful boils on his back, while I had a lovely carbuncle on a forearm.

*   *   *

> And then, from hour to hour,
> We rot and rot,
> And thereby hangs a tale.
> (Shakespeare)

The Column was now a horrid spectacle. Clothing was caked with red clay, equipment was being held together by parachute cord. Hats were green with mildew, and spare bootlaces, normally worn around the hat crown, held wristlet watches suspended from necks – straps had disintegrated. And the queue for medical attention was longer than ever. Glad to leave that repellent red filth, we set off with rain again falling. During the day the mule involved in the spill gave trouble, though carrying only the light rangefinder. Finally he wouldn't budge, so we tied him to a tree with some feed – the bivvy site was not far away. We were now on the summit, close to a huge basha that was at once collared by Brigade H.Q. There was a good view of the Mogaung Plain, and I felt a pang of nostalgia at the English-like landscape. But . . . any lingering doubts were now dispelled. Mustangs and Thunderbolts were celebrating 4th July by strafing Japanese positions from incredibly low altitudes – the rattle of canon-fire and vicious crump of bombs were plainly heard.

It was nearly dusk when the muleteer and I returned for the doki. It had been hurt far more than realised, and was dead. The African wept loudly as he left his pal for the vultures, another poor relic on this ghastly trail.

The Brigade gathered, but Major Carfrae moved on before I could contact him and Jock. A Dakota arrived next day when the summit was mist-shrouded, and the crew unloaded by the only thing the pilot could discern – the big basha, and the very first throw of four 'chutes landed on the roof with loud cracks.

Naturally everyone outside found it amusing, until an
unopened 'chute struck a Burrif sergeant and killed him.

Tons of ammunition, equipment, and clothing were sent, and
soon an enemy patrol probed, wounding one of 43's officers.
Part of 7th Battalion were also involved in a small arms battle,
and with mixed feelings I heard that some of the 12th, including
the Vickers, would relieve them next day. All was quiet when
we arrived to mount the guns near something that riveted my
attention – the newly made-up grave of Captain Haynes of the
7th. On and off, I'd served 20 years, and now the moment of
truth was very near. The sight of that small bamboo cross had
given me involuntary qualms. How would I acquit myself in
front of the Nigerians?

We dug fast, but the Japanese opened up, mortar bombs
whistling over to burst behind us – if the next salvo were
shortened it might be my first, and last, baptism of fire. Nothing
fell very near, and the positions were finished, but with visibil-
ity practically nil we suspended empty tins in the thick bush – a
wasted effort. Before we even took posts a rifle platoon arrived,
and we were sent to another place, with a second lot of digging.
Nothing infuriates Infantrymen more, and Gordon himself was
flaming mad. By the time we were in it was dark, and I
inadvertently tied my hammock to a bamboo already being used
by Harwood. A moment after we'd both settled down, the
hammocks, slowly and gracefully, descended to the mud.

*   *   *

In front of us was the town of Sahmaw, dominated by a tall
factory chimney. I was asked to range on prominent objects, not
knowing whether the instrument had been shaken out of
adjustment. I made the Kamaing–Sahmaw road 4½ miles, so
beyond reach of any Column weapon.

Supplies were dropped all day, visible for miles, but not an
enemy plane appeared. They'd been chased out of the sky by
some U.S. daredevils known, I heard as 'Phil Cochran's Commandos'. The Japanese on the ground must have been hopping
mad, seeing all that lovely grub descending into 'their' territory
and not being able to do a thing about it.

We must be getting near to Stilwell's Chinese. With due
deference, few Europeans could see much difference in Burmese, Chinese or Japanese, and how about the uniforms of
'Merrill's Marauders' – U.S. troops attached to Vinegar Joe?

There was actually a serious suggestion that when doubt existed, something white should be waved – in fact, letting some unknown body see exactly where you were! This daft idea was instantly vetoed. Passwords were then agreed – 'Hong Kong John' would be answered by 'Shanghai Lou'. We couldn't believe it until confirmed, and even then the Africans thought it was a joke, as I told Gordon. 'Right. We'll try them out at dusk stand-to. Make sure they know what's on.' I did just that. Orders were that anything moving in front must be fired upon. We made sure that plenty of bamboo cracked as we bore down on the current look-outs, bosom pals Abdullai Fort Lamy and Bisali Keffi. A hoarse bellow made us jump: "'alt! Oo going?'

'Friend,' called the annoyed Gordon, then roasted Abdullai in English and what he knew of Hausa. He then ordered Bisali to 'c-come', which he did without a thing happening. I heard Gordon breathing heavily and also muffled giggles from the rest of the team. 'Come *on*, Fort Lamy,' said Gordon. 'Challenge!'

'Hong Kong John!' bawled Abdullai, and 'Hong Kong John!' bawled Bisali, huge grin just discernible, but Gordon wasn't amused. 'Sort it out, Dogo.'

That night, as Duty European, I watched enemy vehicle lights on the road; aircraft weren't operating after dark. Suddenly I tensed as a dim shape approached, then raised my carbine. 'Hong Kong John!' No reply, and I added quickly: 'Wannene wannan?' (Who's this?) Still no response, but just in time I recognised a doki, that I caught and tied to a tree. What if I'd shot the poor chap and sent the place into uproar?

*　　*　　*

We advanced next day, the 6th remaining to guard the Brigade's sick. As there was plenty of food to spare, we left it in a heap for them to collect, not suspecting that we were under surveillance. As usual, a section stayed to watch for movement, and saw some when a crowd of Japanese appeared, tossing grenades. Greatly outnumbered, the section hared after us while we wondered what was happening. The enemy ignored the departing Africans and made for the pile of grub. No air drops for them, and they must have been in sore need after milking the villages. At this juncture few of us were bearing the enemy any great hatred. Too full of our own problems!

With Japanese near, Colonel Hughes and 43 led, and almost at once his scouts shot a man who bolted from a chaung, leaving two mules. While looting the body and recapturing the startled dokis, they themselves came under fire from their pals in rear, a little jungle contretemps that caused more curses than casualties! Slowly we advanced, the spreadeagled corpse looking ghastly in the greenish half-light of the chaung, and reached some native huts from which women and children were peering. I felt haunted by the terror in the kids' eyes, and the hostile expressions of the mothers – with their inoffensive country churned into a battlefield they had good reason to feel venomous. Leaving this hamlet, small arms fire sounded ahead and went on until dusk.

Next day, to augment 43's fire power, Macauley's platoon joined them. The enemy had withdrawn overnight, but later firing again began, and Macauley had the task of winkling out a strong force dug into 'foxholes'. This nasty engagement cost the platoon 8 killed and 9 wounded. Macauley won a Military Cross, and Freebody escaped unhurt.

Difficult terrain, so groups bivvied where they stood. With No. 12 astride a chaung, I waded back and forth several times guiding runners. No sleep for anyone, for the road was quite near. Gordon and I took turns with sentries, and at dawn a soaked and miserable Column went on through the mud. Again the Japanese had gone, obviously fighting rearguard actions while supplies went along the road. We entered a narrow ravine – not a man would have lived could the enemy have rolled down explosives. Leaving this claustrophobic trap we hit the plain, and slosh that was kneedeep. It took the Gunners' mules an hour to cross this patch, and we left the R.A.F. party with their dokis sunk to the panniers.

We now shed our 'soft elements' (non-combatants) and turned left towards our objective, a railway station. Soon we encountered tall reeds, then splashed through chaung after chaung draining from the hills, often standing in water while those in front used machetes. Suddenly there was a fusillade of shots, and everyone dropped except a muleteer who wrestled with his scared doki. Soon I rose rather guiltily to help him, for we were on a reverse slope and bullets that seemed to be cracking past our ears were actually well above.

I now had a surprise when Brigadier Ricketts appeared, a deputy no longer. Despite my face fungus he recognised me. 'Sergeant Shaw?'

'Yessir. How are things in front, sir?' I asked daringly.

'Can't tell a thing until we're out of these damn' weeds.' Away he went, and we continued to creep, and stop. Fearing a flank attack, Gordon had the Vickers removed and carried 'three men load'. This meant the guns being mounted, loaded and ready for instant action, and taken along by the three numbers, each gripping a tripod leg. In addition, No. 2 had the spare parts case slung over a shoulder, with No. 3 holding an ammunition box of 250. The total weight was more than enough in the circumstances!

Suddenly violent explosions were added to the small arms fire ahead, then a light plane increased the din. How was Sid, in the thick of it? We were about to form a square when loud shouts were heard, and to our amazement an American liaison officer came out of the bush, having made contact via the plane. Yes, you've guessed correctly – we'd been battling with Stilwell's Chinese, and the heavy crashes had been caused by their new 4.2 inch mortars! Such incidents on manoeuvres at home were hilarious, but not here with the casualties on both sides. And meanwhile the Japanese had been down on the road, either wondering which of their units were in action or, much more likely, laughing their heads off.

*　　*　　*

After the guns were sited I hobbled through the dusk to the nearest chaung. Sid and Hoppy were there, unhurt. We hadn't removed saturated boots for three days, and had to cut socks away, revealing raw patches that were extremely painful. The rain ceased, and there was uneasy sleep, disturbed by probing enemy artillery. At daylight the scouts reported the road unoccupied, and we approached it. Sid and I together for once. 'Mogaung, here we come at last,' I said.

'Not so sure.' And indeed it was right wheel, but with every man glancing to the left as we saw the first road since White City. The surface was littered with smashed stores and pathetic bodies of mules among waterfilled craters. Camouflaged lay-bys held undamaged trucks, but were ignored, and a pile of dried fish also failed to lure us. We proceeded gingerly, praying that there were no mines. During an unexpected halt Sid and I walked over to view a dead Japanese whose pals had departed in a hurry; one of his legs lay a few feet away. 'Look,' Sid exclaimed, 'he's not been searched at all,' and reached towards bulging pouches and pockets that could have been set for a surprise. 'Come off it, Dracula,' I replied, pulling firmly. None too soon, the Column moved.

Our 'vulnerables' weren't where we'd left them, and were contacted by walkie-talkie. The night shelling had approached their bivvies, causing a sharpish 'up sticks and away' in the gloom. At a hurried conference we heard that Mogaung, etc., could be forgotten. Apparently the Japanese, after leaving the road, had occupied a rise just beyond it. This mound was at once named 'Hill 60', and we were allocated positions facing it. On its summit were a huge dead trunk and another big tree shaped like a shaving brush, two prominent landmarks that could be seen for miles. Before starting to dig, Hoppy and I stood appraising the hill for a moment – it seemed much to close for comfort.

'Goodbye Mogaung,' muttered Hoppy. 'Chindit work's finished, Dogo. I guess they'll soon start harassing *us!*'

*   *   *

Hardly had Hoppy spoken when there was a reverberating 'bong' from behind the hill. Everybody froze, then fell prone as a shell whined towards us. It burst on Tait's patch, killing three of his mules. More bongs, and earsplitting crashes that smothered thought but certainly not fear. Between explosions we dug frantically, with machetes, bayonets, fingernails, anything that could scratch. Each projectile landed inside the perimeter, and even the shallowest slit lessened the panicky feeling of naked vulnerability. And myself, who as a starry-eyed schoolkid had vowed to win a V.C.? I dug as fast as anyone.

It stopped, but a party creeping to a chaung for water was at once bombarded. The bush wasn't thick, and obviously movement on our forward slope was being detected; nobody stirred before dark. At the evening conference, we heard that No. 43 would attack the hill next day, aided by 12's machine-guns and mortars, but Gordon and I listened in some bewilderment to our own task. '500 a gun in 30 minutes?' repeated Gordon. 'What's the use of that?'

Miles shrugged; it wasn't his plan. Next morning, despite shelling, we crossed the road and took positions. Corporal Iya Mubi fired one gun and I the other, trying to eke out 500 rounds each in half an hour through weapons capable of firing the number in one minute! At length we were reduced almost to singles, and Corporal Moman Jaruwa, my No. 2, spat disgustedly. 'Wannan ba shi da kau!' (This is no good!) adding that the 'Japans' were laughing at us. But of one thing we were sure – the guns were undamaged by the march.

We ceased firing, and the riflemen advanced, grappling with undergrowth and swamp, and were soon being showered with bullets and grenades – it seemed to go on interminably. Sudden silence; the defenders had withdrawn, but our elation was short-lived. Before 43 could consolidate, the enemy counter-attacked so fiercely that they regained the hill and a section was captured. The African corporal later bolted to freedom but his men weren't so fortunate.

After the initial success, the Brigadier must have been infuriated. Ricketts had said I was 'enterprising', but was himself very unorthodox, typical of most Chindit leaders. No rear funkhole for him – he'd been one of the first on the hilltop. We learned that the Vickers had shredded Japanese laundry drying on bushes, but that was the net gain, with casualties on the debit side. Sergeant Mathews of 43 lay dead on the hill – it hadn't been possible to bring him back.

A small mongrel dog appeared, and we named him 'Spot'. He shared our rations, but his friendliness didn't discriminate, for occasionally he sped uphill, to return with tail wagging furiously.

The guns stayed in position, and next day the Column joined us from their untenable slope. With 43 on our right, and 6th Battalion in reserve, our open left flank had to be closely watched. The moves provoked more shelling, until Chinese Artillery in the rear opened up and silenced it.

Major Carfrae and the 7th were dug in further down the plain, facing a large enemy force. Meanwhile Ricketts didn't remain idle. No. 12 and 66 (a 6th Battalion Column) would attack, but this time after the hill had been blasted from the air. On hearing that, everyone felt confident. We continued to dig in uncomfortably close to the enemy. The bush wasn't very thick, and with only sparse cover Gordon and I beetled around for new gun sites. To our delight, Major Taylor appeared, rejuvenated by the American field hospital. 'Careful, you two,' he admonished, 'you're nearly under observation.'

Correct. Two minutes later there was a spitting sound – a Japanese 'knee-high' mortar used for short ranges. The small, approaching bomb sounded just like someone chuckling, and we threw ourselves flat before it burst 15 yards away. 'Blimey, that was close!' I exclaimed as whizzing metal 'wewed' over us.

'Damn' good shooting!' commented Gordon as we departed for pastures new. After choosing sites, he left for the teams while I retrieved our packs, to find that our former positions were now Column Headquarters. Grabbing our gear, I stumbled away, and seconds afterwards there was another boom from the distant Chinese gun. Suddenly I dropped the packs and flung myself down, for the whine seemed menacingly low. Then a terrific crash. I looked up to see smoke at H.Q., and went back to deadheat with Captain Harison and R.Q.M.S. Bell. Together we stared in horror at a hideous sight. The shell had exploded in the midst of the group, and everyone there died except the Column Commander.

Captain Briggs was almost unrecognisable, but Captain Heap had been killed by the blast, his face as grey as ash. All the African runners were dead except one man obviously in extremis. I used a morphia needle but he went within seconds. If anything could be gained from this ghastly catastrophe, it was that none of those killed suffered pain. Major Taylor was helped to his feet, blood pouring down a broken arm. His escape from death was miraculous. Maybe Briggs had been between him and the explosion.

I was told to bring the Gunners – with shovels – and picked my way between scattered papers, plans of the coming attack to be read to Europeans. People almost disbelieved me, and Gordon was in the depths of despair, for Briggs had been his particular friend. I cheered a little at sight of our own runner, Anton Antonadi, whom I'd thought dead. 'I no be for dat place,' he said. 'Na gode Allah.' (I thank God.)

This time Major Taylor did not rejoin, and after the Gunners had finished their sickening task, Gordon commandeered my rum for them; it must have been appreciated.

Already weakened by wastage of personnel, we had now lost another 8 Africans and 3 of our most important officers, taken by a stray shell, and an Allied shell at that. Not unnaturally, the morale of No. 12 Column sank to rock-bottom.

CHAPTER FIFTEEN

Stalemate

For the third and last time Miles took command. As Hoppy had forecast, Chindit work was over. The Reccy disbanded, and many people were given unaccustomed work. With air support, we still felt confident about the next attack. A thousand rounds a gun, we heard, but Gordon intended to fire as many as possible, for ammo was plentiful. 66 would use only one Vickers, mobile and moving with their Column; someone would have an unenviable job with the weight on that difficult terrain. Just before dawn, beds were hurriedly vacated as shots cracked – just a few nuisance bullets around hammock height . . . definitely not cricket!

To take position the Gunners had to cross the road, and reached it with Gordon and Spot leading. Jabbering began, for it was plain that we'd be seen from the hill. 'If they recognise the Vickers we'll be plastered,' I said.

'Can't be helped. I was pinpointed,' said Gordon. 'I'll go first.' He walked on to the road, upright! Instantly a bullet spat past his head, and like a kangaroo he leaped across, with Spot thinking it no end of a lark, but the rest of us didn't need an order to find a less hazardous crossing.

Reaching 43, we were told bluntly to keep low or the Japanese would pepper the area. Already camouflaged, we crept forward and mounted the guns 200 yards from the enemy. With my mouldy bush hat tasteful with greenery and the Vickers aimed at six o'clock of the shaving brush tree, I awaited the buzz of planes. In vain. An African crawled up to say that the air strike was off – weather at Base impossible. A crushing blow.

Barker's first mortar shattered the depressed silence, and we pumped long bursts into the hill, with Chinese shells helping. The riflemen were now getting as close as they could go to the hilltop, and I'd arranged to signal and help them keep direction in the bush, by making the gun 'stutter'. Later Moman Jaruwa said that 'Dogo he make de gun talk like a man do sing – bom diddy bom bom, bom-bom', and named me 'Sarakin Mai Ruwa' (King of the Machine-Gun).

The Vickers were faultless – no other Infantry weapon could have surpassed their performance after such gruelling treatment. One stoppage only – a broken cartridge case. Iya Mubi and I expended thousands of rounds, the bullets cutting great swathes through the undergrowth and leaving us exposed; we were too busy to become scared. Yet, when we ceased firing and lugged the guns away from the swathes, enemy shots cracked past us. No-one was hit. 200 yards. The defenders were either shocking marksmen or punchdrunk!

Again the platoons forced their way upwards but, unfortunately, the enemy were thoroughly dug in. Like the Gurkhas, they weren't content with slits, but delved deep enough to stand, with bamboo platforms to keep feet dry. With no wire, they cut bamboo stakes with razor-sharp edges, then built snipers' nests and O.P.'s in trees. And, if ordered not to retreat or be taken captive, every fanatic had to be killed – surrender was disgrace.

This was what our weakened platoons faced, and even while the battle was raging I could sense the attack failing – they had no chance. Some reached the stakes, but no further, the enemy pouring fire on every movement. The African sergeant with the mobile Vickers was doing valiant work, but the inevitable happened and the assault was called off.

*   *   *

There, but for the grace of God . . .

On our dispirited way back we met Colonel Upjohn, commanding 66, who told us that No. 12 had suffered heavy casualties, and almost immediately we saw one as four Nigerians approached with a laden stretcher. One of the bearers spoke quietly: 'Sergie Freebody ya mutu.'

'Dead . . . and I was in his original place. I felt sick. But for a twist of fate I'd be on that stretcher now. Freebody had crawled to help a wounded man and was shot through the head. We buried him, with many Africans, at the ill-fated former H.Q., that was now a cemetery. More wounded, including Potter, were evacuated to the field hospital. Five Europeans lost in 24 hours. Adding to our depression, fires were forbidden, and after putting out a listening-post, Gordon felt so uneasy that we entered our hammocks fully clothed and shod, to be jerked awake by a lengthy burst from a machine-gun – no casual shooting. Gordon shouted, and in my hurry I turned the hammock over and struggled like a fish in a keepnet, forgetting that the zip was now on the other side. Frantic, I fought free as a blaze of fire came from the hill – rifles, automatics, mortar spits. 'Take a gun!' yelled Gordon. It was already loaded; I had merely to press the thumbpiece, and was on the point of doing so when just in time I recognised bush hats on the dim figures that were approaching. They were Dan-Boy and the listeners, including Zaki. Something whispered over and there was a red flash and a bang. I felt a searing pain at my knee and ankle, and as it eased a little I saw that Dan-Boy was upright but that the other three had fallen. They moved, groaning. I couldn't discover where Zaki had been hit – he replied with grunts.

The deafening racket ceased, to be replaced by the ominous sounds of people moving through the scrub and along the road; some Nigerians were withdrawing. In the gloom, Gordon and I stared towards the Gunners, who stared back, making no move. 'Guns close together, Dogo,' ordered Gordon quickly and when it was done brought the men into a group just behind, with spare numbers attending the wounded. One uninjured chap began whimpering, a most disturbing sound, until Dan-Boy slapped his face with a noise like a shot; brutal but effective.

Macauley materialised from the left. 'Two sections have hopped it, Hugh.'

'Get the rest together, Mac. If you're left alone, join us.' Mac departed. 'Dogo,' went on Gordon, 'we'll take the guns if we have to go. If we're forced to abandon them, grab your lock. I'll attend to the other. Now have a quick dekko at our right flank.'

Almost at once I tripped over an unattended Bren. Half of Sergeant Lacey's platoon had gone, he told me. Barlow was there, with just one man and all his signals equipment. Several chaps were hurrying along the road, all convinced that the 'Japans' were attacking. I tried to stay them and they ran.

Back at my gun, I imagined every bush to be moving. Dan-Boy, gripping his bomb, was beside me, and Gordon, showing no fear, and with his Captain Kettle beard jutting pugnaciously, was with Iya Mubi. Moans sounded from behind us.

Had the enemy followed up their bombardment, we'd have

been over-run. Probably they were paying us back for our two attacks. Men began trickling back. The panic had begun when one or two had been unable to withstand the volume of fire. The mortars left as one, with Barker and Hoppy vainly trying to stop them. Muleteers departed, but H.Q. remained. Cameron, nearest to the hill, saw his platoon leave en masse. One man returned, and got behind a Bren with Sid. After defiantly emptying a few magazines into the hill, they stayed. What guts to stick there only yards from the enemy. Sid Mew would have made a splendid officer.

At dawn, during a jittery stand-to, there was another wretched moment when Spot made one of his periodic scampers across no-man's land. A single shot sounded, followed by an agonised yelping. Our pal didn't reappear.

The wounded left at stand-down. Bisali Keffi and Audu Damlin were hit in the body, while Zaki had an ugly wound in the jaw – half his teeth had gone. He couldn't reply when I spoke. 'Thank you for everything, Zaki. I hope we meet again.' We never did. Off they went in a jeep. Harwood patched me up. I'd received three small splinters, but the punctures hardly bled. My jungle sores were a greater nuisance. Sid, too, had stopped a bit of shrapnel with his back; like the kick of a mule, he said.

Stalemate. We couldn't attack, and neither could the Japanese by all appearances. I glanced wearily around – would we never get out of this green hell? And soon afterwards came welcome mail, with many more schools' letters. The simple, loving messages helped to preserve my sanity.

*   *   *

Music, the greatest gift we know,
And all we have of Heaven below.

I spoke to Barlow, who was looking ghastly, and he handed me his headphones. News was coming through. The Allies were advancing in Europe and flying-bombs still dropping on England. Then I heard music – Bach's 'Air on the G String', and felt with Keats that a thing of beauty was a joy whatever the circumstances.

Air drops continued, including rice and spuds, of little use without fires. We also took a jaundiced view of leather soles and heels sent without hammer and nails! I got new boots to replace the jungle ones, now extremely porous, and Moman Jaruwa won the ensuing scramble. I warned him of their condition, but from that moment until we lost him I never saw those things off his feet – he'd strut around admiring their length.

The Chinese shelled spasmodically, but the Japanese were now cock-a-hoop, taking full advantage of the impasse. Besides haphazard shots to harry us, they machine-gunned the defenceless Dakotas, and when the dropping site was moved, artillery followed it. Worst of all, they brought in a high-velocity gun that greatly upset the Africans, who were used to hearing a boom, with time to take cover before the shell arrived. This new, low-trajectory horror savoured of ju-ju – a sudden loud hiss being cut off by a stunning crash. The missile was small, but exploded with ear-splitting force, and the first one landed in Lacey's platoon. An African rose and ran, blood pouring from a shattered hand, and half his comrades followed. Lacey stood upright as more shells hissed and burst, and when Gordon and I added our exhortations to his the men stopped and returned.

But now came welcome relief when Mustangs unexpectedly appeared, and dive-bombed the hill while we watched the bursts and huge lumps of earth scattering. Finally the Americans emptied their cannons before roaring away, and there wasn't a sqawk from the hill, or the ju-ju, for the rest of that day.

Under cover of darkness the Column withdrew. Our new gun sites were near a junction on the road, and at dawn there was trepidation. The road here was quite straight, and the point where it crossed the shoulder of the hill was held by the enemy –they had only to fire along the road for the shots to land in our midst, and Gordon asked in vain for another move. An American officer arrived, spotting for the Chinese artillery, and collared a big tree for an O.P. A shelling duel became solo when his telephone line was smashed. Down he came, cursing his luck after locating three enemy guns. 'Never mind,' he called, 'we'll paste 'em when this line's repaired,' then departed in a hurry as the Japanese salvos continued. By a thousand to one chance a shell struck the tree, richocheted and burst. It killed Captain Kettridge, a Brigade officer who was passing and with no hole to dive into.

A yell, and everyone scattered as Japanese appeared on the road and strolled to and fro with sublime arrogance. All could have been wiped out, but we held fire; a Vickers section would have been blasted. The enemy disappeared, glancing over their

shoulders towards us. 'Show's over,' Gordon grunted. 'Get
those guns dug in before dark.' And of course, soon after that
was done, orders to move arrived!

The new position, away from the road, held undergrowth but
few trees. Abu claimed two for his master, leaving only one
other pair suitable for my hammock. A mule had been interred
between them and bones were visible, but at this stage I wasn't
squeamish. These stunted trees had orange-sized fruit with peel
like wood, and every time I turned over in bed there were bangs
on the roof.

Bumping into 43's position, a probing enemy patrol lost a
man, and in the small hours a lone figure approached, armed
with nothing more lethal than a shovel to bury his friend.
Instead of the African listening-post pouncing on the chap, they
shot him full of holes from point-blank range. Major Carfrae's
Column and the enemy facing him made a habit of mortaring
each other before breakfast, and Carfrae also lost a European,
killed by an unopened 'chute.

Sid still being well forward, I crept out for a word during one
lull and noticed interesting happenings on the hill. One fellow
was breaking wood, and another tending a fire. 'Look at 'em!' I
exclaimed in amazement.

'Yes,' replied Sid, peering through the leaves, 'and I could do
with a drop of whatever they're brewing.'

'But . . . they're sitting ducks.'

'You pipe down!' grinned Sid. 'Tacit agreement. We leave
them alone and they don't bother us!'

Point taken! I 'piped down', leaving Sid and Co. to their quid
pro quo. Learning that fires were again allowed, I took tea out to
the post after dark. Suddenly we both jumped as voices
sounded from the hill; 'Mutamen baki, tafi biya,' and astonished
comments burst from Sid's men. 'Stone me!' he said. 'Wasn't
that Hausa?'

'Yes: "Black men go back".' Although the tones were much
too high-pitched to be Nigerian, there was no doubting that the
captured section had been utilised.

Mustangs were now strafing the hill daily, but the enemy
artillery was not silenced. It stopped when it was wet, but
directly the rain ceased we baled water from our slits in
readiness for the inevitable bong. After a time the Chinese
would retaliate, and at least one European would crawl from his
soggy funkhole in delirious relief – life was still sweet.

There were remarkable escapes. A shell ripped hammocks at

the Aid Post, leaving sick men unhurt, and another wounded a
man on the road. Harwood coolly went out to tend him in the
open while other projectiles landed. He and Tait would soon
have even more to do do, for hopes of evacuation from the lake
had been abandoned, and the sick were being escorted towards
us. So much nasty hardware was falling around Tait's patch that
unnecessary movements towards it were stopped, and I was
accosted by an indignant Abu. 'White man himsay no agree for
me see my sick brudder. Himsay must take pass.'

'See Mr Gordon.'

'Mr Gordon he go bath. Sergie Dogo put name for dis?'

Keeping a straight face, I scribbled another, for his effort read:
'Private Abu Bamenda has permission for the proceeding to
pass absent from the military duty for the purpose of the
proceeding'. Off went Abu for the purpose of the proceeding,
and without doubt that scarred road to Kamaing saved the lives
of many; some had to be lifted into the jeep. There was plenty of
food, but the appalling weather was proving more deadly than
the Japanese, and a spate of evacuations began. Cameron left, a
shadow of his former self, and was followed by Barlow, Barker,
Hazelwood and Macauley. All R.A.F. personnel had gone, with
Corporal Cody the one remaining Sapper. When Pomeroy
went, Dickson quit the post of Animal Transport Officer to
assume Second-in-Command, and Miles himself looked
ghastly.

With each European went some Africans, and those remaining had to adapt. Hoppy and I were to lay ambushes with Brens
– queer roles to say the least! The Gunners went first, a Burrif
leading us on a detour before approaching Hill 60 from a flank
and stopping by a junction. I was told to put one ambush a few
yards along a track leading to the right, and the other on the
main one, but another hundred yards nearer the hill. 'You're on
your own now, sergeant,' grinned the Burrif, and left.

'Thanks for nothing, mate!' I thought, then with one team
pussyfooted the longest hundred yards I'd ever known – we
could hear sounds as though defences were being strengthened.
Soon we reached yet another fork and a small sign painted with
Japanese characters, but crept on past bits of discarded uniform
and busted boots before I posted the men quietly. 'If Japans
come, suh, what t'ing we do?' queried Moman Jaruwa, and I
said that if there were only one, to capture him from behind. If
more, to shoot as many as possible, then gudu (run).

'Make I stay for dis place, suh?' pleaded Dan-Boy.

'You stay with *me*, sergie!' What would that blood-thirsty merchant have done if given a free hand? He and I went back to the other team, wrenching away the sign-post en passant. They whispered that there was a 'Japan' in a hole a little way along the path and they thought he was 'mutu'. Blimy, yes . . . *very* mutu, and the second ambush was laid under the mute gaze of the sightless eye sockets.

Brigade translated the sign-post – directing stragglers from the mountains to Hill 60. For sheer cheek it was a classic. Brigade were also holding a prisoner who had surrendered voluntarily. Unprecedented. God help him if his Emperor heard about it!

These ambushes were laid in daylight only, with Dan-Boy and I shuttling between the posts. Once I looked back and noted that his bomb had no pin in it; a stumble and there could have been dire results. One morning the dead Japanese had gone, so Hoppy and I became ultra-cautious for a time. Later there was sudden movement ahead and a loud bang. A bullet cracked past my head and Dan-Boy and I fell flat, but instead of lobbing his grenade he got up shouting angrily – the shot was from one of the escort bringing the Indawgyi sick, and my equilibrium wasn't restored by all the laughter. 'I sorry truly,' said the firer. 'I t'ink you be Japan.'

'Do I *look* like a bloody Japan?' I snarled, clutching my bushy black beard, then the man's grin vanished when Dan-Boy threatened to thump him.

The sick, of all nationalities, were a piteous sight, the worst cases being head-carried by 6th Battalion Nigerians. Some walking were on the point of collapse, but cheered a little on hearing that the road wasn't far away. I now received a great shock when Keevil spoke, for the blonde giant had shrunk and I hadn't recognised him. Sickness was again his enemy.

Near that day's end I was between ambushes when feet suddenly pounded, and there was a 'ping' from the flying lever as Dan-Boy's grenade was flung and he dragged me down. As the explosion half stunned me, he rose and dashed into the bush, rifle ready . . . to return sheepishly. 'Nama, suh.' (meat, or animal.)

He'd been itching for weeks to use that bomb. Explanations at the Column for all the banging brought laughter – all too rare these days.

Rain was now draining into the chaung from slopes holding dead mules, but fortunately we had lemon flavouring to help fight the horrid taste of chlorinating powder. Just then, if you can understand my meaning, our main bit of cheer was the knowledge that the Japanese were even more miserable. We heard that Lentaigne was to visit us, and we waited expectantly. However, like Billy Bunter's famous postal order, he didn't turn up. What a difference it might have made had Wingate been alive to galvanise us!

Spotting for the Chinese guns, a cheeky Yank in a light plane cocked a daily snook at the hill. The enemy had no A.A. weapon, but nevertheless threw everything they had at him without success. They were taking such a pounding with shells and bombs that it was thought they could be withdrawing at dawn and reoccupying at night, but patrols met a hot reception. Sergeant Roberts reached the stakes, and Sid tried to turn a flank until fired upon. He passed the body of Mathews, and said his chaps were game to retrieve it after dark. I told him to include Dan-Boy and myself, for the thought of Mathews lying out there was abhorrent. Miles referred us to Brigade, who refused permission. Understandable, for we were desperately short of personnel now. Death must also be taking toll of the Japanese, for vultures hovered over the hill during dry spells.

Our own wastage continued, and it was a tiny group of white scarecrows that gathered for the evening conferences. Tough Rhodesian Roberts had to leave, with huge jungle sores, and on going along to have my own rot dressed I learned that the indefatigable M.O. had at last collapsed and departed. Captain Graham Tait, actually a son of the Rector of the High School of Stirling. No other mortal could have done more for his men. Harwood had joined up with 43's doctor, who told me (satirically I fancied) that I was the fittest man he'd seen for weeks. Lacey went next, having performed a platoon commander's job since White City. He didn't get an extra penny, but never moaned about it.

Chinese and Indians were now encamped on the road behind us, and there were accidents – on one black day a European, an African and a Gurkha were killed by free drops. As a minor diversion an earth tremor occurred in the small hours; I thought someone was shaking my hammock as a shower of fruit descended.

The only bright moments were when mail arrived, with mine in bulk! What an uplift these letters proved. I also received a magnificent one from young Sylvester – the pro. must have charged him a day's pay!

Dear Dogo Sir,
    Your letter is received, read, and noted. All this time I have
been expecting for your cablegram which shall have tell for me
the joyful news of your return, but now I see that you are not
even prepared. What is all this foolish talk? There never was a
time in which you do not make me happy but not this time. If you
could tell me of your return to Nigeria, I shall be coming to you,
never matter how far it is. I often see you in my dreams, while at
times you have charming smiles and saying things to me. But oh,
Sir, this is not sufficient, it not being a practical one. I wish we see
face to face. Your loveth servant is ever waiting upon you with
warm reception. Many others are saluting you with best compliments, and I express my spiritually divided sufferings with you.
My work is going steadily, and what of yours? It is we hear from
many quarters that you are confounding the Japanese by your
masterpiece of low pressure cunning. Good. Your departure was
actually a blow to me, but as departure is lot to mankind, so I will
harbour this in my heart coolly. May God the Omnipotent guide
you safely to the pink of health. The said watch and fountain pen
I have noted what you said and wish you to succeed, because I
am pocketless. Can we get some pictures, please, against your
homecoming and delayed return? I shall be expecting yours
towards next coming mail. I will close by sending ten times
double hundred greetings from all at Enugu. Though you have
gone, I shall not forget you. In my dreams and prayers, you will
always be remembered.

        Yours in love and service your servant,
        Sylvester Oparah

'Blimey, Dogo! You sure this ain't from a woman?' demanded
Hoppy, reading it.

CHAPTER SIXTEEN

'War is Hell'*

Hoppy reappeared, unusually animated. 'Official rumour. Going out!'

True, and even more interesting when I learned that the 36th Division was encamped 5 miles north. They included the 9th Royal Sussex, and I hadn't seen nephew Tommy Jones since the war began. With permission from Major Miles I set out, carrying only my carbine. Soon I passed the field hospital, constructed entirely of white, uncamouflaged parachuting, dazzling in the sun and an eloquent tribute to the complete mastery of the U.S. Air Force in this area; we hadn't seen an enemy plane for weeks. How lucky we were to have escaped the bombing that could have been the last straw, and how those fellows on Hill 60 must resent the absence of their own kites!

British troops who saw me grinned widely. No haircut or shave for months, trousers rolled up to the knees, bush hat shoved up into a dome for coolth, and every square inch of clothing smothered with rich Burma chocolate. In fact I resembled anything but a member of a corps d'élite.

After favouring me with a prolonged gape, the Royal Sussex Adjutant sent for C.Q.M.S. Jones. Tom was a lance-jack when called up, but now, if we hadn't been on active service, I'd have to stand to attention. He arrived, passing me with a puzzled stare. 'What's up, Tom?' I called.

He came back, then stammered: 'Why . . . you old bleeder!'

'Uncle to you,' I said sternly.

'I thought you were in Nigeria.'

'I was. You won't believe this, but I'm one of the *crème de la crème* – a Shitty Chindit.'

* General William Sherman

'What? *You*, in that lot?'

At his quarters I appraised, and envied, all the signs of a rear supply line – they even had transport to carry their packs. I saw people I'd known of old, and also overheard compliments. I was an old bastard, a bloody ape, and the Wild Man of Borneo . . . the Royal Sussex hadn't changed much! The C.O. walked by, faintly resembling the former Lieutenant Oliver, who'd carried the Colour at Buckingham Palace years before. 'Yes,' agreed Tom, 'that's him.'

'Bet he doesn't recognise one of his escorts!' I muttered, as the C.O. gave an amused backward glance. 'Well, I must get back for stand-to.' A few old pals made a rather rowdy group when seeing me off near H.Q., and I was about to push off when someone referred facetiously to my 'peashooter'. It's an American Underwood carbine,' I told him. 'As for peashooting, the calibre's .30.'

'Yankee, eh,' said Tom. 'Let's have a dekko.' And I should have had more sense than than to relinquish the weapon to someone after Sid's own heart. 'Where's the safety catch?' he asked, handling the carbine lovingly.

'There. It pushes in. Don't touch – look *out*!' So help me if he didn't pull at the trigger . . . bang! A fan of dirt shot up from the road. Stunned silence was followed by a yell of mirth from everyone except Tom, myself, and H.Q. Over came the R.S.M. to take Tom's particulars after giving me a frosty, unnerving glare. It reminded me of Wellington Barracks and the nick. A jeep came along and I thumbed it!

*   *   *

Incredibly, reinforcements had come during my absence. A Lieutenant Clarke joined Sid, and a C.S.M. Booker took Potter's place. We heard the battle plans for the impending Infantry attack. The South Wales Borderers would tackle the left flank, and the Royal Sussex would assault the hill itself. 'Take it from me,' I assured everyone who would listen, 'the hill's going *this* time!'

At sunset I was making up my diary, and didn't move as fast as usual at an enemy bong, then flung myself upon the mule's bones as a dud shell smothered me with dirt. Sid and Gordon ran to help. 'Gosh! Thought they'd got you,' said Sid. 'Did you hear it coming? They say you can't if it's right in line.'

'They're liars,' I grunted. 'I heard that bastard all right.' I began to collect my scattered paper.

'Writing again?' queried Gordon. 'How about a book on this lot?'

'It's an idea, but let me quote: "I have fears that I may cease to be, before my pen has gleaned my teeming brain".'

'Swinburne,' guessed Sid.

'Keats,' amended Gordon.

'You've been on about Keats before,' remarked Sid. 'Why him?'

'He was a Cockney, for one thing. Ain't that good enough reason?'

Another shock that night when my hammock rocked and the voice of Moman Jaruwa spoke urgently. To our disquiet he had been behaving very strangely of late, and now said that while on sentry someone had flung a piece of wood at him. 'Japans don't throw wood, Moman,' I said testily.

'No be Japans, suh. Him inside dis Column. De man want slap me for nutting's sake. Sergie Dogo come look please?' I found nothing, of course, and finally left him muttering to himself and with safety-catch forward. I prayed that he'd also keep the rifle aiming forward!

A big air strike took place on the day before the attack – why not on the day itself? Anyway, it was most spectacular – Mustangs, Thunderbolts, and Mitchells. The last-named dropped some 500 pound bombs, including a stick of duds. Those that did explode flung debris far and wide. Moman, uninterested and with his back turned, saw a chunk fall near him. He glared at me, his thoughts easy to read.

Suspecting that the Sahmaw sugar factory chimney was an O.P., the British Brigadier asked that it be destroyed, and again the Yanks obliged. Not only did they flatten the chimney, but completely wrecked the factory for the second time, just when the Japanese in the rear were ready to restart production. Sugar was a valuable commodity, and they'd been sweating at repairs for months.

All was now set for next day, but during the night Ricketts sent patrols to discover whether the hill had been abandoned. They were there all right, dug in like moles, and resisted furiously. Later, when the attack began, the high-velocity gun opened up – it hadn't been in action for some time and we'd thought it destroyed. As the Royal Sussex struggled through the boggy approaches a short monsoon shower broke. When that ceased they charged, my blood tingling at their shouts. Hill 60 fell, but many Sussex lads fell too. Every defending fanatic perished, for those not killed in the assault destroyed themselves rather than be captured. But, on the left, the South Wales Borderers met a murderous ambush where there was little cover, the enemy blasting them with every conceivable weapon. They were unable to tend the wounded, or even move, until the hill was taken, when all other Japanese, not under 'stay and die' orders, departed hotfoot for Sahmaw.

12 and 43 took over as the Royal Sussex pursued, and an appalling sight lay before us. Some Japanese were cut to pieces by explosions, and one who'd committed hara kiri or asked a comrade to kill him had a bayonet pushed into his eye. There, too, was a small heap of bones that could have been Spot, but at least Mathews could now be given a decent burial.

That was Hill 60, and here are extracts from their officer's diary:

> Owing to the constant artillery fire, the hilltop is now bare of foliage, giving no concealment. Most of us are delirious with lack of sleep and deaf from the thunderous bombings. Some are shell-shocked and dazed.
>
> Our food supply is being bombed away daily. From now we have nothing to eat. We are just existing by drinking river water. It is obvious that men are literally falling from exhaustion, yet we are holding on day after day hoping that help will come.
>
> Sergeant Kinoshita and Corporal Yamada contracted beri-beri. As long as there is a drop of blood left in us we will not give up.

*   *   *

43 collared the summit, and they were welcome to it! Anticipating a counter attack from Sahmaw, 12's Vickers were dug in near the stick of dud 500 pounders – God help us if one were hit. A Royal Sussex man was lying there, and we buried him. Behind the summit were stacks of enemy shells and equipment, and clothing held wads of useless paper money for 'trading' with the Burmese. In one small cave Sid discovered a rusty spring bed – the officer's? There wasn't an item of food anywhere.

In front, strange Africans appeared and began digging, and I went out to pinpoint their positions in case of night-firing. 'Hallo, ye long streak!' I heard, and there stood grinning Jock. He took me along to Major Carfrae, whose beard was as big and bushy as my own. Jock's motto had been 'better safe than sorry'. Leading a patrol, he shot a signaller laying wire, then laid an ambush. Sure enough a party came along and Jock, himself behind a Bren, let them almost reach the weapon. It fired one round and jammed, the Japanese fleeing. 'Did you chase 'em?' I asked, enthralled.

'*Chase* 'em? We were running the ither bluidy way!'

Gordon had found a fellow-countryman in Sid's new officer, so we two were left much to ourselves. We wandered behind the hill, and soon I was wishing we hadn't. Old sites showed that guns had been moved frequently, and several tree O.P.'s gave a full view forward – no wonder the shelling was accurate. Several fox-holes had a *rear* outlook only, so that a bullet in the back rewarded the unwary. Carfrae's men found a wounded Japanese in one of them, and couldn't take him until he fainted.

The left flank, where the South Wales Borderers had been ambushed, was horrifying. The enemy had lined a chaung, and had cut great swathes through the grass with automatics. Flattened stalks showed how trapped men had tried to crawl from the murderous fire – to us it seemed incredible that any had escaped at that point-blank range. Along the chaung bank had been painstakingly dug holes, like caves. Undoubtedly this had been their intended monsoon line, with Hill 60 an outpost that they didn't expect to relinquish.

This ambush must have been hellish for the Borderers wounded, and the dead had been hurriedly placed in craters for the time being, steel helmets marking the spots. By a wrecked limber three mules formed a nightmare group of contorted immobility, one with neck stretched taut in a last paroxysm. Further on, the enemy themselves had had havoc wreaked upon them, with corpses in communal graves only partly covered – the Japanese must have indeed been pressed. Four men lay symmetrically around a small crater, and what the vultures had left was swarming with maggots, the air above a black canopy of flies. Three months before, the stench from that fetid mass would have made me retch, but now I regarded it almost impassively. Someone had performed the nauseating task of searching the bodies; letters and photos were scattered. Family men, like myself. They'd died for their Emperor and Country, but those who extol the 'glory and glamour' of war should have been with Sid and me as we looked upon some of its hideousness – lifeless remains of what so shortly before had been living, breathing humanity. I glanced at Sid; his face was expressionless. This new callousness – what on earth was happening to us? 'God made man in His own image,' I muttered involuntarily.

'What was that?' asked Sid.

I repeated it, indicating the obscene spectacle before us, then the nightmarish tableau of mules. 'And those poor inoffensive animals, Sid. If there *is* a God, wouldn't He end all this?'

'Don't blame God,' was the prompt reply. *'We're* making our own hell. You know, Dogo, I reckon God won't need to come and destroy the world . . . man will do it for Him.' At that, I dropped the controversial subject.

More bodies, and a queer find in a pocket alarm clock bearing the name of a leading London jeweller. Then, as several vultures flapped away, we came to the final horror – a spreadeagled, headless Japanese who'd been cleanly decapitated by a knife, or sword. I grabbed the enemy flag that hung by the corpse – bold characters were painted on it. This souvenir must certainly be hidden to thwart confiscation! There was no sign of the severed head, and Sid looked up at the darkening sky. 'Had enough?'

'Just about!'

Translated later, the words on the flag read: 'Attention all men of the Imperial Japanese Army – Nagasake Regiment – Take Regiment'. It looked as though the man must have offended against the strict Army code and was executed. The flag is now in the Imperial War Museum, London.

Meanwhile, around midnight, some enemy crept towards us with a machine-gun and, with two huge landmarks to help, swept the hilltop with fire. 43 were shot up, and among casualties was R.S.M. Bolland. Confusion was also caused by individual runners coming back to contact their British rear elements, and with a total absence of Hongkong Johns, etc., every response to challenges had to be checked. There were still pockets of Japanese around – the Black Watch surprised a party at breakfast and annihilated them with bayonets. There was Artillery retaliation from Sahmaw, many shells falling on the road, but soon the Japanese in the town realised the danger of being surrounded, and scarpered. A 43 patrol met resistance from only one man, who defiantly lobbed grenades until killed.

While parties were tidying the late battlefield, Sid and I crossed country to explore abandoned Sahmaw. In one house Sid crashed both hands upon the keyboard of a piano, one of the easiest things to booby-trap, I should think. In a bedroom I was confronted by a repulsive apparition – myself in a full-length mirror. After we'd inspected the wrecked factory, in which lay a Japanese blown into three pieces, we returned home in time to find an ailing Hoppy awaiting the jeep, despondent at being evacuated at this late stage. Moman Jaruwa was also there. He'd repeatedly told Gordon that I'd 'thrown things' at him, and Gordon deemed it expedient to send him to the M.O. However, Moman was quite affable. After asking permission to take away the jungle boots he said that he hadn't really objected to 'Sergie Dogo's' bit of play. It was a real tragedy; Moman was a great lad. We could only pray that his treatment would prove efficacious. And now, of all people, Jock came shambling along. 'Hail and farewell,' he growled morosely. 'I'm oot!'

'What? With all that campaign experience?' I said. 'What's up?'

'I wouldna mind if it was something worthwhile . . . bluidy malaria!' To my surprise, Gordon shook hands warmly with Jock. They were both in the Gordon Highlanders and already acquainted, Definitely an occasion, and when I produced my rum-bottle Jock wasn't too ill to take a swig. 'I nearly forgot to tell ye,' he said. 'Your pal Carfrae got an M.C. for bashing that convoy.' The jeep began to jolt away. 'See ye in Bombay!' yelled Jock.

In our waving group was the Padre, still sticking it grimly with 43. He intended holding a memorial service at the cemetery, and I was at my diary when Sid passed on his way there. How could a man remain so unswervingly in his faith after what he'd recently seen? Yet I'd realised long before that my friend was far removed from Shakespeare's 'oath-filled' soldier. His most explosive 'oath' was 'Stone me!' and after the war I wasn't surprised to find that he was an official in the 'Boys' Brigade'. But now, looking after him, I felt strangely envious, also guilty. I hadn't attended a church parade since they'd ceased to be obligatory many years before. Although I hadn't seen much action, I'd had a full share of good fortune since being recalled. Could it all be attributed to luck? Suddenly I was stowing away my diary, and following Sid.

*   *   *

With far too much reserve ammunition to take out, the Gunners were given some practice! The mortars also shed some bombs, until a 'stray' whistled over to fall among 43, wounding two Africans. All 43 gathered on the hilltop and cursed in one ugly voice, and a message came from the British, now chasing the enemy south: 'What's all the bloody racket back there?' We were

then told to *bury* spare ammo, which seemed a criminal waste.
'The men must think we're insane!' muttered Gordon savagely,
as mud was shovelled on hundreds of rounds. He told me to
find out why Gamadadi Ambusa was dodging this chore, and I
discovered the truant busy at an unsavoury place where puddles were greenish. Rain was exposing hastily interred enemy
bodies, and the grinning Gamadadi was searching for gold
teeth.

Gordon and Bell left for a job at the reception camp awaiting
us, and Harwood went to the 6th Battalion, who were sent out
first. Our turn now, and with Mogaung only 14 miles distant
everyone felt cheerful, but although spirits were willing, flesh
proved weak indeed. It was unexpectedly sunny, the hottest
since the monsoon began. Combining with extreme humidity
and a treacle-like road surface, it caused a spate of falling-out
after the very first routine halt. It puzzled me, for I was feeling
very fit – all that sugar I'd been scrounging? I was able to
relieve the staggering Iya Mubi of his pack for a spell. One
after another the Africans stumbled to the verge, and I could
see Miles, in the lead, saving energy by wading through
thigh-deep puddles instead of by-passing them. At the next
stop I told him that more than a hundred were left behind, and
he ordered a long halt. Reaction was taking toll of the strongest
– even young Sid admitted that he'd only just managed to keep
going. After we resumed, Oscar Minas collapsed, and later
overtook us in a jeep. We couldn't afford to lose Oscar, our
eyes and ears.

Failing to make Mogaung before dark, we halted and rested,
setting off again in the small hours when it was moonlit and
cool. Around dawn we crawled into the town that had been our
Mecca for so long; the distance of 80 miles from White City had
taken over three months.

Less than half the 500 Nigerians were left, while of the 40
white men only 6 remained – Major Harry Miles (Devonshire
Regiment), Captain Owen Harrison (Rhodesia), Oscar Minas
(Burmese Intelligence), Sergeant Sid Mew (Essex Regiment),
Corporal Cody (Royal Engineers), and yours truly (Royal Sussex
Regiment). Others who had made the grade were Lieutenant
Hugh Gordon (Gordon Highlanders), Regimental Quartermas-
ter Sergeant Bell (home unit not known), and Sergeant Har-
wood (Royal Army Medical Corps).

Surprisingly, the sun again began blazing – was the monsoon
ending with our departure? We made for the railway, where the

mules were unloaded, and to our consternation and ineffable regret were commandeered by more 14th Army personnel going into action. Before our own trek they had done sterling work with Calvert's Brigade, so this would be their third slog without a break. For those faithful, patient dokis, war seemed indeed a never-ending hell.

CHAPTER SEVENTEEN

Rehabilitation

The train consisted of two wagons and a flatcar, the 'locomotive' being a jeep, modified by the inventive Yanks. 200 bods and the stores were loaded, during which Miles collapsed in the hellish heat. The last African boarded, the signal for a scrambling invasion by Asiatic civilians – one train daily to Myitkyina and they didn't mean to miss it. I'd never seen rolling stock packed like it. Some sat on the steel wagon roofs; must have had asbestos buttocks. I accompanied the driver, who asked for men to sit on the bonnet – weight was needed. Jokingly I asked whether he'd given his 'engine' a name. 'Yes,' he laughed, 'the "Princess of Mogaung"!' Then, to prolonged clapping and cheering, this bizarre journey started, and although the jeep was derailed several times the bonnet-squatters soon replaced it.

At the rest camp near Myitkyina Station, Major Miles was too ill to unlace his boots. Oscar obtained for him a bed and net, with much food for us. The Nigerians had a bonanza when souvenir hunters almost fought for panic maps and other treasures, but my flag remained hidden. Dan-Boy, who probably flogged his spare explosives now there were no enemy to blow up, confronted me with a fistful of notes and said he'd like the little clock. No chance.

Next morning was again dry, with dustclouds, but who cared? That dust was being stirred by Dakota airscrews! True, we might be coming in again, but at the moment were about to leave the horror behind. Miles led, slowly and painfully, and reached the airfield with his weary Column, or rather the remnants of it. 'Forgotten' may be an exaggeration, but to the Second Expedition of Wingate's Force it held more than a modicum of truth. The General's plan was to fly out the Chindits before the monsoon broke, for after reaching safety every survivor was given a letter of appreciation. The first sentence read – 'You have come out from the middle of Burma'. The last – 'Have a good leave'. Although signed by Lentaigne, Wingate's successor, the date 26th April – *before* the monsoon – had not been amended. The letters were issued to us in late August. A consensus of opinion from the 'rank and file' was that many casualties and much privation could have been avoided.

> When you go home, tell them of us, and say –
> For your tomorrow, we gave our today.
> (From the Allied Cemetery at Kohima)

*　　*　　*

Airborne, Sid and I looked through the exit at a glimpse of the Irrawaddy, while a magnificent panorama of jungle-covered razor-backs passed majestically below – exactly like those so recently cussed. 'There's the Chindwin,' said Sid later, as the river for ever associated with Wingate swept into view. 'Y'know, Dogo, I can't realise that we're going out. Wouldn't be surprised if we don't!'

I didn't reply. Just then I was thinking of Freebody, and all those other good fellows for whom there would be no 'getting out'.

Sid spoke again: 'Going down, and wherever it is, I'm not shaving 'til I've found a photographer!' We were greeted by some American newsmen. 'Howdy?' said Sid. 'What's the name of this hole, chums?'

'Dibrughar.'

'Never heard of it. Which country?'

'Assam, buddy.' So we *were* out!

*　　*　　*

I didn't recognise Gordon – first time I'd seen him clean-shaven. I assured him that both guns were complete, and more prepared for another do than myself. A native barber began working against the clock, but we found our photographer. Oscar Minas, chin as smooth as a baby's bottom, plonked himself between us to 'balance' the picture. All our clothing and equipment, with their jungle bacteria, were incinerated, and during a glorious train ride across India we were feted at every stop; at one place they even hung lotus blossoms around our necks!

At Dhond I found that Zaki had left for Nigeria. We all entered hospital for observation – blissful eating and sleeping. I'd lost a stone, little enough compared to others. Teeth were my problem; all the sugar I suppose. I had half extracted and couldn't obtain dentures. Jock entered the ward while we were at dinner. 'Look at 'em! D'ye think this is the bluidy Ritz?'

'Fattening for the next slaughter,' I answered. 'Anyway, I expect you put away your full share.'

'Couldn' keep anything doon for a week. Ye're lucky. Some ha'e meat an' canna eat.'

'Beg pardon?' remarked Sid.

'I should ha'e known a bluidy Sassenach wouldna understand it! "Some ha'e meat, and canna eat, and some wad eat that want it; but we ha'e meat and we can eat, and so the Lord be thankit".'

'Sounds to me like Rabbie Burns,' grinned Sid the Sassenach.

'Right first time!' Jock was a lot livelier than at Hill 60. Soon he departed for his native Aberdeen, and although I wrote there was no response.

Anyway, Jock, wherever you are today, and especially if you married that mysterious lassie, lang may yer lum reek (long may your chimney smoke).

Obtaining some local leave, Sid and I tried golf, but the barefooted caddies had a unique method of speeding up learners whose balls went astray. The kids nipped on ahead to grip the ball with the undersides of their toes and convey it nearer to the hole. Both ingenious and infuriating – we found out too late!

One night I asked Sid to wind the little clock – he was nearest – and the next thing I heard was: 'Well, stone *me*!'

'Wassup?' I asked sleepily.

'Listen. "If lost, please return to Mrs Hooper, 11 Redford Avenue, Coulsdon, Surrey". You've had it, Dogo.'

Nosey blighter! Inquisitive fingers had prised away a stiff bit of card that I'd assumed was for strengthening. Later I learned that the clock had belonged to the lady's son. With the Borderers, he'd been badly wounded in the ambush and forced to abandon his equipment.

Back from leave, I was suddenly accosted by the Gunners, all jabbering at the same time. 'What's up, Dan-Boy?' I asked in bewilderment.

'Suh. Mr Gordon he go lib for die.'

'What? Are you telling me the truth?'

'Yessuh. We tell.'

'When was this?'

'Today, suh.'

It was true. After surviving that back-breaking march, Gordon had suddenly died. Soon, standing by the place where he lay, and numbed by the shock, I felt a hand on my shoulder; Dan-Boy had followed me, and I wasn't ashamed of my tears. Hugh Gordon was not a regular soldier – he worked in a bank – but was one of the finest officers I'd ever met, and I'd met many. Normally quiet and unassuming, he had given unswerving devotion to duty during the most exacting of circumstances. I was haunted by this tragedy.

* * *

The Nigerians spent their leave in batches at a camp near Poona, and I helped with the administration. Having spare time and a typewriter, I began a sustained attack on arrears of correspondence. Not wishing to bore the Camp Commander, Captain Harrison, with repetition, I put school's letters in special envelopes that by-passed his vetting. Soon I was marched before him, to see one of my efforts on his desk, together with a memo from the Base Censor that he read aloud: 'This B.N.C.O.'s letter is returned for your attention, having given a comprehensive account of his Burma experiences.' This puzzled me, for every place-name I'd mentioned had been published in the Command newsletter; some of us had sent copies home. I began to say so, but the Captain stopped me. 'I know, sergeant, and I'm taking no action. Tell me, how many schools are involved?'

'Twelve, sir, plus individuals who write separately.'

'Good God! You're a teacher, I take it?'

'No, sir. May I suggest using carbon copies, then you need only read the original.'

'Thanks very much!' he replied drily, and so the cheery and voluminous correspondence continued, though I wondered what the schools thought of my smudgy carbons; I was a two-fingered typist.

Some of the staff went to Poona races, and after five losers I decided on the last race favourite, putting on all I had left. With no bookmakers, in the melee at the single Tote window I gave the wrong number to find I'd backed an outsider. The hilarity of my companions changed to profane disgust when it won, and I came away with a pocket stuffed with rupees.

After their leave, the men were addressed by an Emir who'd made the long journey to congratulate them. Nigeria was proud of her sons, he told his beaming audience, but on adding that he hoped the war would soon end so that they could return to their villages there was consternation. Whispering changed to jabbering. Wah! Go back to their former primitive existence after all this money, food, and clothing? Nigerians usually love oratory and will listen for hours – but now many were walking away while the big man was still speaking . . . quite unprecedented. Would there be unrest in the Colony after the war? Following the Emir, there was an unsavoury lecture for Europeans, given by a Brigade Intelligence Officer. Although the war at home seemed to be approaching the end, Japan possessed a war potential 'as yet untapped'. Most depressing.

Next, an unexpected turn that caused people to refer to me as a lucky bastard – I was being repatriated! There were a few from other units, but I was probably alone from the 12th. Perhaps I was thought too ancient for another trek; probably correct! But although the prospect of going home was a heady tonic, I again felt much regret at leaving such good friends. That's one of the drawbacks in the Services, whether it's peace or wartime – you're so often saying goodbye to somebody. If only Gordon were alive, so that we could have met at reunions. Sid, Jock, Major Carfrae – unthinkable that I might never again see these grand people.

I joined a mixed crowd at Deolali Camp. It's Army legend that anyone staying overnight at this hole spends the rest of his life 'Doolally Tap' (*non compos mentis*). Hopes of Christmas at home were soon squashed, so I sent over a hundred airgraphs and paid for the lot. At long last, the boat, then infuriating orders confining us to camp the evening before boarding. With many others I used an 'escape route', and around midnight some of us packed a taxi to return. An argument started when a tipsy fellow demanded to be let in, then squatted behind the vehicle – it was necessary for the Indian driver to reverse. Someone noticed that the noisy chap's backside was against the exhaust, and fired the engine . . . I never thought a drunk could move so quickly! The fun wasn't over, for a jeep shot out of a side turning and clipped us, smashing a rear light. It was driven by an American who was also having a good Christmas. Laughingly admitting responsibility, he quietened our voluble driver by producing enough cash to pay our National Debt, with the query: 'How mush ya want, bud?'

CHAPTER EIGHTEEN

Bang Goes My Image

At Port Said the ship was held for two Scots going on compassionate leave, in such a hurry they'd brought only tropical kit. With no battledress on board, they'd arrive at the U.K. in midwinter. One of the crew was working overtime with needle and thread, and as an ex-Guardsman with no lack of swank I ordered Chindit titles to augment the official emblem and green hackle I'd carried in my pack through Burma. These should go down well at the schools. I'd written postcards ready to send on landing, and hoped to visit as many as possible.

An uneventful voyage was enlivened near the end when an 8th Army man, who had foolishly exhibited a very valuable diamond brooch that had been snaffled in Italy, was himself relieved of it by some 'loose wallah'. The infuriated victim secured an interview with the O.C. Ship, who with heavy sarcasm asked whether the skipper was expected to delay disembarkation while 20,000 kits and bodies were searched.

February. Greenock greeted us with a blizzard. First to leave were the two compassionates, still wearing drill but plainly unconcerned. Off they went to Dumfries. When our messdeck emptied, we made deep imprints on the snowbound railway platform, where ladies, bless their Scottish hearts, dispensed mugs of steaming char. In London, people glanced at me and nudged one another – Wingate hadn't yet faded from memory, although one dear old soul, after staring at my shoulder, told her pal that she'd thought Chindits were Chinese.

I hadn't been in my mother's house ten minutes before seven-year-old son and heir took me to a field where lay a dud flying-bomb. 'Don't be scared,' he said, as I eyed the ugly, twisted casing. 'They emptied it. I was hoping you might see one coming over, but they've stopped. You just watched, and if it started to drop you just lay flat. Rockets are worst. You only hear a crash. Dad, you're going bald.'

'Grass doesn't grow on busy streets, Brian.'

'No,' he grinned, 'it can't get through the concrete.' The permissive age had arrived, but he kindly added that the joke wasn't his own – he'd heard it at school. Meanwhile all was buzzing activity at the adjacent Biggin Hill airfield, and later, when a distant rumble of an exploding V2 sounded, people merely hesitated for a moment before walking on.

Within three days all my cards had been answered, one by telegram, and in some difficulty I worked out an itinerary. With a small case containing some essentials and mementoes, and feeling rather excited, I set off. What would these hundreds of youngsters be expecting? Undoubtedly a tall, handsome soldier, à la film and fiction. Well, the hero was tall enough, but thin on top, minus half his teeth, and on the wrong side of 40. Handsome indeed!

First, a convent school in Kent, where I hadn't reckoned to find so much fun and laughter. Then schools in Middlesex, Birmingham, Warwickshire and Staffordshire. In Cheshire 'Uncle Jim' had a deafening welcome, and in County Durham I descended a pit shaft, thankful that I wasn't a miner! Lastly, to distant Devon, where I sat (sideways) at a tiny desk, taking school dinner. My small companion, specially chosen as a London evacuee, was quietly informative in a delicious Cockney/West Country accent: 'Don't git up yet, mate – we ain't 'ad our arters.' Of course, I fell behind schedule, but visited all schools except one in Belfast. At the last, a 'Junior and Infants', the kids sang: 'Will ye nae come back agen?'

There had been one or two hiccups. One boy, assured that his letter had indeed arrived by parachute, asked whether I'd ever felt afraid, then waited in obvious perplexity as I hesitated. Dead silence when I finally admitted being scared on occasion. Again, a girl wished to know whether the stains on the Japanese flag were blood. No, she was told, just immovable monsoon mud. Again disappointment, but the most embarrassing moment was when an eager lad called out: 'Did you kill many Japs with your machine-gun?' Involuntarily I said that I hoped not. Bewilderment as another bit of my image went west – should I have lied?

On my return, Brian was hopping with impatience – my Enugu treasure chest had come. C.Q.M.S. Parry had indeed 'done his best' as promised, stencilling it as 'The Personal

Effects of Sergeant Shaw, Deceased'. Fortunately my repatriation had preceded it! Again the Customs had turned a blind eye.

Back to the Royal Sussex at Clacton; I had an attic to myself in an empty seafront house, and from this monastic eyrie watched the last doodlebugs coming in from over the North Sea. Some were intercepted and blown up with tremendous bangs. Then my odd jobs suddenly ceased. Someone at the Ministry of Information had seen a local news item from a school, and I was asked to give talks to adults. Soon I was being shuttled from one area to another, and at first found it difficult to speak in public until I learned that the moment I appeared in full Chindit regalia they were ready to listen to anything. At one place I was actually given a staff car with lady chauffeur and spoke to an audience of service-women – hundreds of female eyes boring into mine. At a large American camp in East Anglia a loudspeaker built me up as a 'British hero from Burma', and at Bath a guide told me that people outside the Pump Room were queueing to hear *me*; very ego-inflating!

It became routine not to book overnight accommodation. Someone would offer hospitality. The Chindit titles were magical – in buses and trams commuters would insist on paying my fare. But the tour was tiring. One early morning I fell asleep in a waiting room and missed a train. Perhaps I was entitled to a lie-in, for it was my birthday. The last had been spent in White City.

Suddenly Europe was the only thing that mattered, the lectures ending abruptly. The last was at Birmingham Chamber of Commerce, after which I dashed off to the village school at Little Bloxwich, on the edge of the Black Country, where they'd sung: 'Will ye nae come back agen?' I'd a date there to crown the May Queen. I also saw a Victorian instrument of torture called a 'Tawse', used instead of a cane. It was made of leather strips, but being a Junior school, the heaviest punishment was a moderate slap on the palm, with effect more psychological than physical. It had been used only once in the past five years . . . lucky kids.

*   *   *

Back at Clacton, I joined a party escorting German P.O.W.'s back to Newcastle-upon-Tyne. Buying two newspapers, I handed one to the captives, some of whom knew English. They were already aware that their Vaterland was on the point of capitulating, but as they read the headlines I could see no sign of hatred or bitterness. Like ourselves, their thoughts were of home, and an end to all the misery.

When war in Europe ended I was on leave. One place only on such a day – London's west end. The last time I'd traversed Birdcage Walk was 17 years before, leaving the regiment that had just ejected me. Here were the railings, but where was the Guards Chapel? Later I learned of its tragic end. A flying bomb made a direct hit while a service was in progress, and among the great number who lost their lives was the Chaplain himself.

Wellington Barracks hadn't altered, nor the guardroom where I'd set the chimney alight and often stood in scarlet and blue; this fellow on the gate was wearing sombre service dress. Turning away from that nightmare memory of long ago, I made for Buckingham Palace as cheering sounded. They weren't for His Majesty, but merely for the sentries who were being changed. Nobody had hoorayed when I was posted on Buck in the Twenties!

I joined a million others in the Mall, and in Leicester Square found people dancing. Uniformed men, even the mature like myself, were being kissed by strangers. Had I been wearing Chindit regalia I might not have emerged alive. Well, no more air raids, and Dover folk could once again sleep without shells whizzing across the Straits. Six years to beat the Nazis, so how many more to go against all that Japanese 'untapped war potential'? With another monsoon raging in Burma, Sid and co. wouldn't be dancing and kissing.

The excitement was too great, and after a severe malarial relapse I convalesced near Norwich. During a fete in the Cathedral grounds the nurses dressed me as a Teddy Bear to sell raffle tickets. After nearly suffocating in the heat I was saved by an affable gent's wallet – he purchased all my stock.

Although fighting went on in the Far East, the wartime Parliamentary Coalition at home was dissolved. Still disenchanted with politics, I didn't vote in the General Election. Labour won, with a working majority for the first time. How would they use it? Hardly had the King's Speech ended before the Commons erupted to the 'Red Flag', then taunts of: 'We are the masters now.' Shinwell proclaimed that 'anyone else wasn't worth a tinker's cuss', and Bevan referred to 'Tory vermin'. So, Merrie England, gird up thy loins – a new era was about to begin.

Suddenly all this was forgotten for a time when our Allies dropped the atomic bomb on Hiroshima, then another on Nagasaki when the enemy remained defiant. The reeling Japanese surrendered and we could hardly credit that it was all over.

No more war, vowed everyone. Never, never again. But unbelievably hardly had the nuclear dust settled before former comrades-in-arms began snarling at one another in Berlin. Would man's stupidity *never* cease? As far back as 1513 A.D. a peace-lover named Fragiovanni was pleading:

> 'The gloom of the world is but a shadow.
> Behind it, yet within our reach, is joy.
> There is radiance and glory in the darkness
> Could we but see, and to see, we have only
> To look. I beseech you to look . . .'

The poet might have added that if politicians were forced to fight with weapons instead of words, world disarmament would be assured, and that idea recurred to me years later. At a Commemoration Sunday service in Whitehall I felt sickened by the spectacle of political leaders laying wreaths at the Cenotaph, and uttering prayers for world peace, when at the same time we were sending arms to where African was killing African in the ghastly Nigeria–Biafra War. Could hypocrisy possibly go any further?

*   *   *

My chequered military service was about to end . . . or was it? I was being transferred to something called 'Z' Reserve. For Pete's sake! Were they actually expecting another bust-up?

Another exemplary character. I'd now collected two of those, plus a 'Good' and a 'Bad'. I'd settle for the average! Twenty years, four regiments, but overshadowed by that miserable exit from the Welsh Guards.

I nodded frostily to the Redcap outside the Release Centre, and was approached by a little fellow with a van. 'Give yer ten quid for yer box, sarge.' I stared; what was he on about? Inside, the place resembled a huge Quartermaster's Store, but despite tons of stuff there wasn't a trilby to fit my average-sized head, and they finally fobbed me off with a cloth cap – with a button on top. Never having possessed a pinstripe, I chose one. Everything was put in a big carton, for my uniform must be retained against this mysterious 'Z' Reserve. Again I was intercepted. 'Ten quid for yer box.' A tenner was a tidy sum in those days, and I hesitated before declining. 'Look, coupons too,' he wheedled, clawing sheets of them from a pocket; there must have been hundreds.

'D'yer print those yerself?' I asked interestedly.

'Don't be funny, sarge. I'm a dealer and git a quota. If I sold what's in that box —'

'For twenty quid?' I hazarded.

'Twenty? You're barmy!' he said pityingly. 'I was sayin' —'

'Tell yer what,' I interrupted. 'Sell yer a cloth cap cheap – no coupons.'

'Yer bloody won't!'

'It's better than yours – got a button on top.'

'Yer can stuff it!'

I grinned bravely down on his five-feet-nothing, noticed that the Redcap was getting interested, so staggered off. Obviously the spiv would be with us until all rationing had ended. Later, finding that my pre-war togs still fitted tolerably, I put the pinstripe into mothballs against the uncertain future.

* * *

Half an inch, half an inch, half an inch onward,
Nearer the grocer's shop crept the six hundred.
People in front of 'em, people behind 'em,
People all round 'em chattered and wondered.
Never a man afraid, never a girl dismayed,
Oh, what a queue they made –
Gallant six hundred. (With apologies)

Sid, back home, sent two invitations. One to his wedding, the other to be Godfather (!) should the vacancy arise. My former employer told me that I was welcome to restart before my leave expired. With wages plus Army pay the Taxman would find me doubly welcome, but schools' letters weren't decreasing and extra cash for postage would be handy.

Feeling restless after leaving my boss, I made for old East End haunts. A long walk, but if a Boy Scout cum Cadet cum Boy Soldier cum Guardsman cum Infantryman cum Park-keeper cum Chindit couldn't walk, who the heck could?

From the bomb damage en route, Berlin, said to be much worse, must look like a huge ruin. Whitechapel, Mile End, good old Bow. How different from the start of the century when we safely played on roads now teeming with traffic. Here was my tiny, terraced home of years ago, still showing the Zeppelin scars. Eerie. I could hear my mother's shrill: 'Jesse-e-e-e!' as I passed the door. Nearby was one of the German-owned shops looted by a mob in 1916 – I remembered the walloping I got for creeping out to watch it. Now Gran's house, where we'd held such roisterous parties. I looked at the homes of former classmates. Maybury, everyone's pal – his father kept a toffee shop. Prater, a fruiterer's son, equally popular. Legge, who played street soccer in clogs. Our favourite war cry was:

> We are the Knapp Road boys, we are the Knapp Road boys;
> We know our manners, we spend our tanners,
> We are respected wherever we may go.
> When we're walking down the Mile End Road, all the windows open wide;
> We know how to use our feet – Bom-diddy bom-bom, bom-bom,
> We are the Knapp Road boys.

I hadn't entered Knapp Road school since coming out of the gate, clutching my 'character', 30 years before. Could there possibly be any staff who would remember me, a type not easily forgotten? I'd find out, and if my name wasn't on the Roll of Honour board, it soon would be! Ahead loomed a railway bridge, with an ugly, unkempt cemetery beyond, but one prominent silhouette was not there – the big dome under which the hated school-bell had jangled. I stopped, aghast, at a great gap.

An old man slowly approached. 'What happened here, mate?' I asked.

'Doodle-bug done it.'

'Many killed?

'No. Breakfast time before kids arrived. The school got knocked about a bit before that but the doodle-bug finished it. Bastards!'

'It was *my* school,' I muttered.

He peered at me. 'Mine too. Bit before your time though, I reckon, lad. Bastards!' he repeated, and shuffled away.

CHAPTER NINETEEN

A New Era

Depressed, I headed for the Underground, then noticed people lining up quickly at a grocery. Already well-primed by female relatives, I surmised that something worthwhile was about to be sold off ration. 'What are we queueing for?' I asked the chap who'd beaten me by a short head.

'Rabbits.'

'Blast! Got no coupons.'

'Blimey, where've *you* been? No coupons for rabbits, *when* you can find 'em. Not even a bit of offal these days. It's this bleedin' Government.'

'Give 'em a chance, mate,' protested the little fat woman behind me. 'They ain't bin in five minutes.'

'Maybe, missus, but we 'ad plenty o' bread an' spuds when old Woolton was in charge o' grub. Now I've bin told *they're* goin' on ration.'

'Kur . . . *rist*! I 'ope not. I've got me old man and four kids to feed!'

Spasmodic movements. Slow, stop, slow, stop – nothing like the 'Charge of the Light Brigade'. Had I been wearing my lovely hackle I'd have been urged to the front, but those halcyon days were gone for good; I was back with the hoi polloi from whence I'd sprung. The woman whispered. 'I'm afraid you'll only git one rabbit if you're not a regler.'

I whispered back: 'I didn't know grocers sold rabbits.'

'Oh *you* know. This shop's in the know, yer know.'

At last. The counter, but feeling gentlemanly, I gestured to my confidante to precede me. She smiled. 'Nice of yer, mate. Arternoon, Amy. The usual.'

'Arternoon,' replied the girl, pushing forward three carcasses.

Taking the money, she slapped another rabbit on the counter. 'Arf a crown.'

'Er . . . may I have two, please?' I asked, with my most disarming grin.

It failed to impact. 'One each,' exclaimed Amy brusquely.

Flabbergasted, I stared at three beasties being stuffed into a shopping bag, while Amy herself was almost hull-down among rabbits. Then I remembererd that the lady customer was a 'regler', with six tummies to fill. For a fleeting moment I pictured the family at table, each with a poised rabbit at their teeth. 'One please,' I said to the girl, who was looking impatient.

'Taking it like this?' she demanded. 'We're out o' wrappin' paper.'

I gaped at the corpse, lying in an abandoned attitude. 'Sorry, miss. I'll buy a bag.'

Amy opened her mouth, closed it, then groped around near her knees. The transaction was completed, I found the regular waiting outside. 'You *was* lucky to git that carrier, mate.'

'Is there *anything* that isn't scarce?'

'Not a lot. You can bet there's always something that's shoved out o' sight.' She lowered her voice: 'Listen. If yer want another rabbit bad, queue up again. That's allowed at this shop, but o' course us locals don't shout it to the rooftops!'

I thanked her, obtained another rabbit, and felt myself go red when Amy favoured me with a most ostentatious wink. Well, the war had been won, and here we were, queueing for the humble bunny, and with offal and paper bags under the counter . . . that brave new era hadn't yet arrived.

*   *   *

How little they know of England,
Who only England know.

At Charing Cross I kept a firm grip on the bag and precious cargo, then strolled towards the river and Waterloo Station. Hungerford Bridge was an old favourite, and halfway along the narrow pedestrian path I paused, as always. It was dusk, and six years since I'd seen the Thames and surroundings so bright. In the distance was the silhouette of St Paul's dome, and on my left lurked the murky Cleopatra's Needle, its base chipped from a first world war air raid. Towards me slid a powerful tug, red and green navigation lights glowing and smokestack lowered to clear the bridge. She was towing a string of coal barges, probably for the power station at Battersea. As they began to pass under me like ghosts, the railings suddenly vibrated violently as a train thundered by within a few feet of my back.

A Cockney sparrow had come home to roost, and, at that moment, Nigeria and Burma seemed far, far away.

Old Soldiers
Never Die
They only
Fade away

Epilogue

1977. Watching a military parade on television with my wife Edna (my second wife; Florrie had died from cancer many years before) I made a comment as the Welsh Guards appeared; I'd never forgotten the circumstances of my departure. 'Is all that business still on your mind?' asked Edna.

'I'll always feel guilty about that wrongful rejoining in '28.'

'Well, it's time you did something about it.'

'What on earth can I do?'

'Petition the Queen for a pardon.'

'*What*?'

'Why not? She wouldn't have you shot.'

'It could land me in clink.'

'After fifty years?'

'Don't you realise that I could be charged with fraudulent enlistment?'

'I'm sure you wouldn't be – you're nearly eighty. Look, it's the Queen's Jubilee Year. It could catch her at just the right moment.'

Greatly tempted, I took the chance, suggesting to Her Majesty that I might not be as black as painted, and told Edna not to be surprised if redcaps came through the gate. 'I wonder what *will* happen?' I added.

'She'll probably get the mail with her elevenses. After reading yours she'll say to the Duke: "What should I do about this, Phil?"'

'Oh, you think so? And what'll the Duke advise?'

'I reckon he'll say: "Let the poor old blighter have his pardon, Lizzie".'

'Look, it's no joke. You suggested this, and now you're being flippant.'

'No. I'm quite sure he doesn't go around all day calling her
"Your Majesty".'

To my surprise, I received an acknowledgement by return of
post:

Buckingham Palace
31st March 1977

The Defence Services Secretary is Commanded by Her Majesty
the Queen to acknowledge the receipt of Mr J. Shaw's letter
which has been referred to the Ministry of Defence for reply.

*   *   *

Ministry of Defence
4th April 1977

To Mr J. Shaw

Sir,
Please furnish on the enclosed form particulars of your
regimental numbers in all units in which you served.

*   *   *

This done, I now had to sweat while my records from four
different units were scrutinised. 'Don't look so pessimistic!' said
Edna.

Ministry of Defence
30th July 1977

To Mr J. Shaw

Sir,
I am directed to inform you that your petition concerning your
Services record was referred by the Queen to the Secretary of
State for Defence who, by Her Majesty's Command, has given it
careful consideration. Your anxiety is well appreciated, and I
hope it will be a relief to you to know that you have no further
cause for concern.

*   *   *

'Well,' remarked my wife, magnanimously refraining from a
reminder that she had 'told me so', 'Are you any happier now?'

'No need to ask.'
'Good. You'd better write to the Queen and thank her.'

*   *   *

To Her Majesty Queen Elizabeth II   31st July 1977
Buckingham Palace

Your Majesty

Earlier this year I petitioned for a pardon concerning fraudulent enlistment into the Army in 1928, and you Commanded that it be considered by the Secretary of State for Defence. I have now been informed that I have no further cause for concern. May I offer my humble thanks for your kind recommendation? Also, as a staunch Loyalist, may I express my admiration for your quiet courage shown at difficult moments in your recent Jubilee tours?

I am,
Your Majesty's Obedient Servant,
J. Shaw

*   *   *

Balmoral Castle
20th August 1977

Dear Mr Shaw,

I am Commanded by the Queen to thank you for your letter and to say that Her Majesty was delighted that you were granted a pardon for your youthful indiscretions. Her Majesty thought it most kind of you to write, and greatly appreciated the loyal sentiments in your letter.

Postscript

James Shaw spent the last twelve years of his life in a small village in North Wales, where he was a popular and respected member of the community.

Accompanied by his springer spaniel, his tall figure walking the lanes became familiar to animals, children and adults alike.

When he died at the age of eighty two, his passing was mourned by all, and in the little village church, Welsh and English voices joined together to sing

The strife is o'er, the battle done;
                                Alleluia.

General Interest

ON THE WESTERN FRONT
Soldiers' Stories from France and Flanders 1914–18
John Laffin

These stories reflect the Western Front conditions, attitudes and practices of 1914–18, revealing the soldiers' war from first shot to last.

256pp   219mm × 157mm   Illustrated
ISBN 0 86299 242 7 (cloth) £11.95

THE RAMBLING SOLDIER
Edited by Roy Palmer

Down the ages the British soldier has described his life through his songs, his ballads, his letters and memoirs. Roy Palmer has collected the best of these.

320pp   198mm × 127mm   Illustrated
ISBN 0 86299 246 X (paper) £5.95

WAY OF REVELATION
Wilfrid Ewart

A classic account of men in battle praised by Henry Williamson as one of the finest novels to come out of the 'Great War'.

544pp   172mm × 114mm
ISBN 0 86299 288 5 (paper) £3.95

THE MAN THE NAZIS COULDN'T CATCH
John Laffin

The story of a British private soldier on the run and working with the Resistance in France from Dunkirk until the Liberation.

192pp   216mm × 138mm Illustrated
ISBN 0 86299 043 2 (cloth) £8.95

STARS IN A DARK NIGHT
The Letters of Ivor Gurney to the Chapman Family
Anthony Boden
With a foreword by Michael Hurd

A newly discovered collection of letters and an unpublished essay from a creative genius of rare quality and a singularly attractive human being.

320pp   216mm × 138mm Illustrated
ISBN 0 86299 225 7 (cloth) £9.95

A FEATHER ON THE TIDE
Alison Wolff-Wilson

An intriguing story of travel and adventure – from England in the 1920s to the Far East on the edge of catastrophe, from wartime India and post-war Turkey to Hungary just prior to the 1956 uprising.

224pp   216mm × 138mm Illustrated
ISBN 0 86299 169 2 (cloth) £9.95 AC

BADEN-POWELL: A FAMILY ALBUM
Heather Baden-Powell

The story of one of the worlds most remarkable father-figures, by his own daughter, containing a wealth of material from the family albums and coloured sketchbooks previously unavailable to biographers.

128pp   220mm × 255mm   Illustrated
ISBN 086299 273 7 (cloth) £12.95

MAN OF THE VALLEYS
The Recollections of a South Wales Miner
Edited by Mary Paget

The tragedies, the triumphs, the disasters and the drama of life as a miner at the turn of the century are revealed in this the story of William Paget.

224pp   219mm × 157mm Illustrated
ISBN 0 86299 244 3 (paper) £5.95

FLOODSHOCK: THE DROWNING OF PLANET EARTH
Antony Milne

A fully illustrated history of the Earths most violent floods from Noah to the present day looking at the theories, underlying causes, predictions and the possible worldwide response to future disasters.

214pp   246mm × 172mm   Illustrated
ISBN 086299 270 2 (cloth) £12.95